Environmental Assessment
and Development

edited by
Robert Goodland and Valerie Edmundson

The World Bank
Washington, D.C.

The findings, interpretations, and conclusions expressed in this study are entirely those of the authors and should not be attributed in any manner to the World Bank, to its affiliated organizations, or to members of its Board of Executive Directors or the countries they represent.

Because of the informality of this series and to make the publication available with the least possible delay, the manuscript has not been edited as fully as would be the case with a more formal document, and the World Bank accepts no responsibility for errors.

The complete backlist of publications from the World Bank is shown in the annual *Index of Publications*, which contains an alphabetical title list and indexes of subjects, authors, and countries and regions. The latest edition is available free of charge from the Distribution Unit, Office of the Publisher, at the address in the copyright notice or from Publications, World Bank, 66, avenue d'Iéna, 75116 Paris, France.

Robert Goodland is Adviser for Environmental Assessment in the World Bank's Environment Department. Valerie Edmundson is a consultant with the World Bank.

The International Association for Impact Assessment (IAIA) was organized in 1980 to promote the local and global use of impact assessment and to develop international capability in anticipating and managing the consequences of development. IAIA is affiliated with the American Association for the Advancement of Science and is a designated nongovernmental organization of the United Nations.

The Twelfth Annual Meeting of the IAIA took place August 19–22, 1992, at the World Bank. The topic of the forum was "Industrial and Third World Environmental Assessment: The Urgent Transition to Sustainability." This volume contains selected papers from the IAIA meeting.

Library of Congress Cataloging-in-Publication Data

Environmental assessment and development / edited by Robert
  Goodland and Valerie Edmundson.
     p. cm. — (World Bank symposium)
  Includes bibliographical references.
  ISBN 0-8213-2762-3 √
    1. Environmental risk assessment. 2. Environmental risk
  assessment—Developing countries. 3. Sustainable development.
  4. Sustainable development—Developing countries. I. Goodland,
  Robert, 1945– . II. Edmundson, Valerie. III. Series.
  GE145.E57   1994
  333.7'14—dc20
                                                    94-13693
                                                      CIP

Environmental Assessment
and Development

A World Bank–IAIA Symposium

Contents

Foreword

Environmental assessment (EA) at the World Bank began in the early 1970s on an ad hoc basis, and by 1984 EA had become a Bank requirement for all relevant projects. The Bank has since devoted a great deal of effort to assessing Bank-financed projects and, in part because of that work, has made considerable progress in the way it handles environmental issues.

In 1989 the Bank formalized EA requirements in Operational Directive (OD) 4.00, Annex A. This was revised and updated in October 1991 (OD 4.01). The Bank has continued to refine its procedures, has run an accelerated program of EA training for Bank staff and borrowers, and has set up a detailed tracking system for EAs in Bank projects. In addition, the Bank has greatly strengthened its capacity to expedite the EA process through increases in staff and financial resources and production of many publications disseminating Bank expertise on EA. One of the most important of these is still the *Environmental Assessment Sourcebook*, published in the summer of 1991.

In January 1993 the Vice Presidency for Environmentally Sustainable Development (ESD) was formed to provide special leadership in achieving development that would provide long-term prosperity. ESD's mandate was stated as meeting three environmental challenges—food production, urbanization and natural resource management—and bridging three gaps—in knowledge, capacity and attention to social factors. These mechanisms for meeting the urgent goals of sustainability are based on solid environmental, social and economic principles and pragmatism.

While progress has been rapid, there is no room for complacency. We cannot yet claim that all EAs are satisfactory, but the Bank is moving ahead already to a more mature phase of environmental work. The Bank's first review of EA experience in 1992 generated a deepened commitment by the Bank to extending its expertise in assessment and the prediction of environmental impacts to the later phases of supervision and implementation to help strengthen borrower capacity in these areas.

There are other forward-looking activities. In fact, some of the most important lessons learned in recent years are not only about the high cost of environmental degradation and the ultimate loss in productivity, but also about the limitation of project-by-project assessment for addressing this overall degradation of natural resources that puts a country's future at risk economically and socially—as well as environmentally. To properly deal with these problems, a multidisciplinary approach is called for that combines broad environmental policy, institution building, and other aspects of resource management.

In response, the Bank will continue its work in country economic and sector work, technical assistance, project lending, formulation of national environmental action plans (NEAPs), and collaboration with the Global Environment Facility (GEF). Of course, individual lending will continue to be important in borrowing countries, and the Bank will use each opportunity to help governments map out achievable environmental goals that will ensure future resources. An important Bank effort in the near future will be working out NEAPs with governments to focus investments on critical areas. Sectoral EAs will be used more frequently. Finally, our joint responsibility to the global environment will undergird the Bank's continued work with the GEF, particularly in energy planning and development, forest management, and agriculture.

Protecting the global environment will require greater levels of effort and probably restraint within each country and unprecedented levels of information sharing and cooperation between countries. There are many daunting problems that also require adaptation to the changing needs of society as well as unconventional ways for dealing with the new generation of development and environmental challenges.

I am very pleased that the Bank can be instrumental in the wide dissemination of environmental information through this publication. Let me extend my gratitude to the authors represented here and all others who are devoting their skill and energy to the environmental challenges we and succeeding generations face.

Mohamed T. El-Ashry
Chief Environmental Adviser
to the President and
Director of the Environment Department
The World Bank

Editors' Preface

This volume presents selected papers that were presented and discussed at the International Association for Impact Assessment (IAIA) conference on environmental assessment (EA) held in Washington, DC, August 19–22, 1992, and hosted by the World Bank. The meeting was especially timely as a follow-up to the recommendations for EA at the United Nations Conference on Environment and Development (UNCED) in Rio de Janeiro. Some 425 professionals from 45 countries travelled to this conference to discuss the state of the art in EA, evaluate recent innovations, and critically examine the discipline as a means of achieving environmentally sustainable development.

The conference covered a wide range of issues, from economic valuation theory to comparisons of EA procedures in industrial and developing countries to practical assessments of case studies. Several experts on the environment and development examined global patterns of income distribution. All of the findings emphasize that changes can be made—and must be made—to move environmental sustainability from concept to reality.

Sustainable development as advocated in the 1987 Brundtland Commission report, *Our Common Future*, is a complex undertaking that requires a global response and an unprecedented level of effort, knowledge, and international cooperation, particularly between North and South. In the poorest countries, where the ecosystems on which people depend are threatened by population pressures, land and water degradation, deforestation, and other forms of environmental stress, economic development remains the greatest challenge. In industrial countries, where the level of consumption today jeopardizes global sustainability more than population growth, the greatest challenge will be moderating per capita impact. EA has a major role in the difficult counterbalancing of these objectives.

During the past two decades, many industrial and developing countries, as well as international assistance agencies, have adopted environmental assessment procedures to improve the environmental performance of their development projects. In developing countries, narrowly planned investment projects were found to have negative consequences for the environment that not only impeded economic development but also threatened human well-being.

The contributions included in this volume were selected to provide a broad overview of these issues and perspectives. Together they help clarify how the management of our environment can be improved through a better understanding of the interplay between environmental quality, economic performance and social welfare. The papers have been organized around four topics. Part I discusses priorities of sustainable development and introduces specific methods for achieving them, such as environmental accounting, environmental assessment, and strategic environmental assessment. Part II presents case studies of environmental assessment as a major instrument in environmental planning and management in developing institutions, with attention to building EA capacity. Part III discusses the application of the environmental assessment process for specific issues and types of development projects. Part IV examines how the concept of sustainability can be used in the economic analysis of projects and programs, including the treatment of the depletion of natural capital.

Part I begins with a discussion of expanding the scope of environmental assessment to achieve the goals of environmentally sustainable development. Barry Sadler contends that the conventional system of project-oriented environmental assessment is an ineffective response to the current patterns and rate of ecological deterioration. A more integrated approach is required—a second-generation EA process that addresses the source of impacts and is linked to all levels of decisionmaking. Raymond

Mikesell presents an outline for making sustainable development a part of the EA process. The transition to sustainable development will require restoring and then preserving the productivity and full functioning of the natural resource base. This of course is a hard and far-reaching task needing a commitment of effort and funds to avoid or mitigate environmental damage, to restore depleted natural capital such as forests and soil, to substitute for nonrenewable resources, and to compensate future generations for the depletion of natural capital in the present.

Part II presents an overview of environmental assessment processes in selected countries and of case studies on transferring EA technology. Mary MacDonald compares EA procedures in industrial and developing countries and illustrates the value of striving for an international approach that will be strengthened by the combined experience and environmental management goals from different cultures and geographical regions. The assumption that traditional environmental assessments conducted in industrial countries result in more effective management is flawed; in fact, the "best" approach has yet to be found for many difficult issues such as screening, monitoring, and public participation. Nonita Yap discusses the institutionalization of the EA process in Thailand and Canada. She argues that developing countries "on the fast track to industrialization" are often particularly vulnerable to the undervaluation of social and environmental costs in their pursuit of development goals.

Wilson Eedy and Lars Hurlen discuss the development of EA legislation in Indonesia and illustrate how EA has been used for tropical forestry development. Government funding agencies have also supported the development of local environmental regulation, but there is an urgent need to make these laws functional. Josef Leitmann describes the research experience of the World Bank Urban Management and the Environment Program (UMP/E) in the area of rapid urban environmental assessment, which uses comparable case studies to broaden knowledge about issues and options. The objectives of UMP/E are to formulate an environmental management strategy and action plan for cities in the developing world. Basil Savitsky and others discuss the application of Geographic Information Systems (GIS) and gap analysis to provide data on species distribution in Costa Rica. The study evaluates available data sources and develops a GIS framework for prioritizing both

conservation and sustainable development of land areas.

In Part III the authors discuss environmental assessment as it applies to the technical and social issues of dams, tourism, natural hazards, and public participation. Jan Veltrop examines the effectiveness of EA guidelines as a planning tool for the design and management of dams and hydroelectric projects. He discusses ways in which management plans are used to resolve conflicts between water resource development and environmental conservation, based on selected country case studies, and illustrates the advantages of conducting an EA during project planning and design. Cynthia Cook and Paula Donnelly-Roark discuss how the involvement of an informed public and the participation of affected groups in project planning determine the success of environmental assessments as well as of implementation of the project. In Sub-Saharan Africa, the meaning of local participation is problematic, especially where major investment decisions are frequently made by elite groups and broad popular participation in the political process is the exception rather than the rule. Ways to ensure participation have not been well defined, and barriers such as restricted access to information and inadequate linkages to local institutions hinder effective communication. Participation is frequently undertaken too late to have a significant impact on decisionmaking.

Emdad Haque discusses how people in Bangladesh are affected by natural hazards (for example, coastal floods, river bank erosion and droughts) that have seriously hampered the development process, requiring a substantial reallocation of resources from development to relief and recovery. The World Bank and the Bangladesh government have approved a plan to control floods that calls for the construction of high embankments along the major river systems of the country. On the basis of a survey of eight villages, Haque argues that such large-scale structural solutions do not address the entire situation and run the real risk of adverse ecological and social impacts. He advocates an integrative approach involving both small-scale engineering projects and nonstructural indigenous strategies to control floodwater and ensure the conservation of vital natural and cultural resources. Douglas Earl McLaren presents a methodology for assessing negative environmental impacts, including mitigation measures to be taken as part of the EA process, and relevant lessons learned from tourism projects in industrial and developing countries. McLaren believes that when decisionmakers and planners analyze the long-term investment value of tourism projects, they should assess their potential negative effects on the environment and people. A key component of EA in tourism projects is seeking the involvement of local people early on to ensure the development of a more viable and sustainable industry.

In Part IV the authors examine the relationship between environmental assessment and environmentally sustainable development from a macroeconomic, sectoral and project perspective. Joachim von Amsberg argues that in conventional economic analysis, the costs of natural capital are systematically underestimated due to individual short-term incentives of decisionmakers, the presence of externalities, and uncertainties about the functioning of the biosphere. He proposes a sustainability constraint on current economic activities to ensure that the value of natural capital be maintained. Herman Daly proposes that investing in natural capital is fundamental to sustainable development to maximize current productivity and to ensure the future supply. He discusses the practical means of achieving this through defining in context natural capital, various investments, and efficiency ratios.

As these papers and the IAIA conferees discussed, the application of environmental assessment has improved project appraisal and development planning and decisionmaking in general. The project-by-project approach is no longer adequate, however, for the broad environmental policy, institution building, and other aspects of resource management now needed. A more imaginative pursuit of economic ends is required—one that is less resource-intensive and that allows for an increase in the quality of life without a corresponding decrease in environmental quality.

The conference was organized by Robert Goodland and Valerie Edmundson of the World Bank and Gary Williams of the Argonne National Laboratory, Washington, DC. We are indebted to Maurice and Ellen Voland of the International Association for Impact Assessment, Bellhaven, North Carolina, and Sherie Voland-Koob of V-K Enterprises, Washington, DC, who assisted in the preparation and implementation of the conference. From the World Bank Group, significant support came from Michael Cernea, Herman Daly, Mohamed El-Ashry, Jose Furtado, Joan Grigsby, Ishrat Husain, Maritta Koch-Weser, Elizabeth Monosowski, Nimalka Moonesinghe, Philip Paradine, Robert Picciotto, Jane Pratt, Rebecca Russ, and Thomas Walton.

We would also like to thank all the conference participants and especially the contributors to this volume for making the publication possible. To prepare the papers for publication, restructuring was necessary at times—for example, including long annexes and all the tables and graphs would have made the volume too large. Several authors provided updated or follow-up material to their original analyses and, where possible, this new information has been added to the chapters presented here. Nancy Levine and Virginia Hitchcock provided guidance and moral support without which this work would not have been completed. Finally, our sincere gratitude to Jill Kuehnert for producing the expert desktop publishing under a tight deadline and to Charlotte Maxey and Stephanie Gerard for seeing the publication through production.

Contributors

Joachim von Amsberg
Faculty of Commerce and Business Administration
The University of British Columbia
Vancouver, British Columbia, Canada

G. Wesley Burnett
Strom Thurmond Institute
Clemson University
Clemson, South Carolina

Cynthia Cook
Senior Sociologist
Environmentally Sustainable Development Division
Africa Technical Department
The World Bank

Herman Daly
School of Public Affairs, University of Maryland
College Park, Maryland

Paula Donnelly-Roark
Consultant
The World Bank

Valerie Edmundson
Consultant
The World Bank

Wilson Eedy
Geomatics International, Inc.
Burlington, Ontario, Canada

Jorge Fallas
Universidad National
Heredia, Costa Rica

Robert Goodland
Adviser, Environmental Assessment
Environment Department
The World Bank

C. Emdad Haque
Department of Geography
Brandon University
Brandon, Manitoba, Canada

Lars Hurlen
Lura Group
Toronto, Ontario, Canada

Thomas E. Lacher, Jr.
Strom Thurmond Institute
Clemson University
Clemson, South Carolina

Josef L. Leitmann
Urban Planner, Transport, Water, and Urban
    Development Division
The World Bank

Mary MacDonald
Stockholm Environment Institute
University of York
Hoslington, York, United Kingdom

Douglas Earl McLaren
I.C.F. Kaiser Engineers
Washington, DC

Raymond F. Mikesell
Department of Economics
University of Oregon
Eugene, Oregon

Barry Sadler
Canadian Environmental Assessment Research
    Council
Victoria, British Columbia, Canada

Basil G. Savitsky
Strom Thurmond Institute
Clemson University
Clemson, South Carolina

Christopher Vaughan
Universidad National
Heredia, Costa Rica

Jan A. Veltrop
Harza Engineering Company
Chicago, Illinois

Nonita T. Yap
School of Rural Planning and Development
University of Guelph
Guelph, Ontario, Canada

Acronyms and Abbreviations

AFTEN   Africa Region Environment Division (World Bank)

ALARP   As low as reasonably possible

AMDAL   Environmental assessment (Indonesia)

ANDAL   Indonesian Department of Population and Environment

AsDB   Asian Development Bank

AVHRR   Advanced Very High Radiometric Resolution

BAT   Best available technology

bbl   Barrel

BOI   Board of Investment (Thailand)

BRBFPE   Brahmaputra Right Bank Flood Protection (Bangladesh)

CB   Cost/benefit (analysis)

CC   Carrying capacity

CEAA   Canadian Environmental Assessment Agency

CEO   Chief executive officer

CETESB   São Paulo State Environmental Company

CFCs   Chlorofluorocarbons

CH_4 Methane

CIDA   Canadian International Development Agency

CO_2 Carbon dioxide

CZCS   Coastal Zone Color Scanner

DCW   Digital chart of the world

DMA   Defense Mapping Agency

EA   Environmental assessment

EAP   Environmental action plan

EARP   Environmental assessment review process (Canada)

EAS   Environmental assessment study

EC   European Community

ECC   Environmental compliance certificate (Philippines)

ECE   United Nations Economic Commission for Europe

ECODES   National Conservation Strategy for Sustainable Development (Costa Rica)

EdF   Electricité de France

EDI   Economic Development Institute

EIS   Environmental impact assessment

EMDI   Environmental Management Department of Indonesia

EMS   Environmental management strategy

ENDS   Environmental Data Service

ENMOD   United Nations Convention on the Prohibition of Military or Any Other Hostile Use of Environmental Modification

EPM   Environmental Program for the Mediterranean (United Nations/World Bank)

EPWAPDA   East Pakistan Water and Power Development Authority

EQMAP   Environmental quality management action plan

ERR   Economic rate of return

ES   Environmental sustainability

E&SA   Environmental and social assessment

ESAS   External support agencies

ESRI   Environmental Systems Research Institute

EUROSTAT   European Statistical Office

FAP   Flood Action Plan (World Bank)

FAO   Food and Agriculture Organization of the United Nations

FEARO   Federal Environmental Assessment Review Office (Canada)

FFWP   Food for Works Program (Bangladesh)

FPCO   Flood Plan Coordination Organization (Bangladesh)

GDP   Gross domestic product

GEF   Global Environment Facility

GEMS   Global Environment Monitoring System

GIS   Geographic Information System

GL   Gigajoule

GNP   Gross national product

GPS   Global Positioning System

GRID   Global Resource Information Database

ha   Hectare

HCCs	High-consumption countries	OEPP	Office of Environmental Policy and Planning (Thailand)
HYV	High-yielding varieties	OMS	Operational Manual Statement (World Bank)
IADB	Inter-American Development Bank		
IAIA	International Association for Impact Assessment	ONC	Operational navigational charts
IBRD	International Bank for Reconstruction and Development (World Bank)	ONEB	Office of the National Environmental Board (Thailand)
ICC	International Chamber of Commerce	PEL	Project evaluation level (Indonesia)
ICOLD	International Commission on Large Dams	PIL	Project initial evaluation level or new plan (Indonesia)
IEE	Initial environmental evaluation	PPF	Project Preparation Facility (World Bank)
IFIs	International financial institutions		
INBIO	Instituto Nacional de Biodiversidad (Costa Rica)	PWP	Public Works Program
		R&D	Research and development
ITCPD	Indian Town and Country Planning Department	RED	Regional Environmental Division (World Bank)
IUCN	International Union for the Conservation of Nature and Natural Resources	ROR	Rate of return
		RWP	Rural Works Program (Bangladesh)
km	Kilometer	SAR	Staff Appraisal Report (World Bank)
km^2	Square kilometers	SEA	Strategic environmental assessment
LCCs	Low-consumption countries	SECAL	Sector adjustment loan (World Bank)
m	Meter	SEI	Stockholm Environment Institute
m^3	Cubic meters	SEQRA	State Environmental Quality Review Act (New York, United States)
MAF	Million acre-feet		
MDBs	Multilateral development banks	SIA	Social impact assessment
MEIP	Metropolitan Environmental Improvement Program (United Nations/World Bank)	TAGPE	Technical Assistance Grant Program for the Environment
		TM	Task manager or thematic mapper
MFIs	Multinational financial institutions	TORs	Terms of reference
MJ	Megajoule	TP	Throughput
MMK	Manmade capital	TPD	Tons per day
MSS	Multispectral Scanner	UMP	Urban Management Program
MW	Megawatt	UMP/E	Urban Management and the Environment Program
NAFTA	North American Free Trade Act		
NASA	National Aeronautics and Space Administration (United States)	UNCED	United Nations Conference on Environment and Development
NEAP	National environmental action plan	UNCHS	United Nations Center for Human Settlements
NEB	National Environmental Board (Thailand)	UNDP	United Nations Development Programme
NEPA	National Environmental Policy Act (United States)	UNECE	United Nations Economic Commission for Europe
NEQA	National Environmental Quality Act (Thailand)	UNEP	United Nations Environmental Programme
NESDB	National Economic and Social Development Board (Thailand)	UNESCO	United Nations Educational, Scientific and Cultural Organization
NGO	Nongovernmental organization	USAID	United States Agency for International Development
NK	Natural capital		
NUREC	Network for Urban Research in the European Community	USNRC	United States National Research Council
OD	Operational Directive (World Bank)	UVb	Ultraviolet rays
ODA	Overseas Development Aid (Canada)	WCED	World Commission on Environment and Development (Brundtland)
OECD	Organization for Economic Cooperation and Development		
OED	Operations Evaluation Department (World Bank)	WHO	World Health Organization

Part I
Environmental Assessment and Development

1

Environmental Assessment and Development Policymaking

Barry Sadler

The practical contribution that environmental assessment (EA) can make to informed decisionmaking is acknowledged in Principle 17 of the Rio Declaration on Environment and Development.[1] During the last twenty years, EA has been adopted and adapted by a growing number of countries and international agencies. It has evolved, in the process, into a comprehensive and versatile instrument for development planning and resource management. New demands are being made on EA by the international agreements signed at the Earth Summit and by the endorsement of Agenda 21.

In that context, the practice of EA is constrained by certain well-documented deficiencies. By most measures, conventional (that is, project-oriented) EA is a self-limiting and ineffective response to current scales and rates of ecological deterioration. More proactive, integrated approaches are required—in effect, a second-generation EA process that moves beyond the "impact fixation" to address the causes of unsustainable development. These are located at the "upstream" phase of the decisionmaking cycle, in the macro-economic policies and development programs pursued by governments of all political stripes.

What is termed strategic environmental assessment (SEA) is a promising approach to ensure that policymaking[2] takes account of sustainability principles (Sadler 1986, 1990a; Wood and Djeddour 1992). A number of countries have recently introduced elements of this approach, and more appear likely to do so. To date, however, practical experience with SEA of policies, plans and programs is limited, with critical issues yet to be resolved.[3] These include the proposed scope of this approach, its role and relationship to other policy instruments in decisionmaking; and the appropriateness of relying on the methods and procedures of project EA.

This chapter will address these issues by analyzing relevant inter-relationships in process development, as indicated by the following key questions:

- What is the rationale for SEA? What is its proposed role in decisionmaking?
- What institutional opportunities and constraints are encountered in introducing SEA into development policies, plans and programs? How might this approach reinforce environmental accountability in the economic and central agencies of government?
- How do different countries and institutions define SEA and link it with sustainability concepts and strategies? Which frameworks show promise for structuring this approach in relation to different levels of decisionmaking (policies, plans and programs)?
- How adequate are existing EA methodologies and techniques for SEA? Which other policy tools might be adapted to that purpose?
- Where do we go from here with research and development? How might process development draw on advances in environmental and ecological economics (for example) to design a more integrated approach consistent with sustainability principles?

Rationale for SEA

The axial relationship of EA and policymaking is often misunderstood. Impact assessment is a particular form of policy analysis, with a characteristic purpose and approach. By definition, this approach is concerned with identifying, evaluating and mitigating the potential consequences of proposed decisions, and strives to be rational, systematic and integrated. EA and its related components—social impact assessment (SIA), risk analysis, and so forth—initially develop to augment the deficiencies of economic techniques in accounting for the qualitative and intangible effects of major developments. This generic process of EA has evolved considerably in a relatively short period of time and is, "one of the major innovations in policymaking" (Bartlett 1988).

SEA may be seen as a logical extension of this trend, particularly in industrial countries with well-established EA systems. However, it applies equally to developing countries (Biswas and Geping 1987). A recent study lists a dozen general advantages of introducing SEA (Wood and Djeddour 1992). These stem from two sources of interest: overcoming the limitations of conventional project EA; and promoting more integrated approaches for assessing and evaluating the sustainability of development policies, programs and plans.

Strengthening EA

There is no basis in the principles of EA for overlooking policies, programs and plans. Quite the contrary. The preoccupation to date with *project* EA is de facto rather than de jure. For example, from the outset of the U.S. National Environmental Policy Act in 1969, EA was meant to test, inform and reorient federal decisionmaking (Caldwell 1982). Section 102 (2) (c), in fact, refers to coverage of "proposals for legislation and other major Federal actions significantly affecting the environment." The language of intent is also broadly drawn and permissive in initial EA laws and policies established by other countries, such as Australia and Canada (see Clark 1981). Canadian guidelines, for example, call for the application of the process "as early as possible in the decisionmaking process."

In reality, this has not happened. With certain exceptions, EA is applied as a project planning and mitigation tool, focussing on questions of how (rather than whether or where) development should take place. This circumscribed role in decisionmaking works effectively within an integrated policy and planning context in which prior-order issues of justification and alternatives are resolved in a phased manner. Where this framework does not exist or is incomplete, which is typically the case, project-by-project impact assessment is constrained by limited information about the larger opportunity costs of development proposals. Under these circumstances, it becomes difficult to evaluate the real significance of predicted impacts, or just what is being lost or forgone (Sadler 1986).

In response to this problem, the scope of EA has progressively been extended to policy and planning concerns. Several of the process trends represent prototype forms of SEA. Several key examples are:

• EAs of major projects have opened questions of need, alternatives and siting to public scrutiny and examination (Sadler 1984).

• Programmatic (or class) assessment is conducted in the USA and the Province of Ontario, Canada, to review the effects of economic development programs, new technologies, and even wildlife conservation strategies (Sigal and Webb 1989).

• Areawide assessment is utilized to identify the regional consequences of sectoral and multiple use development proposals and to gain initial policy and planning clearances (Ballard and others 1982).

• Cumulative effects assessment is a more recent and comprehensive version of the above innovations; it is concerned with incremental, synergistic and cross-media effects of development patterns on ecosystem and landscape functions (Canadian Environmental Assessment Research Council and U.S. National Research Council 1986).

• State of Environment Reporting is a comprehensive, national assessment of resource and ecological trends, conditions and responses to the stresses induced by development activities (Bird and Rapport 1986).

Despite such advances, resource and ecological deterioration is now pervasive, and is expressed on regional and global as well as local scales. Acid rain, biodiversity loss, and climate warming are well documented examples of changes that are impairing the productivity and habitability of the earth (Brown and others 1990). In effect, these and other cumulative effects of development activity have seeped through the institutional cracks, and now threaten to become overwhelming and irreversible. The decisions and actions that escape EA, from new development policy and program initiatives to routine land use practices, greatly outnumber those that are subject to review (Boothroyd 1990; Rees 1990).

An explicit, formalized approach to SEA forms part of an integrated response to these issues. It should realize the following interrelated benefits: (a) encourage review of the potential environmental effects associated with all development proposals, from policy to project levels; (b) permit more systematic consideration of need and alternatives, for instance, whether a development program to address an energy shortfall should emphasize energy conservation or supply extension, and which is the best practicable environmental option, hydro or fuel fossil generation; (c) facilitate identification and management of cumulative impacts; and (d) catalyze the reorientation of EA as a sustainability instrument.

Promoting Sustainability

The transition to a sustainability agenda, called for by the World Commission on Environment and Development (1987), carries important implications for the theory and practice of EA. Ecological and economic considerations, for example, must be treated on the same level and the same time in decisionmaking. The standard environmental agenda that focuses on the symptoms of deterioration and unsustainability must be complemented by an anticipatory strategy that addresses the source of these effects, which are found in economic growth policies and assumptions. Such a shift in emphasis demands two key innovations: translating the principles of environmental sustainability into operational terms, guidelines and such as policy performance indicators; and redesigning the architecture of EA and related processes to give effect to these new "rules of the game."

To ensure sustainability, all development options and activities must be adjusted to and be consistent with the "carrying capacity" of the global biosphere and regional ecosystems. Paragraph 9a of the World Bank's Operational Manual Statement (OMS) 2.36 *Environmental Aspects of Bank Work* provides a formal statement of this goal: "to ensure that each project affecting renewable natural resources (as a sink for residues or as a source for raw materials, for example) does not exceed the regenerative capacities of the environment" (Goodland and Daly 1991). At present, scientific understanding is insufficient to permit before-the-fact predictions of whether and when significant thresholds will be crossed, that is, the "operating point" at which cumulative stress of use and activity will cause irreversible change or structural breakdown in natural systems (Kay 1991). Ecological capacities or limits may be interpreted only in qualitative terms of "acceptable" change and risk.

A formal approximation for environmental sustainability is non-liquidation of natural capital, that is, resource stocks and the ecological processes essential for their continued productivity and regeneration. This criterion links long-established conservation principles with new modes of economic valuation of the source and sink functions and services performed by natural systems. Natural capital is now considered by ecological economists to be a complementary and limiting factor of development, rather than freely available and substitutable with manmade capital. On the basis of this interpretation,

Goodland and Daly (1991) have elaborated output and input rules for environmental sustainability. The output guide deals with assimilative capacity; the input guide with regenerative capacity for renewable resources and replacement rates for exhaustible resources.

These precautionary principles may appear demanding and onerous, and they clearly are if strictly applied at the individual project level. Few development proposals would go forward under a strict criterion of non-liquidation of natural capital. Natural capital, however, is an aggregate concept that refers to multi-function ecosystems, rather than to single resources or specific sites. It is most appropriately operationalized at a net or programmatic level (Pearce, Markandya and Barbier 1989) and in a bio-regional context (Sadler and Jacobs 1990). At this scale, cumulative environmental impacts may be thought of as a drawdown of natural capital, which must be offset by an equivalent investment in resource conservation, rehabilitation or enhancement. In-kind impact compensation measures, as well as conventional, mitigation terms and conditions, should be applied to non-conforming development activities (that do not meet the no net loss rule).

Maintenance of natural capital and carrying capacity and in-kind impact compensation are concepts that grew from existing approaches to resource and environmental management. Other examples include air and water quality standards and pollution emission "bubbles," no net loss of habitat policies, and sustained yield fish and timber allocation systems. Such approaches, of course, are tremendously difficult to extend to aquatic and terrestrial ecosystems, where output and input rules for sustainability encounter complex interdependencies among resource uses, energy throughputs, and mass balances (Daly 1989). The point here is not to grasp a theory of the impossible but to promote the art of the practical, which involves creatively employing "best guess" science to implement prudent rules of thumb that help guarantee sustainability.

A second-generation EA process is needed to support this new modus operandi (Sadler and Jacobs 1990). The building blocks of this emerging model are outlined in figure 1-1. In this framework, EA is identified as a generic approach that encompasses two scales of analysis (EA and SEA) and their linkage with other policy instruments. EA is applied to all classes of economic activity with potential resource or ecological effects and is linked (with risk

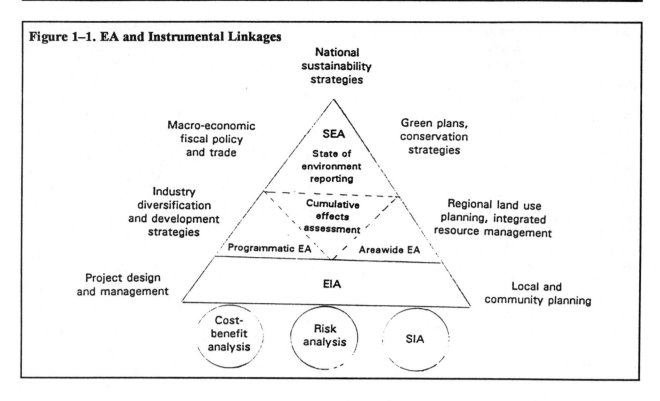

Figure 1–1. EA and Instrumental Linkages

assessment, SIA, and cost-benefit analysis), into comprehensive project review to ensure sustainability. SEA extends the principles of EA to cover the development policies, plans and programs that govern the conversion and depletion of natural capital. This embryonic approach must now be coordinated with other strategies and instruments for environment-economy integration (as shown in figure 1-1).

In this context, SEA may be seen as a vector for moving from the standard to the sustainability agenda. Specifically, this process can help to: instill and integrate environmental goals and principles into the highest levels of policymaking; ensure that economic and fiscal agencies are responsible and accountable for the environmental consequences of their choices and actions; and promote long–term changes in attitudes and assumptions about economic growth. When comparing these, the key point to note is the progression from EA-based approaches toward more integrated methods of environmental-economic principles.

Evolving Approaches to SEA

The approach taken to SEA will vary with purpose and context and a number of initiatives are either in place already or are under consideration. When comparing these, the key point to note is the progression from EA-based approaches toward more

integrated methods of environmental-economic analysis.

In many developing countries, however, various constraints impede the introduction of EA and, by extension, SEA (Abel and Stocking 1981). Major barriers include lack of resources, shortage of requisite skills, and an absence of environmental laws or a failure to enforce them (Kennedy 1988). In response, international aid programs are now beginning to directly address the problems through environmental requirements, training and institution-building. These efforts provide important and timely opportunities for demonstrating and adapting EA practice to the requirements of developing countries (Marshall and others 1988). However, because the experience in developing countries is limited, the following analysis is selective and largely restricted to industrial countries.

Overview of SEA Experience

The United Nations Economic Commission for Europe (UNECE) has established a task force to study the frameworks, procedures, and mechanisms for applying EA principles to policies, programs, and plans. A draft report is being circulated among member countries for comment (UNECE in preparation). Provisional conclusions are that SEA is necessary and feasible, and it will be most effective when applied at the earliest possible stage of policy evolution. This approach is seen as providing an added capability for anticipating and highlighting potential problems and assisting long-term planning. It is expected that the final report will recommend that SEA should reflect, as much as possible, elements of project EA (for example, screening, scoping, the evaluation, and documentation). So far, only a few member countries have institutionalized SEA or equivalent processes.

A commitment to this approach is part of recent reforms to the Canadian EA system. The *Canadian Environmental Assessment Act* (1992) prescribes the process for project assessment; and although policy and program assessment is not covered, it is required by cabinet directive (Government of Canada 1990). This is a major departure from previous practice. Draft guidelines are under preparation and were discussed at two recent international workshops, involving Australia, Canada, and New Zealand (1991) and Canada and the Netherlands (1992). In present form, the proposed approach relies heavily on EA-based procedures.

By contrast, the United Kingdom guidelines on Policy Appraisal and the Environment recommend the application of extended benefit-cost analysis (U.K. Department of the Environment 1991). Environmental effects are to be considered with other economic and social factors during the design of policy options—with a view to clarifying trade-offs and identifying a preferred alternative. In effect, impact assessment and policy analysis are merged into environmental-economic evaluation. The recommended approach also draws on risk assessment. Scientific uncertainties regarding environmental impacts are to be handled according to precautionary principles, such as reducing "acceptable" risks "as low as reasonably practicable" (ALARP).

In Australia, the commonwealth and state governments have various discretionary provisions pertaining to SEA. The Resources Assessment Commission Act (1989) provides a mandate for public inquiry into resource allocation conflicts at the industry or sector level. The Resource Assessment Commission is required to promote an integrated approach to development and conservation, to take account of economic, environment and social equity values to the community, and to settle disputes "as far as possible." Other strengths of this process include its potential for comprehensive, independent review of policy options (Craig 1989). The Resource Assessment Commission process is examined further in the next section.

A further level of integration is the application of SEA as part of an integrated policy and institutional framework for sustainable development. To date, very few countries have adopted such an approach:

• The New Zealand Resource Management Act (1991) has replaced a plethora of planning and regulatory statutes with a single law with one purpose: to promote sustainable land and resource use. Previously required only for major projects, EA now must be applied to most resource consents and to urban and regional plans. The processes and mechanisms for integrating EA and planning practices are still being designed. Future directions will be strongly influenced by the policy guidelines on sustainability that are established, the extent to which regional plans are directed at managing cumulative environmental impacts, and the effort that is put into retraining personnel (Dixon 1991).

• The Netherlands National Environmental Policy Plan is the most radical strategy for sustainability proposed by an industrial nation (Ministry for Housing, Physical Planning and the Environment 1989). It calls for drastic reductions in many industrial emissions and wastes, backed by clean-up of contaminated soils to restore and maintain environmental carrying capacities within the time frame of a generation. A mix of policy, economic, regulatory, and negotiation measures are deployed to reduce risks and impacts at source (by closing raw materials-production-waste cycles). EA is not specifically discussed in the Plan; however, the Dutch Evaluation Committee recommended in 1990 that EA be applied to concepts introduced in the Plan and to land reconstruction plans (the basis of physical planning in the Netherlands).

Regional and sectoral EAs are part of the operational requirements of the World Bank (1991) and other lending and aid agencies. Environmental profiles, national conservation strategies and similar approaches are also widely promoted to provide a sustainability context for review of development policies (Halle and Furtado 1988).

Several developing countries have implemented or adopted conservation-based development models. For example, Costa Rica's National Conservation Strategy for Sustainable Development (ECODES) outlines a series of policies, programs, and action plans for biodiversity and wildlands protection, integrated land and water management, reforestation and related initiatives (Solis 1992); Bhutan and the Maldives have adopted eco-tourism strategies based on strict capacities to regulate visitor numbers and activities.

Other relevant trends center on international training, networking, and research activities to strengthen EA in developing countries. These are now beginning to include SEA. The organization of special sessions and workshops at conferences and meetings held by the International Association for Impact Assessment (IAIA) are recent initiatives. The Indonesian Ministry of the Environment and IAIA, for example, have collaborated in studying options for applying SIA concepts to population policy issues. In developing countries, SEA could be accelerated by international agreements on institution-building for sustainable development initialled at the Earth Summit.

Options for Tiering and Linkages

Experience to date with SEA exemplifies the potential range of choice for process development. What may be termed the standard model of SEA involves the application of EA procedures to review policy, program, and planning proposals. SEA also may be employed to support, as well as check, policy design

or to integrate it with other instruments as part of a comprehensive realignment of decisionmaking processes to make them fully consistent with sustainability principles. These alternatives are not, of course, mutually exclusive. Policy review and design are closely interrelated, and the phased development of SEA can contribute to their further integration.

A tiered (or vertically integrated) process of policy, program and plan review is usually recommended by proponents of SEA (see Wood and Djeddour 1992). Tiering means simply the sequential process of addressing issues and impacts at the appropriate level and with the degree of effort required for decisionmaking, and is already a familiar concept in EA. For example, screening identifies the level of examination necessary for different types of projects and classes of activity. The extension of tiering to focus and coordinate SEA and EA as complementary activities should prove cost-effective. Relevant experience with this approach in California is discussed by Bass (1991).

Figure 1-2 illustrates the tiering of SEA and EA to facilitate a systematic review of key issues (justification, alternatives, and mitigation) in energy development. Each stage establishes ongoing requirements and directions for the next phase of

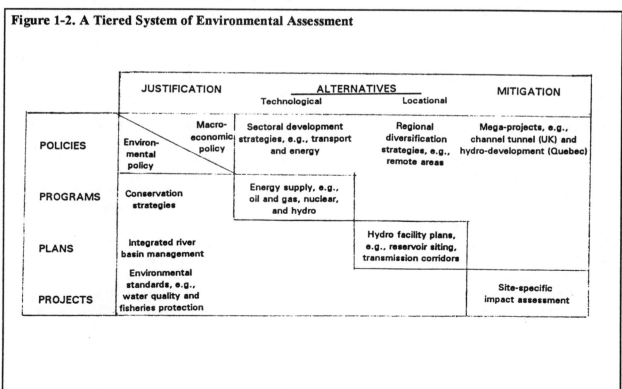

Figure 1-2. A Tiered System of Environmental Assessment

analysis. The decisionmaking "staircase" is framed by a portfolio of economic policies (the horizontal box) that also will be subject to SEA. A comparable group of environmental policies (the vertical box) provides an initial benchmark against which reviews may be conducted. This framework corresponds with a disciplined and adaptive approach to EA, one that permits a certain degree of substitution of effort between different levels (Sadler 1986).

SEA may also be linked (or horizontally integrated) with other policy and planning instruments (identified in figure 1-1), and directed toward "full-cost accounting" of natural capital losses. Environment-economy integration might be instituted initially at the macro-policy level by comparing state of the environment reports with national economic accounts, and then systematically advanced through the preparation of green plans and sustainability strategies (see IUCN, UNEP, and WWF 1991). Industry sectors that have major environmental impacts should be reviewed to identify problem areas and to propose practical solutions, with targets and time frames for implementation. This approach is exemplified by the report of the Australian Ecologically Sustainable Development Working Groups (1991). Finally, full-cost accounting of development programs must be "ecologically grounded" by regional planning that adjusts land uses to resource potentials (Richardson 1989) and provides an integrated context for project assessment (Sadler and Jacobs 1990).

Of course, tiered, integrated EA systems that link policy and project appraisal are difficult to design and apply. The following example indicates how existing SEA and EA elements might be recast into a "second-generation" process to ensure sustainability:

• Screening of economic and development policies for their conformity with sustainability goals and principles (for example, identifying environmentally perverse subsidies).

• Preliminary assessment of environmental costs of development programs to identify low-impact, resource-efficient energy, transportation and manufacturing strategies.

• Areawide assessment to establish resource and land use zoning systems for regional development.

• Extending project EA to identify in-kind compensation for loss of natural capital (for example, offsetting residual fish and wildlife losses in one location by rehabilitating habitats elsewhere).

Institutional and Methodological Challenges

Many institutional and methodological barriers stand in the way of the introduction of SEA. A practical strategy of process development must take into account the realities of policymaking, as well as the limitations imposed by current tools and techniques.

Policymaking, according to Doern (1990) "is often examined simplistically," and environmental issues in particular would prove the responsiveness and adaptiveness of policymaking. They are typically complex and controversial, cutting across a range of values, interests and policy sectors, and often result in trade-offs through a political process of bargaining and compromise (O'Riordan 1976). The point emphasized here is the multi-faceted nature of economic and environmental policymaking and the permutations of process and outcome that may require practical account in SEA.

Prerequisites and Provisions for SEA

All countries (and agencies) have a characteristic political and organizational culture of policymaking: the customary institutional arrangements (laws, rules, conventions, etc.) that frame strategy, guide choice, shape analysis, and influence judgement. Several interrelated aspects of political culture bear on the transition from EA to SEA (O'Riordan and Sewell 1981):

• The character of the policymaking process, whether it is open or closed, pluralistic or elitist, innovative or traditional (for example, how would it introduce analytical techniques and mechanisms for dispute settlement).

• The level of political accountability, measured by due process, access to information, and recourse to the courts.

• The degree of activism and influence of interest and community groups, reflected by their ability to mobilize resources, undertake critical analysis, and generate political pressure.

These dimensions provide an initial framework for analyzing whether and under what circumstances SEA may be incorporated into policymaking.

POLITICAL AND BUREAUCRATIC RESPONSIVENESS. These factors will determine whether SEA is applied (political) and the effectiveness of the process followed (bureaucratic). Political will is the main (perhaps only) precondition for institutional reform. However, the responsiveness of bureaucracy to the introduction of SEA can dictate the tempo and thoroughness of process implementation. For example, the Canadian government's directive on policy and program assessment (1990) was to be "implemented immediately," but the process has every appearance of in fact being introduced slowly and unevenly. Many of the central agencies and line departments of government, reportedly, still have serious reservations about the impact of this initiative on their jurisdictional responsibilities, as well as practical concerns with proposed procedures.

From a sustainability perspective, SEA may gain maximum leverage on decisionmaking by being used to review the macro-economic policies that initiate and give direction to subsequent programs, plans, and projects. Yet the incorporation of SEA at this stage also seems more likely to be controversial and complicated than at subsequent levels. Policy determination is the prerogative of ministers and their most senior advisors who guard their turf zealously and have the power to block or co-opt reforms. This will certainly be the case if questions of confidentiality or constitutionality are raised by, for example, the pre-release of budget information or the possibility of Cabinet decisions being opened to scrutiny. Often, however, the reluctance to open policymaking to systematic assessment extends to all contentious issues. In these circumstances, public involvement remains the best counterweight against political and bureaucratic discretion.

SCOPE OF COVERAGE. As noted previously, the policy-making process does not necessarily correspond to the idealized, hierarchical sequence outlined in figure 1-2. It is more realistic to think of policymaking as a complex filtration process in which the range of choice tends to be channelled along preselected lines by ideology, convention and technical bias (O'Riordan 1976). Decision cycles "back upward" as well as "flow downward" and are affected by events in contingent policy sectors. Often, development policies are molded implicitly by the precedent of large–scale projects or the accumulated weight of incremental choices and activities. These processes are exemplified by recent environmental reviews of major energy and water development schemes (Sadler 1987; 1990a,b).

In most cases, the result is a "nested basket" of interdependent public policies (Sproule-Jones 1989), characterized by a mix of "top-down" strategies and "bottom-up" preemptions. A differentiated process of SEA will be necessary in order to achieve a reasonable coverage of actual policy structures. For present purposes, three policymaking configurations may be identified:

• *Routine decisions (policy as usual).* Routine policies tend to reflect past precedent and, typically, contain little recognition of environmental consequences. A wide array of conventional economic development and resource management programs have cumulative effects on the "source and sink" capacities of natural systems. Examples include agricultural expansion policies that lead to wetland habitat losses or irrigation programs that cause salinization of soils. In this context, environmental audits of policies and programs should be conducted on an "impact priority" basis. Other less environmentally significant sectors could be dealt with through annual or occasional policy audits.

• *Strategic choices (policy initiatives).* Policy innovations may be introduced in response to political crisis or to set out developmental priorities. These should be subject to immediate application of SEA. Recent Canadian proposals, for example, call for SEA to be integrated with the preparation of Cabinet memoranda. Each year, "about a thousand such decision and policy cycles occur" (Doern 1990), although only a limited number warrant close environmental review. More to the point, the annual budget should be seen as an "environmental statement" (MacNeill, Winsemius, and Yakushiji 1991). It outlines the spending decisions that in aggregate will serve to either increase or reduce the natural capital of a country, and affords a "single window" of opportunity for application of SEA to economic and development policy.

• *Overriding priorities (policy definition).* The key priorities of governments, whether driven by ideology or events, define the direction of policy. In some cases, they are exemplified by structural, mandate-defining decisions, which carry a high political profile. Often, these decisions will be off-limits to environmental assessment or subject only to defensive, after-the-fact review. Respective examples are the Free Trade Agreement between the United States and Canada (where the environmental implications went unassessed), and the subsequent tri-country North American Free Trade Agreement (where an ex-post SEA is under preparation by Environment Canada). Looking ahead, international trade negotiations are shaping the economics of global and regional sustainability and must be restructured to proactively consider environmental concerns (French 1992). SEA can be applied to good effect in this regard.

PUBLIC INVOLVEMENT. This might be the litmus test of the utility and effectiveness of SEA. Public consultation has driven many of the recent EA process innovations and has helped to promote accountability in government decisionmaking. There is good reason why public scrutiny and input should be an integral part of SEA, with certain exemptions to safeguard Cabinet and fiscal confidentiality.

Key questions in public involvement are: who will be consulted, at what stage in the process, and with which methods? The record on this first question is mixed but encouraging. On the one hand, much development policymaking still takes place behind closed doors, and involves a relatively small number of power holders and brokers who set the agenda or depart from it to placate vested interests. On the other hand, important innovations have occurred in opening energy and resources policy to wide-ranging consultation (Sadler 1985) and in establishing collaborative forums for environmental dispute settlement (Tryzna and Gotelli 1990). There are also indications that these processes are being institutionalized. An important example is the roundtable movement in Canada, which attempts to involve all sectors and interests in an ongoing dialogue on the "response necessary for the transition to a sustainable society" (National Roundtable on the Environment and the Economy 1992).

This experience, allied to that in project EA, provides a sound basis for public involvement in SEA. It also indicates the different forms that this relationship can assume. Some aspects of policy review may require little more than public scrutiny. Others will lend themselves to wide-ranging public consultation, or to mediated negotiations and other consensus-building dialogues. A disciplined approach to public involvement in SEA is suggested by the policy typology outlined below.

Procedures for SEA

Initially, SEA procedures can be adapted from those for project EA. A flexible, cost-effective approach will be necessary, rather than a doctrinaire equation of SEA as EA. Senior EA administrators at the 1991 Australia-Canada-New Zealand workshop warned that the latter strategy would be counterproductive. Wherever possible, SEA and project EA should be complementary processes (see figure 1-2). SEA

procedures should be drafted with this principle in mind and streamlined to avoid duplication of activities best undertaken at later stages:

• *Initiation and screening* establishes the level of analysis required indicating whether no action is needed or whether a full or preliminary EA should be undertaken.

• *Analysis and reporting* covers the main steps involved in conducting full or preliminary assessment and preparing a statement of environmental effects (a succinct, policy-relevant interpretation of findings). Preliminary assessments will establish the protocols and arrangements for further analysis of programs, plans and projects; full assessments will result in a policy proposal being revised or given environmental clearance.

• *Monitoring and follow-up* includes overseeing the implementation of decisions made at the second stage, including continuity and integration with subsequent phases of program, plan or project assessment.

A flow chart for the application of SEA is outlined in figure 1-3, and generic procedural guidelines for each stage of decisionmaking are annotated in box 1-1.

The flow chart and accompanying procedures are intended to serve only as starting point for further discussion and specific applications. The proposed guidelines, for example, reflect the principle of self-assessment by initiating agencies. Self-assessment is based on the premise that proponents of a policy or project are in the best position to integrate environmental considerations into decisionmaking. It is usually bolstered by other mechanisms to ensure compliance with procedures and promote effective implementation. These mechanisms will assume particular importance with regard to SEA because of its potentially controversial nature. At the policymaking level, for example, social values assume greater prominence and decisions are more open-ended, less technical than in project EA. It will also be necessary to specify what constitutes appropriate standards of performance for SEA.

Methods and Techniques of Analysis

At the policy level, the scientific and technical uncertainties associated with impact assessment become written much larger. SEA can be generally expected to deal with chains of environmental effects and consequences that are less concrete, and more attenuated than those encountered at the project level. This context of analysis, at a minimum, indicates the need for adaptation of current EA methods and techniques. It may also require more far reaching adjustments; such as the integration of EA tools with those of policy analysis. An initial perspective on these questions can be derived from operational experience with project EA.

LESSONS FOR PROJECT ASSESSMENT. EA has undergone extensive methodological development. Several comprehensive reviews have been undertaken of the scientific basis, technical content, and analytical techniques of the field (Beanlands and Duinker 1983; Caldwell and others 1983; Environmental Resources Ltd. 1984; Sadler 1987). These studies underline the continuing methodological limitations of EA despite recent advances. Scientific understanding is insufficient to make accurate predictions of the environmental impacts of development activity, and this deficiency has been compounded by the relative lack of monitoring and follow-up. As a result, an adaptive, integrative approach to EA still remains prescribed in the literature, rather than applied in practice (Sadler 1988).

The adaptive approach, pioneered by Holling and others (1978), seems well suited to SEA. It provides an intellectual framework for analysis that is explicitly aimed at coping with uncertainty to assist policy design. A range of techniques are mobilized to understand environment-development interactions and consequences. Many of these are applied already in EA. By definition, however, adaptive EA orchestrates methods and techniques in a continuing, trial and error evaluation of management options (rather than applying them to a conventional, one-shot impact prediction). The emphasis is on an interactive policy dialogue, in which analysis aids negotiation and vice-versa.

At the policy level, the traditional "before and after" project framework for EA will be difficult to apply. EA audits indicate (not unexpectedly) that the accuracy of impact predictions tend to be inversely related to the scope and complexity of environment-activity relationships under investigation. The

---

Box 1-1. Draft Procedural Guidelines for SEA

Initiation and Screening

• Policy initiating agencies must screen all proposals *as early as possible* to identify their potential environmental consequences.

• They must also determine (if necessary in consultation with the supervisory authority) whether the initiative will be subject to preliminary or full SEA.

• A full SEA may be required for policies that are not divisible into discrete programs, plans and projects (for example, immigration and fiscal policies), or that have global or cumulative environmental effects that may be only or best dealt with at the policy level (for example, emissions and climate warming; urban development and habitat/landscape conversion). A preliminary SEA will be supplemented by more detailed impact analysis at a later stage (for programs, plans or projects).

Analysis and Reporting

A preliminary or full SEA may encompass the following activities:

• Describe the purpose, objectives and context of the proposed initiative, including the options reviewed or under consideration.

• Scope the direct and indirect environmental linkages, consequences and trade-offs of the proposed policy, and/or the main alternatives, including, wherever possible, magnitude, probability, timing and location of occurrence.

• Assess the relative and net significance of potential effects in relation to sustainability guidelines, environmental standards, etc., and identify risks of irreversible or unacceptable ecological changes (for example, loss of species, reduction in biodiversity).

• Identify options and measures for mitigation, amelioration and compensation (including in-kind investments of natural capital) of environmental effects, and where necessary, a benefit-cost and sensitivity analysis.

• File a draft SEA statement for review and comment by the competent authority, designated agencies and other interested parties.

• Submit final report and recommendations to policymakers in a decision-relevant format.

Monitoring and Follow-Up

• Policy initiating agencies are responsible for implementing the decisions made at this stage, including environmental terms and conditions for proposals and protocols for further assessment.

• The supervisory authority will oversee these arrangements and may make additional provisions as necessary to ensure continuity and integration with program, plan and project assessment.

• SEA statements will be treated as an initial scoping exercise for purposes of ongoing impact analysis.

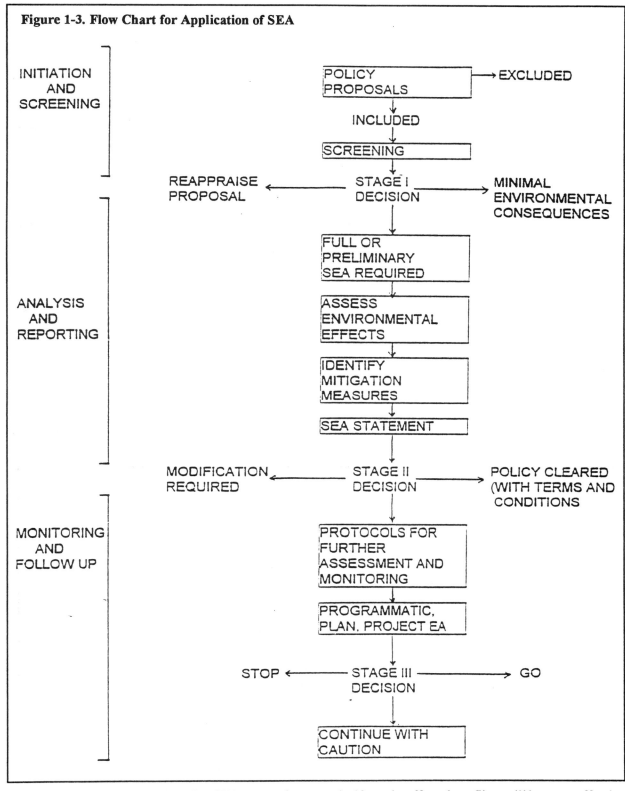

Figure 1-3. Flow Chart for Application of SEA

extended time and space scales of an SEA means that even more factors will affect the results of policy review, often in unforeseen ways. Under these circumstances, relatively simple methods that help clarify trade-offs and conflicts will be most effective for initial analysis, rather than the application of more complicated models (de Jongh 1988). This approach also establishes the basis for an iterative process of analysis tailored to the longer time frames and less onerous information requirements of policymaking (Wathern 1988).

AN INITIAL TOOL KIT. The analytical tasks involved in conducting an SEA can be structured in order to manage the uncertainties described above and link this approach firmly to decisionmaking requirements. For this purpose, the environmental effects of policy proposals may be classified into three categories: implications, issues, and impacts. Each category corresponds with and facilitates choice of methods of analysis. This typology is consistent with and exemplifies the tiering strategy and draft procedures introduced earlier. It also lends itself to a stepped methodology, beginning with the tools of policy analysis and ending with those of impact assessment. In fact, these two analyses make up the basic tool kit for SEA (Wood and Djeddour 1992).

Policy and planning techniques that may be applied include: forecasting and scenario building, simulation exercises, decision trees, geographic information systems and resource suitability analysis, multi-criteria evaluation, goals-achievement matrix, and planning balance sheet (see Nijkamp 1980; McAllister 1980). EA and risk evaluation techniques that seem useful include matrices and checklists, systems and impact modelling, best/worst case estimates, and sensitivity analysis (see Bisset 1988; Cohrssen and Corvello 1989). In addition, there is both opportunity and incentive to incorporate economic techniques into this list (Whitney 1985), especially given recent advances in estimating environmental values and integrating a sustainability criterion into cost-benefit analysis (Pearce and Turner 1990).

The above sources, though separate, are not mutually exclusive. SEA will probably require combined methods of policy, impact and economic analysis, and must integrate these with consultation and negotiation techniques. Public involvement may be solicited passively or actively, informally or formally, and employ a variety of methods: surveys, open houses, meetings, hearings, workshops, advisory and Delphi groups, policy dialogues, and roundtables. Guidelines on the application of consultative methods have been prepared for EA practitioners (see Praxis Ltd. 1988) and for use by all parties in project and policy reviews (Sadler 1980). Recent experience with practical approaches to environmental mediation and other alternative dispute resolution mechanisms is also well documented (see Susskind and Cruikshank 1987).

Three Case Studies

In the final analysis, the application of methods and procedures for SEA is best illustrated by practical example. The problem, of course is that there are few prototype studies on which to draw. With certain qualifications, the three cases reviewed below indicate the analytical scope and tasks involved in reviewing the environmental implications, issues, and impacts, respectively, of economic and development policy.

Environmental Assessment of the Federal Budget

The Environmental Assessment of the Federal Budget is somewhat misnamed by its authors (Resource Futures International 1991). It is a preliminary commentary on the environmental implications of Canadian government expenditures and is limited to three major sectors (energy, agriculture and industrial policy). Even so, the conclusions of the analysis highlight important discrepancies between stated commitments to environment-economy integration and fiscal priorities. The real value of this exercise lies in demonstrating the value of scrutinizing annual budgets as environmental statements and illustrating what can and should be done.

The examination of expenditures was conducted with reference to four principles of sustainability:

• Anticipation and prevention of environmental problems (do expenditures encourage emphasis on energy efficiency or soil conservation?).

• Environment-economy integration or full cost accounting (do sectoral programs subsidize environmental deterioration?).

• Equal competition of options (are government interventions biased against low-impact energy or agriculture?).

• Least-cost planning (in the case of energy) and support for environmental values (in the case of agriculture and industry).

The "quick turnaround" response to a budget release (followed in this case) may be improved by adapting resource accounting methods (see Pearce, Markandya and Barbier 1989). A trial balance sheet, for example, might be drawn up of defensive or conservation allocations versus conventional economic growth expenditures. Subsequently, net or sector estimates of environmental damages (or projected adjustments for natural capital depreciation) could be developed by an expert group. This approach, heavily hedged with qualifications, is also suggestive of a surrogate assessment of the environmental 'impact' of a budget. More proactively, "green budgeting" might employ the type of interactive policy exercise now recommended for building scenarios of sustainability (see Brewer, 1986).

The Forest and Timber Inquiry

This study by the Resource Assessment Commission (1991) of the multiple, often controversial, issues associated with the use and management of Australian forests provides important lessons for SEA. It combined industry and government submissions, public hearings, and independent technical analyses. The methods employed included: resource capability, tenure and use inventories; evaluation of forest management strategies and institutional arrangements; wood supply and demand projections; and economic, social and environmental trend analysis. Of particular methodological interest were: (a) the review of the environmental effects of logging, covering soil productivity aquatic systems, flora and fauna, nutrient recycling, and the function of forests as a sink for sequestering carbon dioxide; (b) the survey of the social and cultural uses and values of forests and community attitudes to management issues; and (c) the identification of five strategies of forest use and management, ranging from maximization of timber production to no further logging of native species. These policy alternatives were designed to facilitate public choice and canvass response, including comment on the methodology used in scenario building.

Further specification of the scenarios in sustainability language would have been helpful, especially for the intermediate options (business as usual, industry growth and revitalization, and transfer of timber production from native forests to plantations). In addition, there were and are potential opportunities for conciliation and mediation, or perhaps even arbitration of residual controversies. For example, opinion is still polarized over preservation versus use of old-growth forests, especially for areas with potential heritage significance. A "test-case" negotiation and agreement or ruling in the context of the strategy finally adopted by the government(s) may prove worthwhile, and would be consistent with the Resource Assessment Commission's mandate to settle disputes "as far as possible."

EA Panel Review of Beaufort Sea Hydrocarbon Production and Transportation Proposal

The EA panel review of the Beaufort Sea Hydrocarbon Production and Transportation Proposal combines elements of policy, program, plan and project review (Federal Environmental Assessment Review Office 1984). This hybrid process, unprecedented to date in Canada and possibly elsewhere, reflected the sheer magnitude of the $40 billion proposal for Arctic offshore and onshore oil and gas production. An enormous range of environmental and social issues were at stake, virtually amounting to a choice of future for Northern Canada and especially for its indigenous peoples. The task of identifying the potential impacts of the development scheme was undertaken and extended into the policy arena by both design and implication—not least because the proposal was referred for review in preliminary or concept form with many provisional components that were dependent on unproven technology.

A multi-component review process included both conventional and innovative approaches and methods. For present purposes, there were three notable features: (a) extensive public review of a seven-volume environmental impact statement (EIS) of the biophysical and socio-economic effects and risks associated with the proposed development; (b) policy and institutional analysis of government planning and management capabilities; and (c) ex-post evaluation of process effectiveness.

The evaluation confirmed the importance of a phased, integrated approach to strategic and project EA (Sadler 1990a). In the Beaufort Sea case, the EA process led to the introduction of conservation (later sustainability) strategies and regional land use planning. These components, ideally, should guide project review. Where they are absent, the preparation of an environmental management strategy (EMS) rather than EIS can provide an initial framework for guiding planning and analysis of regional development schemes. The recommended approach is analogous to the negotiation of "commitment packages" in the Netherlands, which include a schedule of studies and contingency plans explicitly designed to cope with uncertainty (de Jongh 1988). Large-scale development schemes that require extensive, phased EA should be explicitly treated as research and management experiments, with monitoring and audit protocols designed to facilitate learning from experience and improving understanding and practice (Sadler 1987, 1988; Davies and Sadler 1990).

The Beaufort Sea review points to certain adaptations of EA methods that are required at the regional scale. For example, the linkage of scoping and negotiation techniques can help in the identification of ecological values, and in clarifying the issues and trade-offs at stake. Subsequently, resource sensitivity mapping is useful for delineating development impact zones; regional characterization of ecological processes facilitates initial judgements about risk variability and cumulative effects; and impact hypotheses focus current understanding of "cause and effect" relationships among proposed development activities and potential ecological losses (for example, behavior of oil spills under ice-fast versus open-water conditions, and the short and long term repercussions on "slow-recovery" Arctic marine systems). This conceptual framework, which is most appropriately built through interactive science workshops, establishes the basis for ongoing research, impact analysis and monitoring programs (see Cornford, O'Riordan and Sadler 1985; Everitt, Birdsall and Stone 1986).

Conclusions and Recommendations

SEA of policies, programs and plans provides an important avenue for improving project EA and redirecting the total approach to meet sustainability imperatives. By itself, SEA likely will be insufficient for this larger purpose. Ideally, it should be part of or lead to the design of integrated, adaptive environment and economic decisionmaking, in which a range of analytical and consultative instruments are employed.

Recent experience illustrates the range of SEA options that are either being applied or are under consideration. These include a "standard" model, based on the adoption and adaptation of EA procedures and methods. It is also evident that this approach must be tailored to the realities of policymaking, rather than to normative assumptions about how this process should work. Salient lessons, in this regard, can be drawn form institutional analysis and from limited case experience with prototype SEA. This chapter has proposed several preliminary classifications and guidelines for generic process development—which probably will be soon overtaken by emerging practice.

At present, the status of SEA is analogous to that of EA in the early 1970s. With the benefit of twenty years of experience, theorists and practitioners should be in a better position to both initiate and capitalize on the launching of SEA. In the initial phase, careful monitoring and evaluation will be critical to both advancing and disseminating tried and tested approaches. Experimental research should be at the forefront of SEA process development, rather than be an afterthought—as it was for much of the evolution of EA. No doubt, the development of this approach will be a long haul with much resistance, but so was the road from NEPA to Principle 17 of the Rio Declaration.

Several immediate and interim research priorities for advancing SEA can be identified:

• The relationship of SEA and sustainability must be translated into operational terms (rather than explored in generalities). Natural capital, for example, is an important organizing concept for this purpose; it now requires specification as rules for the conduct of SEA and EA.

• Further case studies are required of the effectiveness of alternative policy and EA-based procedures and methods for SEA (rather than drafting shopping lists of techniques). In relation to institutional realities of decisionmaking, it is important to understand what works, what doesn't and why.

• Subsequently, comparative studies of initial experiences with formal and informal SEA processes will help improve the productivity and facilitate the dissemination of this approach. These studies could be launched through formal channels, such as UNECE, or through professional networks for information exchange, such as IAIA.

• Pilot and demonstration projects will be particularly helpful for "hands on" applications of SEA in developing countries. Such "experiment and learn" approaches can also be used in extending SEA to social equity concerns.

• Looking ahead, education and training will become progressively more important as SEA evolves. Professional and technical learning can be accelerated by integrating these processes with the research strategies identified above.

Notes

1. Environmental impact assessment, as a national instrument, shall be undertaken for proposed activities that are likely to have a significant adverse impact on the environment and are subject to a decision of a competent national authority.

2. Policymaking, simply defined, is what governments choose to do or not do (Dye 1972). This process encompasses a range of interrelated decisions, substantive and symbolic,

general and specific, and public and secret. For present purposes, the relationship between different levels and types of decision making is important to understanding the options for SEA.

3. In this paper, policies, plans and programs are characterized as a logical hierarchy of activities. At the top of the pyramid are the policies or the statements of intent and purpose, that give direction to planning, programming and project development. The reality of policymaking, of course, is more complicated, as discussed in this chapter.

References

Abel, N., and M. Stocking. 1981. "The Experience of Underdeveloped Countries." In T. O'Riordan and W.R.D. Sewell, eds., *Project Appraisal and Policy Review* New York: John Wiley and Sons.

Ballard, S.C., M.D. Devine, T.E. James and M.A. Chartock. 1982. "Integrated Regional Environmental Assessments: Purposes, Scope and Products." *Impact Assessment Bulletin* 2: 5-13.

Bartlett, R.V. 1988. "Policy and impact assessment: an introduction." *Impact Assessment Bulletin* 6: 73-74.

Bass, R. 1991. "Policy, Plan and Program EIA in California." *EIA Newsletter* 5: 4-5.

Beanlands, G.E. and P.N. Duinker. 1983. *An Ecological Framework for Environmental Impact Assessment in Canada*. Halifax: Dalhousie University, Institute for Resource and Environmental Studies.

Bird, P.M., and D.J. Rapport. 1986. *State of the Environment Report for Canada*. Ottawa: Environment Canada.

Biswas, A.K. and Q. Geping, eds. 1987. *Environmental Impact Assessment in Developing Countries*. London: Tycooly International.

Boothroyd, P. 1990. "On Using Environmental Assessment to Promote Fair Sustainable Development." In P. Jacobs and B. Sadler, eds., *Sustainable Development and Environmental Assessment: Perspectives in Planning for a Common Future*. Hull: Canadian Environmental Assessment Research Council.

Brewer, G.D. 1986. "Methods for Synthesis: Policy Exercises." In W.C. Clark and R.E. Munn, eds., *Sustainable Development of the Biosphere*. New York: Cambridge University Press.

Brown, L. 1990. *State of the World*. New York: Norton/Worldwatch.

Caldwell, L.K. 1982. *Science and the National Environmental Policy Act*. Birmingham: University of Alabama Press.

———. 1983. *A Study of Ways to Improve the Scientific Content and Methodology of Environmental Impact Analysis*. PB 83-222851. Springfield, Virginia: National Technical Information Service.

Canadian Environmental Assessment Research Council and US National Research Council. 1986. *Cumulative Environmental Effects: A Binational Perspective*. Ottawa and Washington DC.

Caring for the Earth. 1991. Gland, Switzerland: IUCN- The World Conservation Union, UNEP- United Nations Environment Program, WWF- World Wide Fund for Nature.

Clark, S.D., ed. 1981. *Environmental Assessment in Australia and Canada*. Vancouver: Westwater Research Centre.

Cohrssen, J.J. and Covello, V.T. 1989. *Risk Analysis: A Guide to Principles and Methods for Analyzing Health and Environmental Risks*. Washington DC: Council on Environmental Quality.

Cornford, A.B., J. O'Riordan, and B. Sadler. 1985. "Planning, Assessment and Implementation: A Strategy for Integration." In B. Sadler, ed. *Environmental Protection and Resource Development: Convergence for Today*. Calgary: University of Calgary Press.

Craig, D. 1989. "Sustainable Development and Indigenous People." In *Environmental Practice - Sustainable Development*. Proceedings of Second National Conference. Canberra: Environment Institute of Australia.

Daly, H.E. 1989. *Sustainable Development: Towards an Operational Definition*. Washington, DC: The World Bank.

Davies, M. and B. Sadler. 1990. *Post-Project Analysis and the Improvement of Guidelines for Environmental Monitoring and Audit*. Environment Canada Report EPS 6/FA/1, Ottawa.

de Jongh, P. 1988. "Uncertainty in EIA." In P. Wathern, ed. *Environmental Impact Assessment : Theory and Practice*. London: Unwin Hyman.

Dixon, J. 1991. "Idea and Action: Understanding Planning Practice." Paper presented at the Regional Resource Futures Conference, University of Waikato. Hamilton, New Zealand.

Doern, G.B. 1990. "Canadian Environmental Policy: Why Process is Almost Everything." *Commentary* 19: 1-11.

Dye, T.R. 1972. *Understanding Public Policy*. Englewood Cliffs: Prentice Hall.

Ecologically Sustainable Developing Working Groups. 1991. *Final Report*. Canberra: Commonwealth of Australia.

Environmental Resources Ltd. 1984. *Prediction in Environmental Impact Assessment*. The Hague: Ministry of Public Housing, Physical Planning and Environmental Affairs.

Evaluation Committee. 1990. *Towards a Better Procedure to Protect the Environment-Summary*. Report No. 3. The Hague.

Everitt. R.R., D.A. Birdsall, and D. Stone,. 1986. "The Beaufort Sea Monitoring Program." In R. Lang, ed. *Integrated Approaches to Resource Planning and Management*. Calgary: The University of Calgary Press.

Federal Environmental Assessment Review Office. 1984. *Beaufort Sea Hydrocarbon Production and Transportation Proposal*. Report of the Environmental Assessment Panel. Hull.

French, H.F. 1992. "Strengthening global environmental governance." In L. Brown, *State of the World 1992*. New York: Norton/Worldwatch.

Goodland, R., and H. Daly. 1991. "Approaching Global Environmental Sustainability." *World Development* 2:35-41;3:64-71.

Government of Canada. 1990. *Federal Environmental Assessment: New Directions*. Ottawa: Supply and Services Canada.

Halle, M. and J. Furtado. 1988. "The Role of National Conservation Strategies in Attaining the Objectives of the World Conservation Strategy." In P. Jacobs and D.A. Munro, eds., *Conservation with Equity: Strategies for Sustainable Development*. New York: Cambridge University Press.

Holling, C.S. 1978. *Adaptive Environmental Assessment and Management*. New York: John Wiley and Sons.

Kay, J.J. 1991. "The Concept of Ecological Integrity, Alternative Theories of Ecology and the Implications for Decision Support Indicators." In *Economic, Ecological and Decision Theories*. Ottawa: Canadian Environmental Advisory Council.

Kennedy, W.V. 1988. "Environmental Impact Assessment and Bilateral Development Aid: An Overview." In P. Wathern, ed., *Environmental Impact Assessment: Theory and Practice*. London: Unwin Hyman.

MacNeill, J., P. Winsemius, and T. Yakushiji. 1991. *Beyond Interdependence*. New York: Oxford University Press.

McAllister, D.M. 1980. *Evaluation in Environmental Planning*. Cambridge, MA.: The Massachusetts Institute of Technology Press.

Marshall, D., B. Sadler, J. Wiebe, and L. Wolfe, L. 1988. "Final Statement on Impact Assessment for International Development." In *Proceedings of the International Workshop on Impact Assessment for International Development*. Vancouver: International Association for Impact Assessment.

Ministry of Housing, Physical Planning and Environment. 1989. *National Environmental Policy Plan*. The Hague: SDU Publishers.

National Roundtable on the Environment and the Economy. 1992. *Annual Review, 1991-1992*. Ottawa: National Roundtable Secretariat.

Nijkamp, P. 1980. *Environmental Policy Analysis: Operational Methods and Models*. Chichester: John Wiley and Sons.

O'Riordan, T. 1976. "Policymaking and Environmental Management: Some Thoughts on Processes and Research Ideas." *Natural Resources Journal* 16: 55-72.

O'Riordan, T., and W.R.D. Sewell. "From Project Appraisal to Policy Review." In T. O'Riordan and W.R.D. Sewell, eds., *Project Appraisal and Policy Review*. New York: John Wiley and Sons.

Pearce, D., Markandya, A. and Barbier, E. 1989. *Blueprint for a Green Economy*. London: Earthscan.

Pearce, D.W., and R.K. Turner. 1990. *Economics of Natural Resources and the Environment*. Baltimore: The Johns Hopkins University Press.

Praxis Ltd. 1988. *Public Involvement*. Ottawa: Federal Environmental Assessment Review Office.

Rees, W.E. 1990. "Economics, Ecology and the Role of Environmental Assessment in Achieving Sustainable Development." In P. Jacobs and B. Sadler, eds., *Sustainable Development and Environmental Assessment: Perspectives on Planning for a Common Future*. Hull: Canadian Environmental Assessment Research Council.

Resource Assessment Commission. 1991. *Forest and Timber Inquiry Draft Report*. 2 vols. Canberra: Australian Government Publishing Service.

Resource Futures International. 1991. *Environmental Assessment of the Federal Budget*. Ottawa, Canada.

Richardson, N. 1989. *Land Use Planning and Sustainable Development in Canada*. Ottawa: Canadian Environment Advisory Council.

Sadler, B., ed. 1980. *Public Participation in Environmental Decision Making: Strategies for Change*. Edmonton: Environment Council of Alberta.

———. 1984. "Project Justification in Environmental Planning for Major Developments." In J.D. Wiebe, ed., *Environmental Planning for Large Scale Development Projects Final Report*. Calgary: Canadian Petroleum Association.

———, ed. 1985. *Environmental Protection and Resource Development: Convergence for Today*. Calgary: University of Calgary Press.

———. 1986. "Impact Assessment in Transition: A Framework for Redeployment." In R. Lang, ed., *Integrated Approaches to Resource Planning and Management*. Calgary: University of Calgary Press.

———, ed. 1987. *Audit and Evaluation in Environmental Assessment and Management: Canadian and International Experience*. 2 vols. Ottawa: Environment Canada.

———. 1987. "Energy Development on the Arctic frontier of Canada: An Analysis of Project Decision Making." In *Environmentally Sound Development in the Energy and Mining Industries*. Aberdeen: Centre for Environmental Management and Planning.

———. 1988. "The Evaluation of Assessment: Post-EIS Research and Process Development." In P. Wathern, ed., *Environmental Impact Assessment: Theory and Practice*. London: Unwin Hyman.

———. 1990a. *An Evaluation of the Beaufort Sea Environmental Assessment Panel Review*. Ottawa: Federal Environmental Assessment Review Office.

———. 1990b. "Sustainable Development and Water Resource Management." *Alternatives* 17(3): 14-24.

Sadler, B., and P. Jacobs. 1990. "A Key to Tomorrow: on the Relationship of Environmental Assessment and Sustainable Development." In P. Jacobs and B. Sadler, eds., *Sustainable Development and Environmental Assessment: Perspectives on Planning for a Common*

Future. Hull: Canadian Environmental Assessment Research Council.

Sigal, L.L., and J.W. Webb. 1989. "The Programmatic Environmental Impact Statement: Its Purpose and Use." *The Environmental Professional* 11:14-24.

Solis, V. 1992. "Conservation-based Development in Costa Rica." In B. Sadler, ed., *The Greening of Business: Industry Response to the Environmental Challenge*. Vancouver: GLOBE 92.

Sproule-Jones, M. 1989. "Multiple Rules and the Nesting of Public Policies." *Journal of Theoretical Politics* 1 (4): 459-477.

Susskind, L., and J. Cruikshank. 1987. *Breaking the Impasse: Practical Approaches to Resolving Public Disputes*. New York: Basic Books.

Tryzna, T.C., and I.M. Gotelli. 1990. *The Power of Convening: Collaborative Policy Forums for Sustainable Development*. Sacremento: California Institute of Public Affairs.

United Kingdom Department of the Environment. 1991. *Policy Appraisal and the Environment*. London: Her Majesty's Stationery Office.

United Nations Econoimc Commission for Europe (UNECE). In preparation. *Application of the Principles of Environmental Impact Assessment to Policies, Plans and Programs*. Geneva: UNECE Environmental Series.

Wathern, P. 1988. "An Introductory Guide to EIA." In P. Wathern, ed., *Environmental Impact Assessment: Theory and Practice*. London: Unwin Hyman.

Whitney, J.B. 1985. "Integrated Economic-Environmental Models in Environmental Impact Assessment." In V.W. MacLaren and J.B. Whitney, eds., *New Directions in Environmental Impact Assessment in Canada*. Toronto: Methuen.

Wood, C. and M. Djeddour. 1992. "Strategic Environmental Assessment: EA of Policies, Plans and Programs." *Impact Assessment Bulletin* 10: 3-23.

World Bank. 1991. *Environmental Assessment Sourcebook. Vol. 1. Policies, Procedures and Cross-Sectoral Issues*. Technical Paper 139. *Vol. 2. Sectoral Guidelines*. Technical Paper 140. *Vol. 3. Guidelines for Environmental Assessment of Energy and Industry Projects*. Technical Paper 154. Washington DC.

World Commission on Environment and Development. 1987. *Our Common Future*. Oxford: Oxford University Press.

2

Environmental Assessment and Sustainability at the Project and Program Level

Raymond F. Mikesell

A review of the World Bank's "Operational Directive on Environmental Assessment" (World Bank 1991) suggests that most of the elements stressed in the literature on sustainable development are covered in current Bank environmental assessment (EA) procedures. They include not only the standard adverse environmental impacts on health and safety arising from air, water, and soil pollution, but also the adverse impacts on biological diversity, soil productivity, tropical forests, wildlife, and tribal peoples. What do we mean then by introducing sustainability as a criterion for environmental assessments of projects and programs? A conventional EA looks mainly at the potential environmental damage of a project rather than how the project promotes or impairs sustainable development. Some projects clearly promote sustainability, say, by restoring the soil or by reducing damage to the natural resource base arising from other economic activities.

This chapter suggests how EA might be used to assess the net contribution of a project or program to sustainable development. It is recognized that sustainable development is a process encompassing the entire economy (or the global economy) in its relationship to the natural order. A full assessment of the contribution of a project to sustainable development would require an analysis of the role of the project in the context of all other economic activity. Such an analysis would require more information than is available to those conducting the EA and would involve a macroeconomic analysis of the economy. Questions concerning the optimal sectoral allocation of resources cannot normally be dealt with in project evaluation. Nevertheless, an analysis at the microeconomic can reveal a great deal about the compatibility of a project or program with sustainable development. In addition, an EA might take into account the conclusions of a sectoral or overall analysis of an economy in its relationship to the natural resource base.

Natural Resource Sustainability Criterion

The most objective and potentially measurable criterion for sustainable development is the preservation of the productivity and full functioning of the natural resource base. This may not ensure inter-generational equity, but it would provide future generations with the same natural resource capital for producing goods and services, and with the same life support and amenity services provided by the natural environment. The natural resources to be sustained for use by future generations are broadly defined to include everything on the land, the oceans, and the atmosphere that supports and gives meaning and enjoyment to human life. One way to apply the sustainability criterion in EA is to measure the impact of the project on the natural resource base and to include the negative impacts in the social costs and the positive impacts in the social benefits. All unabated environmental impacts, such as pollution of the atmosphere, the oceans, the waterways, and the land would be internalized so that they become a part of the social costs of the project. All natural resource depletion, such as the extraction of minerals, deforestation, and ocean fishing, would be charged as social costs, while any increase in renewable natural resources would be added to the social benefits. This constitutes an application of full environmental and resource accounting to the EA procedure (Commission on Environmental Accounting 1991).

We may recognize three categories of natural resources for purposes of analyzing the environmental and natural resource impacts of projects. The first consists of *exhaustible resources* that are inputs into the productive process, for instance, fuels and mineral ores. These are fixed in amount, but their quantity is unknown. Mineral reserves (amounts that can be economically extracted) can be increased by discoveries and by new technologies for extracting and processing. The second category consists of *renewable resources*, such as forests, agricultural soil, fish, wildlife, and surface and groundwater. These resources provide a flow of goods for consumption and inputs into the productive process. This flow can continue indefinitely provided the resources are not overused or damaged and provided restorative measures are taken following depletion. The third category consists of the *life-support resources* for the planet: all levels of the atmosphere, rivers, lakes and oceans, wetlands, and ecosystems. These resource assets support economic activity, serve as a sink for waste, or provide aesthetic values. These resources cannot be expanded by man, but their functions can be impaired—and in some cases the damage or destruction is irreversible. Many of the resources in the second category and most of those in the third are common property resources that are not traded in markets. Hence, their value can only be imputed from the value of the services lost or the social damage caused by the natural resource impairment. This complicates the problem of assigning costs to projects whose construction or operation depletes or degrades natural resource assets. Yet there are ways of estimating these costs. The development of a statistical base for environmental and resource accounting is in its infancy, but the introduction of its use in EAs would promote research in methodology and the accumulation of data.

How can estimating the social costs of natural resource depletion and degradation in the EA of a project help to determine whether the project is in conformity with the sustainable development criterion? First, assigning the full environmental and resource costs to projects will cause those with the largest adverse environmental impacts to bear relatively higher social costs—and therefore a lower priority in the allocation of capital. In cases of severe impacts, the projects may be shown to be infeasible because their social costs exceed their social benefits. Second, environmental assessment would reveal the total amount of financing required for the project to meet sustainability conditions. Frequently, projects are underfinanced and the operators lack the funds to correct or compensate for environmental damage. Some of the financing should be used in the project itself for restoration and replacement of renewable resources. Another portion of the financing might be available for restoring or protecting natural resources not directly associated with the project. For example, funds accumulated from mining or transportation projects might be used to establish wildlife reserves

or to restore damage done to land by past projects. A third portion of the financing might be paid into a fund that would earn interest for future generations to compensate for the depletion of natural resource capital that cannot be restored. Initially, I shall assume that the interest on such a fund could compensate future generations for the net loss of natural capital caused by the project during its period of preparation and operation. Later on, I shall discuss the limitations of this assumption.

Categories of Natural Resource and Environmental Assets

EXHAUSTIBLE RESOURCES. The social costs of extracting minerals should include the loss to future generations of the natural capital consumed by the present generation. Assuming no new discoveries of the exhaustible resource extracted by a mining company (say, a nonfuel mineral) and assuming no change in the real cost of extraction, the price of the mineral will rise in accordance with the Hotelling rule (1931), that is, the real price over time rises at a percentage rate equal to the discount rate.[1] The price of a mineral will rise until it reaches the price of a substitute material, or if there is no substitute material, the cost of an alternative technology. However, if new discoveries are continually being made, the resource price may rise slowly over several generations, or the resource price may remain constant or even fall, as has been the case with the real price of several nonfuel minerals over the past two decades. The amount required to compensate the next generation for the loss of resource capital is the increase in the average price of the mineral during the period of the project to the average price in the next generation, times the amount of depletion. The amount required to compensate future generations after the resource price has risen to the price of a substitute equals the difference between the average resource price during the project period and the price of the substitute material, times the amount of depletion during the project.

For example, the cost of providing a future energy substitute for the fossil fuel used in creating and operating a project may be substantially higher than the price of the fossil fuel at the time of depletion. In this case, the amount to be accumulated with the depletion of the fossil fuel should be large enough to cover the increased cost of an equivalent amount of renewable energy (solar power for instance) when the fossil fuel is exhausted. The depletion fund could be used for the research and development (R&D) and construction of an alternative energy facility.

The social costs of extracting minerals should also include restoring the land disturbed by mining or well drilling and repairing damage to forests, rivers, and groundwater. These costs, along with the cost of the annual depletion of the mineral should not be discounted to determine their present value at the time the mining project is initiated. Rather, both the depletion and the mine restoration costs should be charged annually throughout the project and discounted at the same rate of interest that the depletion and restoration fund is earning. The annual interest on the fund will offset the discounting used to determine the present value of the social costs of the project, so that at the termination of the project the fund will be sufficient both to restore the land damage and to provide interest to compensate future generations for the depletion of the natural resource capital. The analytical basis for this procedure is contained in recent publications (Mikesell 1992; El Serafy 1989).

RENEWABLE RESOURCES. The social cost of depleting renewable resources is readily dealt with by including in project costs the cost of a program of sustainable yield, including the interest on invested capital over the maturation period. In the case of harvesting a primary forest, the trees that have taken hundreds of years to grow should not be treated as free goods, but the cost of growing them should be imputed at the full social cost. This same approach to project costs should be applied even if reforestation is not planned but the land is to be used for other purposes. Sustainability requires that the value of the resource capital be maintained for future generations. If harvesting the forest also involves the loss of a valuable ecosystem and/or wildlife, the loss of these values should be included in the social costs of the project. Ecosystems, wildlife, and areas providing recreational amenities are exhaustible resources and should be treated accordingly in estimating project costs.

LIFE-SUPPORTING RESOURCES. Determining the social costs of projects attributed to the damage done to life-support environmental resources is the most difficult problem in full resource accounting. There may be little basis for estimating the monetary cost of certain types of environmental damage, such as destruction of the ozone by chlorofluorocarbons (CFCs) or destruction of wetlands or old-growth ecosystems. Where the social costs of such damage are known to be very high but undetermined, they should be embodied in the social costs associated with the project by estimating the cost of avoidance. For example, by adding the cost of avoiding emissions of harmful gases, or of reducing them to tolerable levels, the environmental costs of a project can be reflected in total project costs. The degree to which emissions generated by a specific project should be reduced can be based on the percentage by which all emissions of the same type need to be reduced to achieve some global or regional target for all emissions sources. Thus the cost to be internalized need not depend on any specific determination of the social cost of the environmental damage. The global targets for limiting greenhouse emissions may be based on an estimate of how much the atmosphere can absorb without unacceptable damage to the earth's climate. This knowledge would provide the basis for an estimate of the marginal cost of reducing emissions, which could then be used to determine the fully internalized cost of a project that emitted environmentally damaging greenhouse gases.

Assessing the Sustainability of Projects

ACCOUNTING FOR ENVIRONMENTAL COSTS. To summarize, for a project or program to be compatible with sustainability, the following conditions must be realized:

• Depleted renewable natural resources must be restored or the social cost of adequate compensation to future generations for the loss of natural resource capital must be included in the social cost of the project.

• Compensation to future generations for depleted nonrenewable natural resource capital must be included in the social cost of the project.

• Damage to life-supporting natural resources and environmental assets must be avoided, or the cost of avoidance included in the social cost of the project.

• The compensation included in the social cost of the project may take the form of either contributions to the quantity and/or quality of natural resource assets equivalent to what has been depleted or damaged by the project, or the accumulation of a fund sufficient to offset the loss of income to future generations resulting from the depletion of natural resource capital associated with the project.

This approach differs from conventional EA by including in the social costs of a project an amount sufficient to compensate future generations for the present generation's depletion and degradation of natural resource capital. This is a logical extension of the current practice of including in project costs expenditures for sustainable-yield forest management, compensation for the destruction of wetlands and wildlife habitat by replacement in other areas, and the restoration of land disturbed by mining and other economic activities. Compensation by investing in other projects that may offset adverse impacts of the first project is widely recognized as a method of internalizing the environmental damage. An example is planting trees or preserving a forest that would otherwise be destroyed to compensate for the creation of greenhouse gases by a new power plant.

LIMITS TO COMPENSATION. Including in project cost the cost of compensating future generations for the loss of natural resource capital assumes that the cost is internalized by a tax on a private project or by a compulsory payment made into a depletion fund in the case of a public project. The accumulation of a fund designed to compensate future generations for the loss of resource capital by substituting financial capital for the natural capital has been questioned by some environmental economists who point to the limitations on such substitutions. For example, there may be no substitute for environmental assets damaged by the generation of waste beyond absorptive capacity. Also, it may be impossible to provide substitutes for amenity-producing resources such as old-growth forests, ocean beaches, and scenic rivers. There is also the possibility that the productivity of capital may decline as natural resources are exhausted, so that the accumulated depletion fund will not replace the real loss from depletion. On the other hand, given technological progress, capital may be more productive in the future than it is today.

Herman Daly (1992) has argued that because production of manmade capital assets requires natural resource inputs, there may be little substitution of capital for natural resources in the production function. However, an important use of capital is for supplying technology that will increase the productivity of all inputs in the production process, and for substituting more abundant natural resources for those that are scarce. In this way capital can substitute for natural resources. Improved technology can reduce natural resource inputs required for a given level of economic output, and can reduce waste or render waste less harmful to the environment. Nevertheless, there are severe limits on the degree to which compensation in the form of financial capital can substitute for the loss of certain kinds of natural capital.

As a technological optimist, I believe the more serious problems will arise from damage to the life-supporting and amenity-producing environmental assets rather than from the depletion of minerals and energy sources. Technological progress may well enable future generations to substitute the most abundant materials on the earth's surface for scarce nonfuel minerals and generate almost unlimited supplies of cheap energy. The greatest impediment to sustainable development is maintaining the quality of the environmental assets that support and give meaning to life. The social costs of depleting or degrading these assets attributed to projects should, therefore, be based on the cost of avoidance rather than on the estimated loss to future generations. The accompanying taxes or other charges required to internalize these social costs should be designed to limit the use or damage to what might be regarded as consistent with sustainable development. There would still be a considerable accumulation of funds from both the depletion of minerals and environmental damage, but there will be a large and increasing need for capital for global natural resource preservation, for reducing waste, and for increasing the productivity of natural resource inputs in the production process. It is plausible that a century from now over half the world's capital investment will be required for this purpose to assure global sustainability. This shift in the allocation of capital investment will reduce the rate of growth of consumption, especially in the industrial countries, which must supply the bulk of the savings and investment, but I do not believe it will necessitate a no-growth world.

ENVIRONMENTAL RISK. Environmental risk should also be factored into project costs just as risk is provided for in any prudent financial feasibility study. Most resource projects involve some risk of unexpected environmental damage, with mining, large dams, forestry and resettlement projects among the most risky. Probabilities of unexpected damage and the average value of the damage could be determined from case studies of similar projects. Where there is no basis for determining probability of unexpected environmental damage, worst case scenarios might be used as a basis for estimating the highest conceivable cost from this source. Such estimates are often useful in project assessments, especially where projects are marginal.

Overall Resource Allocation and Sustainability

Sustainable development depends on the overall allocation of productive resources and not simply on project compatibility. EAs should, therefore, take into account the effects of the allocation of additional investment in the project's sector on sustainable development. This assumes the existence of a macroeconomic analysis of the economy oriented to promoting sustainable development. For example, in some countries new agriculture and rural development programs may contribute much more to sustainable development than additional power or urban infrastructure. This does not necessarily mean that all power projects should be shelved, regardless of their compatibility with natural resource conservation. It does mean that power should be given a lower priority than the agricultural sector and this should be noted in the EAs for power projects.

Conclusions

The approach to EA outlined in this chapter is based on a definition of sustainability as the preservation of natural resource capital for future generations. Whether this satisfies the objective of intergenerational equity is more an ethical than an economic issue. At any rate, I believe this is the only concept of sustainability that can be applied at the microeconomic level to projects and programs. This approach avoids the pitfalls of tampering with the social rate of discount and of formulating intergenerational welfare functions (Norgaard 1992). It also avoids the question of the substitutability of manmade capital for natural resource capital raised by Herman Daly (1992) and others. However, such questions cannot be dealt with at the project or program level.

Identifying and estimating all the environmental and natural resource costs in the EA of a project could have important advantages for promoting sustainable development. First, by including these costs in the social cost of a project, projects that are less compatible with sustainability will tend to have a lower priority and in some cases may be shown to have a negative net present social value. Second, environmental costs can be compared with remedial actions that will avoid or mitigate the adverse impacts, or with the net social costs of alternative projects that will serve a similar purpose. Third, such investigation would indicate the amount of compensation required to offset the loss of the natural resource capital resulting from the project.

Much of the information needed for assessing the social cost of natural resource depletion and environmental damage is already provided by a comprehensive environmental appraisal of a project. However, if the estimated loss of natural capital is to be treated as a social cost to the project, environmental assessment must do more than just identify possible environmental hazards. Some evaluation of the relative importance of the environmental harm, whether by estimating the monetary cost or comparing the environmental harm with the cost of modifying the project or the cost of an alternative project that would avoid the harm, is essential if the assessment is to prove useful. I have argued that sustainability requires treating natural resource depletion and damage as a social cost in the same way that air and water pollution, soil depletion, or loss of forest reserves are treated as social costs. Indeed, many of the categories of environmental harm evaluated in environmental assessment constitute a loss of natural resource capital.

I recognize that sustainable development is a macroeconomic problem and cannot be achieved by project evaluation and selection alone. A full determination of the conformity of a project or program with sustainability requires macroeconomic analysis at the national and global levels. But without applying sustainability criteria at the project and program levels, sustainable development may be little more than a policy goal without procedures for implementation.

Notes

1. If real extraction costs rise with production, the resource price will rise more rapidly as will the social cost of depletion. Just the opposite will occur if real extraction costs decline, as has been the case with copper and certain other metals over the past several decades.

References

Commission of Environmental Accounting. 1991. *Taking Nature into Account: Proposed Scheme of Resource and Environmental Accounting*. Stockholm: Ministry of Finance.

Daly, Herman E. 1992. "From Empty-World Economics to Full-World Economics: Recognizing An Historical Turning Point in Economic Development." In Robert Goodland, Herman E. Daly and Salah El Serafy, eds., *Population, Technology and Lifestyle: The Transition to Sustainability*. Washington, DC: Island Press.

El Serafy, Salah. 1989. "The Proper Calculation of Income

from Depletable Natural Resources," in Y.J. Ahmad, S.L. Serafy, and E. Lutz, eds., *Environmental Accounting for Sustainable Development*. Washington, DC: World Bank.

Hotelling, Herold. 1931. "The Economics of Exhaustible Resources." *Journal of Political Economy* 29 (4): 197-275.

Mikesell, Raymond F. 1992. "Project Evaluation and Sustainable Development." In Robert Goodland, Herman E. Daly and Salah El Serafy, eds., *Population, Technology and Lifestyle: The Transition to Sustainability*. Washington, DC: Island Press.

World Bank. 1991. "Environmental Assessment." Operational Directive 4.01. Washington, DC.

Part II
Case Studies of Environmental Management
In Industrial and Developing Countries

3

What's the Difference: A Comparison of EA in Industrial and Developing Countries

Mary MacDonald

Environmental assessment (EA) is one approach to integrating environmental issues into economic decisionmaking and, as such, may prove to be a valuable tool for planning sustainable development. Although EA is currently practiced in many countries, no two countries have adopted precisely the same procedures for preparation or implementation of EA (Wandesforde-Smith and Moreira 1985; Horberry 1984; Carpenter 1981). In any country or region, however, the effectiveness of EA as an environmental management tool will always be limited by political context—that is, by the degree to which the relevant authorities are willing or able to make environmentally sound development a genuine priority.

Although many lessons have been learned regarding issues, such as appropriate EA methodologies and the misuse of EA to give the appearance but not the reality of environmental protection, an ideal approach to environmental assessment does not currently exist. Our understanding of the process and its links to sustainable development continues to evolve, yet, repeatedly, we hear calls for specialized approaches for EA in the developing countries such as scaled-down or low-cost EA strategies (Burdge 1990; Fuggle 1989; Biswas and Geping 1987; Chambers 1987; Lohani and Halim 1987; Carpenter 1985; Roque 1985; Munn 1982). This often leaves the impression that the traditional full-blown EAs carried out in many industrial nations are the standard against which all other approaches to EA should be judged.

This chapter attempts to demonstrate that almost all of the concerns regarding EA are universal and that to claim otherwise is to contribute to the myth that the industrial countries have many answers to environmental dilemmas that only need to be shared with the South. A discussion of the problems associated with EA in developing countries will be followed by a brief overview of the EA experience in industrial countries. Examples of areas of potential differences are explored, including knowledge of

EA, the legal requirement for EA, public participation, and conflicting economic and environmental goals. Finally, conclusions are drawn regarding the benefits of learning from the application and interpretation of EA in developing countries.

EA in Developing Countries

Personal observations in Zimbabwe revealed that those responsible for preparing or reviewing environmental assessments (for example, government personnel or environmental managers of multinational corporations) apparently are concerned that the EAs conducted in developing countries do not equal the high standard of those in industrial countries (Calver 1992; Nixon 1992; Sithole 1992). The author reviewed five EA documents prepared in Zimbabwe including three for mining projects (Environmental Consultants 1990; ULG 1990; Whitlow 1990); one for a hydroelectric dam (Du Toit 1982; Mutizwa-Mangiza and others 1990) and one for an oil pipeline (Feruka-Harare Pipeline 1991). This review indicated that most of the traditional steps of EA preparation were followed: project description, identification of relevant areas of the environment, prediction of potential impacts and identification of appropriate mitigation measures. However, alternatives to the proposed project were not considered, and there was no suggestion of a monitoring program to determine the actual impacts of a proposal once an operation was up and running. In only one case (the hydroelectric dam) was the local community consulted or given an opportunity to review the work. All the reports were prepared by only one or two authors who were either geographers or biologists, although there certainly is expertise available in Zimbabwe for assembling a multidisciplinary team in biology, zoology, anthropology, agriculture, sociology, geology, hydrology, and various fields of engineering.

These EAs were different from EAs prepared by, for example, consultants under the *Environmental*

Assessment Act in the Province of Ontario, Canada. All the EA documents were shorter than any environmental impact statement (EIS) the author has encountered from Canada, the United States, or the United Kingdom. They were not comprehensive nor particularly detailed, and they did not appear to make use of any sophisticated presentation devices (such as desktop publishing). However, in all but one case, the EAs were written in a concise style with a clear indication of information that was not available and a discussion of uncertainty regarding any predictions of future impacts.

Unlike in Ontario, EA is not institutionalized into the planning process in Zimbabwe. New legislation is being developed, but there is not yet a formal requirement for the findings of an EA to be made available at each stage of decisionmaking, nor are decisionmakers required to demonstrate how an EA affected their final decision. Also lacking are provisions for a public hearing to relate EA to project approval.

There are a number of often-cited reasons why the EA experience in industrial countries cannot be repeated in developing countries:

• The conflict between pursuing environmental considerations and much needed economic development (Fuggle 1989; Biswas and Geping 1987; Horberry 1985).

• The financial costs of conducting a full-blown EA are too high (Biswas and Geping 1987; Munn 1982).

• Data for identifying and predicting potential impacts are not available at an appropriate level of detail (Yap 1990; Fuggle 1989; Lohani and Halim 1987).

• The expertise for conducting a comprehensive EA is not available (Nixon 1992; Lohani and Halim 1987; Roque 1985).

• EA is a technology developed in the North and therefore contains cultural values that make the transfer of EA to the South difficult (Tolba 1991; Biswas and Geping 1987).[1]

In the author's experience, none of these problems, except the last, is limited to EA in developing countries.

EA in Industrial Countries

Over the last twenty years EA has been continuously refined and revised in countries such as the United States, Canada, and the Netherlands, who were among the first to enact environmental assessment legislation. One example of this relates to the importance of public consultation during the EA process. The first impact studies involved very little, if any, public discussion of the work in progress or the final EA document. Today, however, some practitioners feel that the emphasis on public consultation has grown to the point where the definition of relevant areas of investigation (that is, what constitutes a significant impact) is often determined by the general public—in some cases irrespective of the findings of scientific studies (Brouwer 1989; Kennedy 1989).

The perception that EA is a highly effective environmental protection tool in the industrial world is held to be true by many members of the public who will often demand an EA for domestic projects and, increasingly, for international development agency projects in the name of responsible environmental management. This view appears to be shared by development institutions and agencies such as the World Bank (1991), the Asian Development Bank (1991) and the Canadian International Development Agency, who are increasing their commitment to environmental assessment in the early stages of project design and as a requirement for project approval.

While EA has been useful for predicting and avoiding the negative impacts associated with the building and operation of some projects in industrial countries, it is far from being a problem-free device for anticipating and avoiding potential environmental difficulties. Practiced on a project-by-project basis, EA is often used as an end-of-pipe solution rather than an early planning technique. Project-based EA can limit the consideration of alternatives and long-range impacts. For these reasons, greater attention is now being paid to conducting EA of broader plans and programs (Wood and Dejeddour 1992). As we have heard so often, EA is only a tool and cannot be a replacement for enlightened and enforced environmental policy (Armour 1991).

A 1988 study of EA in Canada (Needham and Swerdfager, 1988) surveyed public interest groups, academicians and EA professionals. The findings revealed a number of recurring problems concerning: post-development auditing, process implementation costs, process development and support costs, scoping procedures and methodologies, consideration of cumulative impacts, soundness of science in EA, provision of intervenor funding, legal standing of EA, accessibility of information, and timing of EA during program or project development. These concerns are similar to those raised for developing countries.

Comparison of EA Experience in Developing and Industrial Countries

There are many differences between industrial and developing countries with respect to EA that may be more apparent than real, as illustrated above. However, some aspects do warrant further consideration, including knowledge of the EA process, EA legislation, public participation, and competing goals of economic growth and sound environmental management.

Knowledge of the EA Process

The International Association for Impact Assessment (IAIA) and other organizations demonstrate that there are a large number of individuals with the capability to design, conduct, review and evaluate EAs. For historical reasons, the majority of these individuals are from countries of the North. Although this is slowly changing, the major portion of teaching about environmental assessment takes place in industrial countries. Organizations such as the British Council, the United Nations Environment Programme (UNEP), the United Nations Educational, Scientific, and Cultural Organization (UNESCO), and the Commonwealth Secretariat have been a source of funding for students in developing countries to travel to universities in North America and Europe where the fundamentals of EA are taught. The concept of EA is not a difficult one to grasp nor does conducting an EA require highly sophisticated equipment, but learning from long-term EA experience can be valuable for those countries instituting a similar process.

There are a great number of highly educated, locally born, professional people in developing countries working on areas related to EA. The current problems of EA will benefit from the fresh perspectives these individuals bring to some of these areas of concern. Because EA is a technique developed and practiced in the North, it may include values and traditions, such as some of the modes of communication used for public participation, that are not compatible with conditions in developing countries. However, a locally modified approach to EA will not necessarily result in an EA that is of any less value to decisionmakers in terms of sustainable development. In general, broader applications and experiences with EA across different cultural and geographical settings offer the promise of a better understanding of EA practice.

Legal Requirement for EA

One area where industrial countries are ahead of developing countries is in making EA a formal requirement of program and project planning. There is no legal basis for EA in many developing countries. The EAs carried out are often initiated by external agencies or corporations, although this is changing. Some industrial countries that do have environmental assessment legislation undermine the effectiveness of the law by not applying it to plans or programs, failing to offer procedural guidance to help tie EA to the planning process, giving exemptions to controversial projects, or simply allowing the relevant legislation to be ignored.

The European Community (EC), for example, has had a Directive on environmental assessments of major projects since 1985. As recently as late 1991, the United Kingdom has been accused of neglecting to "fully transpose the Directive into national laws" and to have failed to undertake environmental assessments for projects likely to give rise to "significant effects" (ENDS 1991). Devising and promulgating environmental assessment laws increases the likelihood of EA being used for planning decisions, but there is no guarantee that this will occur in either industrial or developing countries.

Public Participation

The results of public consultation will differ very little from no public consultation at all, if information is only presented to the public for review and the suggestions or comments received during an open public meeting do not affect any change in the direction or conclusion of the EA. In industrial countries with democratic political traditions, the public is generally given ample opportunity to provide comments and review materials throughout the EA process. The distinction must be made, however, between public *presentation* of EA information and public *participation* in the final statement on the environmental viability of the undertaking. Participants involved in consultation during EA often express a "lingering doubt" that any real changes occur in the project due to public input (OEAB 1987).

The lack of true representation in many governments, in itself, poses an obstacle to citizens attempting to give input into environmental decisionmaking. In some parts of the world, political situations such as single-party governments may strongly discourage any public opposition to major development projects, making those who have concerns regarding a proposal afraid of the reprisals that may result from speaking out. Incorporating the voiced concerns and information provided by the public during EA preparation remains problematic in both industrial and developing countries. Among other factors, this may be the result of a reluctance on the part of some experts to accept and respect information from those with less formal training, or it may stem from the subjective nature of some of the concerns of local citizens that are difficult to verify or mesh with the often technical and scientific focus of an EA.

There are many tools and methods for initiating and publicizing opportunities for public participation in the EA process, such as telephone, television, radio, newspapers and leaflets delivered door-to-door. However, some are not suitable for areas where poverty precludes ownership of or access to audio-visual equipment or where illiteracy prohibits the use of printed material. In poorer regions, collecting information may require the investigator to meet with community leaders, obtain their permission and agreement for co-operation, publicize a proposed meeting by word-of-mouth and collect and disseminate information at a public meeting through the use of as many visual aids as possible (for example, drawings and models).

Traditional methods of gathering and sharing information in less-developed regions may also prove to be useful in industrial countries where public involvement in decisionmaking is not particularly advanced. It has been pointed out that not only is public involvement of the type discussed above important for identifying the public's concerns regarding a proposed project, but in some cases it may be one of the only methods for obtaining information about local conditions such as location, type, and extent of plant and animal species, or details of flooding patterns (Yap 1990).

Work on defining sustainable development has begun to include looking at various forms of communication used in indigenous societies and attempting to understand how the values inherent in current forms of communication, particularly mass media, may either enhance or diminish positive interactions with the environment (Hanson and Régallet 1992). Increased involvement of the public in the EA process in developing countries may aid in gaining greater knowledge for devising a communication strategy for sustainable development.

Economic Growth and Environmental Management

It is certainly true that when economic growth takes precedence over all other development goals it creates a tension between economic and environmental concerns. Many governments and businesses of the South openly state that economic development is their chief goal, but is this situation unique to developing countries? How many roads, dams, industrial developments, or natural resource extraction schemes in industrial countries have been stopped by a national or regional government for environmental reasons, particularly after the completion of an EA? The answer is very few. The conclusion to be drawn here is that the primary difference between industrial and developing countries with respect to placing economic goals ahead of environmental ones, is that this situation is clearly articulated in the South, while in the North it is not, even though economic growth remains the highest priority in industrial countries.

Those who advocate a distinct approach for EA in developing countries generally agree that "environmental evaluation procedures in developing countries must accept the inevitability and desirability of infrastructural and industrial growth" (Fuggle 1989). Following on this is the belief that economic development must be the number one priority in the developing world and that the luxury of placing environmental concerns foremost in development decisionmaking can only be realized in the industrial world (Sithole 1992; Kunene 1992). How often, however, are businesses of the North prepared to place environmental concerns above economic ones where a trade-off arises?

The International Chamber of Commerce (ICC) has recently published *A Business Charter for Sustainable Development* that includes a list of environmental principles for environmental management. Among these principles is a commitment to: recognize environmental management among the highest corporate priorities; assess environmental impacts before starting a new activity or project and before decommissioning a facility or leaving a site; and develop and provide products and services that have no undue environmental impact (Willums and Golüke 1991).

ICC encourages members to conduct EAs of various undertakings but qualifies this by encouraging products and services with no undue impacts without giving a clear indication of what constitutes an undue impact. At what point would a manufacturer from anywhere in the world determine that the negative environmental impacts of one of his or her products was excessive and therefore cease production? Developers in the North may be willing to consider environmental issues more fully than in the past, but the reality is that economic concerns will always dominate with this group, since economic growth or profitmaking is their *raison d'être*.

Conclusions

The problems encountered with the substantive goals and procedural requirements of EA vary only slightly between industrial and developing countries. The traditional full-blown EA that many proponents in developing countries are reluctant to attempt, usually for financial and timing reasons, is not suitable for many situations even in industrial countries (for example, a slight realignment of a road, construction of a low-rise block of apartments), although the most appropriate EA methodology for a project or a plan must always be considered on a case-by-case basis.

Much of the EA carried out in developing countries is not "second best" to EA work in the North: it is simply a different approach. Considering all the problems associated with conventional approaches to EA, it seems reasonable to assume that some of the experiences arising from EA applications in developing countries will provide learning opportunities that will improve and enhance EAs practiced in industrial countries.

Financial limitations in developing countries often necessitate a cursory scoping of the issues that may result in an inability to predict significant environmental impacts associated with an undertaking; but, again, this problem is not limited to developing countries (Dickman 1991; Berkes 1988; Schindler 1978). Even highly experienced consultants from industrial countries are forced by budget constraints to limit their studies.

A real discussion of the language and concepts of sustainable development is only just beginning. The importance of assigning a country to a particular category based on its economic strength may fade as the search for genuine indicators of social and environmental wellbeing causes current obsessions and prejudices to be questioned.

The genuine value and direction of economic growth, its relationship to social equity, and how these concerns can be understood within the context of the wellbeing of the environment are questions at the heart of the current debate on sustainable development. EA, alone, will not facilitate the integration of these factors in either the developing or industrial world. The context within which EA takes place, the manner in which it is implemented, as well as how closely it imitates both the present and future reality, will ultimately determine its value for sustainable development in all parts of the globe.

Notes

1. Biswas and Geping define technology in its broadest sense to include plans, patents, designs, trademarks and copyrights, as well as hardware, such as boilers.

References

Armour, A. 1991. "Impact assessment and the planning process: a status report." *Impact Assessment Bulletin* 9:27-33.

Asian Development Bank 1991. *Environmental Risk Assessment.* Manila, Philippines.

Berkes, F. 1988. "The Intrinsic Difficulty of Predicting Impacts: Lessons from the James Bay Hydro Project." *Environmental Impact Assessment Review* 8:201-220.

Biswas, A.K., and Q. Geping. 1987. *Environmental Impact Assessment for Developing Countries.* London: Tycooly International.

Brouwer, H. 1989. "Operationalization and Specification of EIA Concepts: Discussion." In H. Paschen, ed., *The Role of Environmental Impact Assessment in the Decisionmaking Process.* Berlin: Erich Schmidt Verlag.

Burdge, R.J. 1990. "The Benefits of Social Impact Assessment in Third World Development." *Environmental Impact Assessment Review* 10(1, 2).

Burdge, R.J. and Robert A. Robertson.1990. "Social Impact Assessment and the Public Involvement Process." *Environmental Impact Assessment Review* 10(1, 2):81-90.

Calver, H. 1992. Personal Communication. Consulting Engineer, Anglo American Corporation. Harare, Zimbabwe.

Carpenter, R.A. 1981. "Balancing Economic and Environmental Objectives: The Question is still How?" *Environmental Impact Assessment Review* 2:175-188.

——. 1985. "Collaboration among American and Third World Environmental Professionals: Constraints and Opportunities." *The Environmental Professional* 7:285-288.

Chambers, R. 1987. "Shortcut Methods in Social Information Gathering for Rural Development Projects." In Khon Kaen University, ed., *Rapid Rural Appraisal.* Khon Kaen, Rural Systems Research and Farming Systems Research Projects,.

Dickman, M. 1991. "Failure of an Environmental Impact Assessment to Predict the Impact of Mine Tailings on Canada's Most Northerly Hypersaline Lake." *Environmental Impact Assessment Review* 11:171-180.

Du Troit, R.F. 1982. *A Preliminary Assessment of the Environmental Implications of the Proposed Mupata and Batoka Hydroelectric Schemes, Zambezi River.* Harare, Zimbabwe: Ministry of Natural Resources and Tourism.

Environmental Data Services (ENDS). 1991. "Brussels Ups the Stakes on Environmental Assessment." *Environmental Data Services* 201:14-17.

Environmental Consultants 1990. *Sencol and the Environment: Proposed Environment-related Activities in connection with the Sengwa Colliery Project.* Harare, Zimbabwe.

Feruka-Harare Pipeline: Environmental Statement. 1991. Harare, Zimbabwe.

Fuggle, R.F. 1989. "Integrated Environmental Management: An Appropriate Approach to Environmental Concerns in Developing Countries." *Impact Assessment Bulletin* 8(1 and 2):31-45.

Hanson, A.J., and G. Régallet. 1992. "Communicating for Sustainable Development." *Nature and Resources* 28:35-43.

Horberry, J.A. 1985. *Status and Application of Environmental Impact Assessment for Development.* Conservation for Development Centre, IUCN, Gland, Switzerland: International Union for the Conservation of Nature.

Kennedy, W. 1989. "Operationalization and Specification of EIA Concepts: Discussion." In H. Paschen, ed., *The Role of Environmental Impact Assessment in the Decisionmaking Process.* Berlin: Erich Schmidt Verlag.

Kunene, I.D. 1992. Personal Communication. Senior Ecologist, Natural Resources Board. Harare, Zimbabwe. Ministry of Natural Resources and Tourism.

Lohani, B.N., and N. Halim. 1987. "Recommended Methodologies for Rapid Environmental Impact Assessment in Developing Countries: Experiences Derived from Case Studies in Thailand." In A.K. Biswas and Q. Geping, eds., *Environmental Impact Assessment in Developing Countries.* London: Tycooly International.

Munn, R.E. 1982. "Environmental Impact Assessment in Developing Countries." *Mazingira* 3/4:6-9.

Mutizwa-Mangiza, N.D., J.T. Du Toit, M.F. Mushay Andebvu, R.B. Gaidzanwa, J.C. Nkomo, and T. Mubvami. 1990. *The Zambezi Valley Environmental Impact Study: A Review.* Harare: Zimbabwe: Ministry of Natural Resources and Tourism.

Needham, R.D. and T.M. Swerdfager. 1988. "Environmental Impact Assessment: Recurring Concerns in Canadians Experience." *The Operational Geographer* 7:3-7.

Nixon, J. 1992. Personal Communication. Managing Director, Rio Tinto, Harare, Zimbabwe.

Ontario Environmental Assessment Board (OEAB). 1987. *Review of South-western Transmission System Environmental Assessment.* Reasons for Decision and Decision. Toronto.

Roque, C.R. 1985. "Environmental Impact Assessment in the Associations of South-east Asian Nations." *Environmental Impact Assessment Review* 5:257-263.

Schindler, D.W. 1978. "The Impact Statement Boondoggle." *Science* 192:509.

Sithole, B. 1992. Personal Communication. Ecologist, Natural Resources Board, Ministry of Natural Resources and Tourism. Harare, Zimbabwe.

Tolba, M. 1991. "Facilitating Technology Transfer in the Interests of the Global Environment." *Conference on Technology Transfer and the Global Environment: Motives and Mechanisms.* World Resources Institute, London.

ULG Consultants. 1990. *Environmental Impact Study for Seismological Survey in the Zambezi Valley - Final Report.* Mobil Oil Company. Harare, Zimbabwe.

Wandesforde-Smith, G., and I.V.D. Moreira. 1985. "Subnational Government and EIA in the Developing World." *Environmental Impact Assessment Review* 5:223-237.

Whitlow, R. 1990. *Review of the Environmental Impact of the Freda-Rebecca Mine on the Bindura Area.* Cluff Mineral Exploration. Harare, Zimbabwe.

Willums, J.O., and U. Golüke. 1991. *Second World Conference on Environmental Management.* International Chamber of Commerce. Rotterdam, The Netherlands.

Wood, C., and M. Dejeddour. 1992. Strategic Environmental Assessment: EA of Policies, Plans and Programmes." *Impact Assessment Bulletin* 10:3-22.

World Bank 1991. *Environmental Assessment Sourcebook.* Vol. 1. Policies, Procedures and Cross-Sectoral Issues (Technical Paper 139). Vol. 2. Sectoral Guidelines (Technical Paper 140). Vol. 3. Guidelines for Environmental Assessment of Energy and Industry Projects (Technical Paper 154). Washington, DC.

Yap, N.T. 1990. "Round the Peg or Square the Hole? Populists, Technocrats and Environmental Assessment in Third World Countries." *Impact Assessment Bulletin* 8:69-84.

4

Environmental Assessment:
The Process in Thailand and Canada

Nonita T. Yap

The effective integration of environmental protection objectives into the legal and public administration systems of most low consumption countries (LCCs) is rather recent. The institutionalization of environmental assessment (EA) as a planning tool remains exceptional. A number of factors probably contribute to this lag: the high costs involved in undertaking EA; the lack of environmental expertise in LCCs; and the length of time needed for EA that delays project implementation (Lohani 1988; Biswas 1989).

The institutionalization process, however, has begun and is likely to continue due to a combination of internal and external pressures. Among the external forces is the funding requirement for preproject environmental assessment increasingly imposed by multilateral financial institutions (MFIs) and bilateral assistance agencies.

Legislation recently passed by the Canadian Parliament reflects this trend. Bill C-13 [now, Canada Statute, Chapter 37][1] specifies that Canadian Overseas Development Aid (ODA) projects be subjected to an environmental impact screening in the planning stage and where warranted, submitted to a mediation or review panel. ODA's assessment of projects would be undertaken "in accordance with the principles and practice of international law." Bill C-13 provides for the use of alternate impact assessment procedures "in recognition of the foreign nature" of the project, provided that the procedure "meets the basic goals and objectives of Canadian environmental policies."

Canada's dilemma and response parallel that of other donor countries and international financial institutions (IFIs). The increasing interest among donor countries and lending institutions in harmonizing environmental assessment procedure is therefore not surprising.

In Southeast Asia, Thailand is one of Canada's important development partners. It has the fastest growing economy in the region and is of considerable interest to international development agencies and environmental organizations. Countries on a fast track to industrialization are seen as particularly vulnerable to the undervaluation of social and environmental costs in their pursuit of development objectives.

Thailand is one of the few LCCs that has developed the necessary policy, legal and institutional framework for environmental planning, impact assessment and management. A comparative analysis of the EA process in Thailand and Canada could thus be useful. Such a comparison may also be interesting at this time because both countries recently introduced legislation that effectively restructures the practice of EA.

This chapter compares and contrasts the EA process in Thailand and Canada; analyzes the trends emerging in LCCs; and identifies some EA issues or areas where donors and IFIs could allocate their resources with greater cost-effectiveness.

Cross-Country Comparison of EA Procedures

The Old Systems and the Impetus for Change

THAILAND. Institutionalization of the EA process in Thailand began with the proclamation of the Enhancement and Conservation of National Environmental Quality Act in 1975. It established the National Environmental Board (NEB) first under the Office of the Prime Minister and later under the Minister of Science, Technology, and Energy. The Office of the National Environment Board (ONEB) served as the Secretariat (Chia 1987).

Section 17 of this Act gave the Minister of Science, Technology and Energy the power to set up standards and indicators of environmental quality except in areas under the jurisdiction of other ministries. Section 17 also allowed the Minister to prescribe the categories of projects that required an Environmental Impact

Statement (EIS). In July 1981, such a list was proclaimed (see table 4-1). For projects deemed by the ONEB as having potentially significant environmental impacts, the Board negotiated with the licensing agency or project proponent. The preparation of an EA applied to private sector projects where a license or permit was required (Pratsith-rathsini 1991).

There were conflicting opinions about whether the legal requirement applied to public sector initiatives. One interpretation was that if projects and activities were proposed or funded by a government agency, state enterprise or joint venture, ONEB negotiated with the agency. According to this interpretation, some public sector projects were subject to an EA for

the pragmatic reason that the National Economic and Social Development Board (NESDB)—the board that submitted all development proposals to the Cabinet for final approval—had agreed in principle that such projects would undergo EA and the EA Report would be submitted to ONEB for approval. The NESDB had further agreed that the comments of the ONEB would be incorporated into the project document submitted to the Cabinet for approval (Pratsith-rathsini 1991). Another opinion was that this discretion applied only to projects approved by the Cabinet before issuance of the Proclamation List of 1981 and that all projects on the list were automatically subject to EA.[2]

The old law was considered flawed in several

Table 4-1. A Comparison of EA Processes in Thailand and Canada

Thailand	Canada
1. Part of Omnibus Legislation on Environmental Conservation.	1. Backed by separate EA legislation.
2. Environmental enhancement and conservation are defined as the objectives of EA; (no mention of sustainable development).	2. Promotion of sustainable development defined as one of the objectives of EA.
3. Projects requiring EA are listed (only one list).	3. Has both a Mandatory Study List and an Exclusion List.
4. EA requirement applies to public and private setor projects or activities in the List.	4. EA requirement does not apply to private sector projects or activities unless federal funding or federal Crown Land is involved.
5. EA TORs decided on and prepared by project proponent.	5. TORs prepared by the government.
6. Public participation not integrated in the EA process.	6. Public participation integral part of EA.
7. Scope of EA at considerable discretion of project proponent.	7. Scope of EA determined by TORs and public input in scoping process.
8. EA paid for by the project proponent and EA Report considered property of proponent.	8. EA paid for by proponent but all project-related documents are public.
9. Environmental quality information may be accessed by the public except where security or property or business rights may be affected (Summary of EA Report may be accessible).	9. All project-related documents are public.
10. Allows for "standard" or "class" assessment.	10. Allows for Class Assessment and Prototype Assessment.
11. NEP or OEPP only "comments" on EA Report; decision to approve or disapprove resides with the Cabinet (for public sector projects) or with the Ad Hoc Experts Committee (for private sector projects).	11. Decision on project approval or rejection resides with the Minister of Environment.

Source: The author.

respects. Environmental policy analysts and environmental organizations noted the NEB's lack of substantive and enforcement authority. The EA process was also criticized for being closed: it was paid for by the project proponent, considered a property of the proponent, and was not open to the public unless the project proponent volunteered to make it available (CIDA 1991). Even in cases where parts of an EIS were leaked to the public, as happened occasionally, there was no mechanism that would allow the affected community to request more information.

The impetus for change came from a coalition of forces and concerns. The 1988 floods in the south, land subsidence and river pollution from salt mining in the northeast, and public controversy over hydroelectric dams and reforestation projects dramatically increased public awareness of the deteriorating state of the environment and the threats to the country's natural resource base. It mobilized university students and urban professionals to form alliances with nongovernmental organizations (NGOs) and affected rural communities. This lent greater sophistication to the arguments for change. In an attempt to address some of these problems, the Anand government that came to power after the 1991 coup introduced new legislation, the Enhancement and Conservation of the National Environmental Quality Act (NEQA).

CANADA. Canada began using EA as a planning tool about the same time as Thailand, in 1974, and closely following the adoption of EAs in the United States. However, unlike EA procedures in the United States that were enshrined in the National Environmental Policy Act, EA in Canada did not have a legislative basis.

The consequences of this legislative vacuum and inherent weakness of the process itself became evident and were the object of criticism by environmental professionals and activists during ten years of implementation. The process was updated in 1977 and attempts were made to further strengthen it in 1984 when Environmental Assessment Review Process (EARP) Guidelines were issued by an Order-in-Council. However, difficulties persisted particularly in relation to other federal agencies and to Crown Corporations that were explicitly exempted or whose responsibilities were not defined in the Guidelines.

In 1987, the Canadian government initiated a series of consultations with special interest groups such as the private sector, NGOs, native groups, and environmental professionals, and decided to legislate and strengthen the environmental assessment process. The recent court decisions on the Rafferty Alameda Dam in the province of Saskatchewan and the Old Man River Dam in Alberta, which showed that EARP Guidelines were legally enforceable, further strengthened the argument for formal legislation.[3]

Definitions of the Environment

Under Thailand's Enhancement and Conservation of National Environmental Quality Act (NEQA), "environment" refers to "natural things which form the physical and biophysical conditions surrounding man and man-made things."

Canada's Bill C-13 defines "environment" as "the components of the Earth, and includes (a) land, water and air, including all layers of the atmosphere; (b) all organic and inorganic matter; and living organisms; and (c) the interacting natural systems that include components referred to in paragraphs (a) and (b)."

Criteria for EA Requirement

Section 17 of Thailand's NEQA of 1975 gave the Minister of Science Technology and Energy the power to list categories of projects requiring an EA. Under NEQA, the Ministry was renamed the Ministry of Science Technology and Environment and this mandate was retained for the Minister under Section 46. However, under the new legislation, the Minister may grant exemption from EA (with NEB approval) to projects and activities if an EA has been undertaken on previous projects or activities of similar type, size, or site. The exemption is granted "provided that the proponent of such project or activity shall express to comply with various measures prescribed in the environmental impact assessment report which is applicable as the standard for assessment."

Canada's Bill C-13 on the other hand provides for two types of lists: a Comprehensive Study (Mandatory) List and an Exclusion List. The Exclusion List is subject to review every five years. The legislation also allows for class assessment.

Scope of EA

THAILAND. Section 46 of NEQA explicitly grants the Minister, "with the approval of the National Environmental Board, the power to specify, by notification published in the Government Gazette, types and sizes of projects or activities, likely to have environmental impact." Section 10 further grants the NEB "the power to require government agencies, state enterprises and private persons to deliver documents relating to the examination of impacts on environmental quality and documents or data concerning the projects or workplans of such government agencies, state enterprises and persons for its consideration. . . The Board may recommend remedial measures to the Cabinet."

CANADA. Bill C-13 applies only to projects where "a federal authority (a) is the proponent of the project and does any act or thing that commits the federal authority to carrying out the project in whole or in part; or (b) makes or authorizes payments or provides a guarantee for a loan or any other form of financial assistance to the proponent for the purpose of enabling the project to be carried out in whole or in part."

A "federal authority" is defined as "a Minister of the Crown in right of Canada," an agency of the Government of Canada or other body ultimately accountable to a Minister of the Crown, a department or departmental corporation set out under the Financial Administration Act. The EA legislation therefore applies to all projects funded in full or in part by the Canadian International Development Agency (CIDA). Development projects within Canada, on the other hand, need to comply solely with provincial EA requirements unless the project (a) involves federal funding; (b) has potentially demonstrable impacts on federal-administered lands and waters; and/or (c) has potential impacts on international conventions, that is, protocols to which the Canadian government is a signatory.

Where both federal and provincial governments are involved in a project, the federal government has traditionally deferred to the provincial EA system. This changed in 1989 with the Canadian federal court decision on the Rafferty Alameda Dam in Saskatchewan. The court interpreted the federal EARP Guidelines as enforceable regulation binding on the Crown. This has resulted in a tremendous increase in the use and influence of the federal process (Robinson 1991). The significance of this change may be measured by the fact that during 1991 there were thirty-five federal environmental assessment Panel Reviews, whereas during the ten years prior to the Rafferty Alameda decision, the average was one or two Panel Reviews a year.[4]

Implementing Agency

THAILAND. Under the old law, the Office of the National Environmental Board through its Environmental Impact Assessment Division had the responsibility and the authority to review EAs and recommend changes and to attach mitigation measures as conditions for approval, if necessary. Section 18 stipulated that the official with the legal power to grant a license had an obligation to submit the EA Report to ONEB before granting the license. The EA Report had to be approved by ONEB before the project could be implemented. ONEB had ninety days to complete its review, and failure to respond to the proponent beyond this period was considered approval for the project to go ahead.

The new legislation, NEQA, upgraded the status of NEB to Cabinet level, with the Prime Minister (rather than the Deputy Minister) serving as Chair, and the Minister of Science Technology and Environment as one of the two Vice-Chairs. The other Board members include: the ministers of key agencies such as Finance, Industry, and Agriculture; the Secretary-General of the NESDB; the Board of Investment (BOI); and Permanent Secretaries of related agencies. Up to eight positions were reserved for "members qualified in environmental matters" of whom "no less than half shall be representatives from the private sector."

The Secretariat of the NEB, ONEB, has been abolished and replaced by three departments: the Office of Environmental Policy and Planning, the Department of Pollution Control and the Department of Environmental Quality Promotion. These three departments report to the Ministry of Science Technology and Environment.

There are two separate tracks in the approval process, one for private sector, and the other for the public sector projects. The EA for public sector projects must be undertaken during the Feasibility Study, and the Report filed with and reviewed by the NEB. The NEB may ask the opinion of the Office of Environmental Policy and Planning (OEPP) or other experts. The Report (with the comments) is then submitted to the Cabinet for decision.

For private sector projects, the EA Report is to be submitted simultaneously to the OEPP and to the licensing/permitting agency. Section 48 does allow the proponent to submit an initial environmental evaluation (IEE) rather than an EA Report.

As indicated in figure 4-1, the OEPP can only "comment" on the EA Report; the decision to approve or disapprove the Report lies with an Ad Hoc Experts Committee. The OEPP has fifteen days to comment on the "correctness" of the EA and another fifteen days to make a complete review. The Ad Hoc Experts Committee, which includes a representative of the

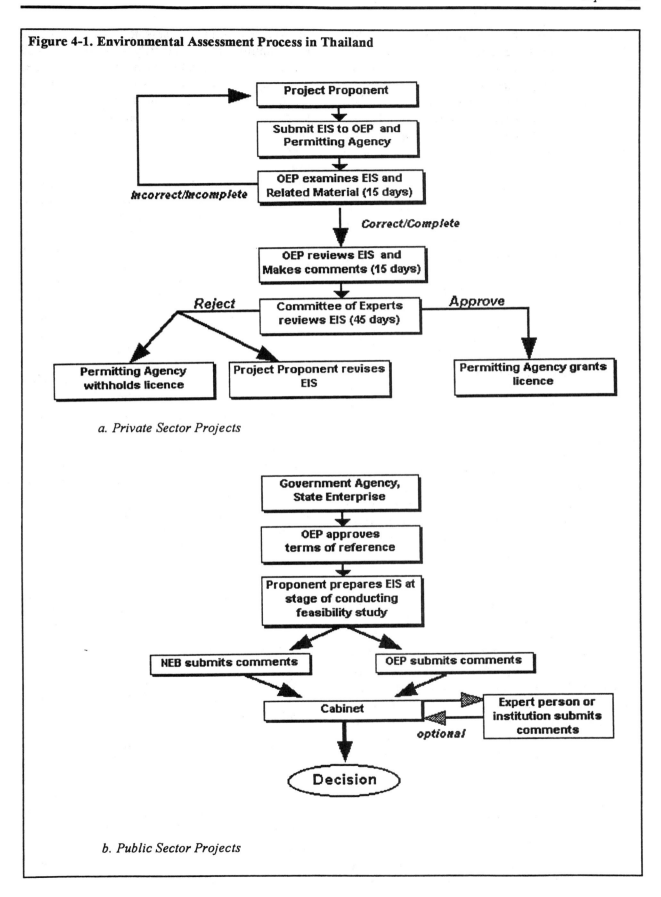

Figure 4-1. Environmental Assessment Process in Thailand

a. Private Sector Projects

b. Public Sector Projects

licensing or permitting agency, must complete its review within forty-five days or the EA Report is considered approved. If it is rejected, the EA Report is either revised or repeated and resubmitted to the Committee. An additional thirty days are allowed for this second review.

CANADA. In Canada, the EARP Guidelines were implemented by the Federal Environmental Assessment Review Office (FEARO). Under Bill C-13, FEARO has been taken out of the Federal Department of Environment and forms the core of a new and independent agency, the Canadian Environmental Assessment Agency (CEAA), which will implement the legislation. The decision to approve or reject the project resides with the Minister of Environment.

Bill C-13 continues to exclude private sector projects unless federal funds or federal lands are involved. "Federal lands" means (a) lands belonging to the Crown; (b) internal waters, fishing zone, and territorial sea within the meaning of the Territorial Sea and Fishing Zones Act; (c) any exclusive economic zone created by the Government of Canada; (d) continental shelf; and (e) reserves and other lands subject to the Indian Act.

This definition of "federal lands" effectively extends the application of the EA review process to predominantly private sector-funded or provincially-funded projects. This definition was unsuccessfully challenged by a private corporation in the Province of British Columbia in 1988, and more recently by the Province of Quebec over the Great Whale Hydroelectric Project. It continues to be a major source of conflict between the federal and provincial governments.

Who Undertakes the EA?

In Thailand the Terms of Reference (TORs) for the EA are decided on and prepared by the project proponent but approved by OEPP. Section 51 of NEQA grants the Minister the authority to require that the EA Report be prepared by licensed specialists. These are generally firms with at least four staff, one being a technical specialist and three having an undergraduate degree in the sciences. An ad hoc committee has been set up to approve the registration of specialists or consulting firms. In Canada no such restriction applies. The TORs are set by the CEAA and open to public bidding.

In Canada, no such restriction applies. The TORs are set by the CEAA and open to public bidding.

Criteria for EA Review

In Thailand, the major criterion for reviewing the EA is whether or not the project design will meet existing environmental quality standards. Where none exists standards of other countries are used. In theory, the EA looks at four impact dimensions: socio-economics, ecological resources, quality of life, and human use. The major review criterion in Canada is whether the EA complies with the TORs, which are also subject to public comment.

Public Participation

THAILAND. Public participation in EA was not institutionalized in the old system nor is it required in the new legislation.[5] Some in the government argue that public interest is taken into consideration through the potential representation of NGOs on the National Environmental Board, which reviews the EA for public sector projects. NGO representatives may also be invited to the Ad Hoc Experts Committee that reviews the EA Report for private sector projects. Others consider that making the EA Report or its Executive Summary public is sufficient notification. The new legislation does have some provisions that have implications for local communities and public interest groups with respect to development projects.

The Environmental Quality Management Action Plan developed under Section 37 decentralizes the environmental protection decisionmaking process. It enforces of laws relating to "pollution control, nature conservation, natural resources and cultural environment" in local (provincial and subdistrict) governments. The NEB is setting up four regional offices for this purpose.

Of equal if not greater significance is Section 6, which grants rights and duties to individuals "for the purposes of public participation in the enhancement and conservation of national environmental quality." These include the right to:

• Be informed and obtain information and data from the government on "matters concerning the enhancement and conservation of environmental quality, except where the information or data involves officially classified material, such as secret intelligence pertaining to national security, or secrets pertaining to rights to privacy, property rights, or the rights in trade or business which are duly protected by law."

• Be remedied or compensated by the state in case of damage or injury from pollution.

• Petition or lodge a complaint against polluters where violation is witnessed.

• Cooperate with and assist government officials in the performance of duties relating to the enhancement and conservation of environmental quality.

Under Section 8, NGOs and nonprofit organizations or juridical persons directly engaged in activities concerning environmental protection or conservation "without any objective to be involved in politics" may register with the Ministry of Science Technology and Environment. Registered NGOs may request government assistance to carry out the following:

• Organize volunteers to assist in implementing conservation laws.

• Mount public relations and environmental education campaigns.

• Initiate environmental protection and conservation projects.

• Conduct environmental protection and conservation research.

• Provide legal aid to victims of pollution.

NGOs may also propose nominees to represent the private sector in the NEB. Registration of NGOs may be revoked if their activities cause "disturbances or [are] contrary to public order or unsuitable."

Sections 8 and 37 appear to provide a window of opportunity for the public to participate in environmental protection and resource management. As will be shown in a later section, communities are indeed using this window.

CANADA. In sharp contrast, the Canadian EA process has always been fairly transparent. One of the objectives of Bill C-13, according to the Preamble, is to "facilitate public participation in the environmental assessment... [by] providing access to the information on which assessments are based." The legislation has opened up the process by allowing public input early in the scoping and public review phase.

Constraints

THAILAND. There have been and will continue to be disadvantages arising from relying on the List of categories of projects that would require an EA.[6] First, the List does not include new areas of major economic activities with serious social and

environmental implications. Important examples include industrial tree plantations, currently a mainstay of forest policy, and reforestation programs such as the recently suspended Khor Jor Kor.[7] These were not included in the List and have been the subject of intense public controversy. Community opposition has occasionally escalated to violence, such as the burning of government nurseries and plantations by villagers in Buriram (TURA-CIDA 1991), and the recent clashes in Nakhon Ratchasima between the military and park encroachers. A third of the three hundred or so families who were relocated in September 1991 decided to leave the state's designated resettlement area because of "frustration over unfulfilled government promises." They camped in the grounds of a nearby temple and in June this year returned to their old village in Tab Larn National Park in an attempt to prepare land for the planting season. Confrontation with the army ensued (Bangkok Post 1992g).

Second, the List places emphasis on large-scale projects and overlooks the cumulative impacts of many relatively small projects. The subsidence from small-scale mining activities that resulted in severe river pollution in the northeastern provinces show that cumulative impacts can be significant. Failure to consider these impacts continues to take its toll. The sequential development of a deep sea port on Si Chang Island and rock mining in the Chon Buri province have caused visible impacts on the social and cultural environment, and may possibly pose a risk to human health. This has led island residents to demand the prosecution of the rock mining plant owner and the cancellation of a proposed solvent plant in Si Chang and deep sea port in the Chon Buri mainland. The promise of a technical school and 4,000 jobs for the residents does not appear to have mollified the opposition.

Finally, the EA process as defined in the legislation assumes that the interest of the public or affected communities can be articulated adequately by NGOs or environmental professionals. This assumption, while understandable, may prove simplistic nevertheless.

There appears to be a genuine lack of confidence on the part of government officials and environmental professionals in the ability of local groups to participate in an informed and meaningful way as part of the project planning. When asked "whether or not the failure to inform and involve the local communities early in the assessment process had not proven too costly," as evidenced by several cases of abandoned projects in the country, the responses ranged from "no, we cannot have the public; every time we have the public we get a mob," to "if you involve the public too early, they will always say 'no' to the project; they can have a role in implementing the relocation" to "the tribals are overly exploiting the environment anyway." Even the participation of NGOs on the NEB or the Ad Hoc Experts Committee would appear to come rather late in the process.

CANADA. The EARP Guidelines have been criticized for being focused only on projects, which effectively excludes from examination policy questions and project alternatives, and places the assessment process late in the project cycle. Bill C-13 does not effectively address these issues.[8] Environmental NGOs have noted two areas of concern regarding Bill C-13. One is that the legislation provides no guarantee for full and automatic "public disclosure of impact-related project documents, which is necessary for a credible and fair environmental review."[9] A second concern is the perceived ambiguity in the mandate and composition of Joint Review Panels.[10] According to critics, the limitations were imposed and rationalized by the "sovereignty" issue.

CIDA is now in the unenviable position of drafting the regulation that may clarify these issues. The regulation will define the essentials of the EA procedure to be followed for CIDA projects. The procedure would have to meet, as well as be perceived as meeting, the "basic goals and objectives of Canadian environmental policies" while at the same time allowing for a cost-effective design and timely delivery of projects that promote Canadian foreign policy objectives. This is CIDA's principal institutional mandate.

Whether or not CIDA succeeds in this task remains to be seen. There are some who would argue that the task is an impossible one because the objectives of environmental protection and foreign policy cannot be fully reconciled. It is arguable that the final adjudication between these conflicting public policy objectives would vary from case to case with the outcome determined largely by the relative strength and strategies of the political actors involved.

A more fundamental but evitable weakness of the Canadian EA legislation lies in the fact that while "the promotion of sustainable development" is explicitly defined as one of the objectives of the legislation, the definition of what constitutes the "environment" remains restricted to the biophysical dimension. There are admittedly many and frequently divergent definitions of sustainable development (see for example Redclift 1991, 1992). There is no consensus on what needs to be sustained, for how long, and over what area. However, what is common among all definitions and principles advocated so far is a recognition of the interdependence between the biophysical and human system dimensions and its relevance to the pursuit of sustainability.

Under Bill C-13, potential impacts on the human system are included in the assessment *only* if they are caused by the environmental effects of the project. This either reflects an institutional failure to fully analyze and understand the different dimensions and planning implications of sustainable development, or it illustrates the inability of public institutions and public servants to innovate, take risks, and accommodate complexity, uncertainty and flexibility in project-related decision criteria and the decisionmaking process.

Other Observations

THAILAND. There is greater use of IEE than EA in Thailand (Lohani 1988). Some analysts see this as positive in that collection of data runs concurrently with the technical feasibility study and is tailored to the major impacts anticipated (Ouano n.d.). NEQA imposes compliance monitoring of mitigation measures on facilities and projects.

CANADA. IEE has been an integral part of the Canadian EA process, but until Bill C-13, neither the criteria used in decisionmaking nor the outcome were open to the public. Bill C-13 calls for a "follow-up program" for "(a) verifying the accuracy of the environmental assessment of a project and (b) determining the effectiveness of any measures taken to mitigate the adverse environmental effects of the project."

Neither the Thai nor the Canadian legislation effectively integrates cumulative impacts in the assessment process (see table 4-1).

Trends in EA in LCCs

More and more LCC governments will institutionalize environmental assessment. The trend is irreversible. There will continue to be pressure from donors and IFIs. Eventually, however, it will be the internal forces—principally, the stronger, unequivocal evidence of environment-development interdependence and a public that is better informed by the mass media—that will sustain the momentum.

How will the content and process of EA look in these countries? To borrow from an earlier publication on institutionalizing EA, will LCC governments "round the peg or square the hole?"[11]

Technical Dimension

Some governments will define a technologically elaborate and sophisticated system, seemingly "squaring the hole." In Southeast Asia, we see this in the People's Republic of China and to a certain extent, in Indonesia. Others will put in place a modified, technically more modest process. Some of the modifications will be creative; others will appear to be a simple "cutting of corners," at least initially. Thailand, Malaysia and the Philippines appear to be taking this route. The Philippine EA, implemented under severe political, institutional and resources constraints, is nevertheless dynamic, and its application is creative and responsive. The changes prudently introduced through administrative order rather than legislative channels include: (a) "social acceptability" as an additional criterion for granting the Environmental Compliance Certificate (ECC) needed for project implementation; (b) the setting up of an Environmental Guarantee Fund by the proponent to cover the cost of potential accidents; (c) multipartite coordination of the compliance monitoring program with the regional offices of the Department of Environment and Natural Resources, Local Government Units, Nongovernmental Organizations and Peoples' Organization; and (d) Emergency Response Program as part of the EIS.

Political Dimension

Some governments will formally acknowledge the need for and accommodate public input in different stages of the assessment; others will not. Looking again at Southeast Asian countries, the Philippines, Indonesia and Malaysia explicitly indicate public participation in the EA process, whereas China and Thailand do not.

Operationalization

Whether EA is operationalized and effectively internalized in the public administration system as officially prescribed, will ultimately depend on many factors. No doubt one of the variables is the assistance LCC governments will receive in training the necessary cadre of practitioners and in establishing the necessary ecological database.

Given the current sluggishness of the global economy, it is not likely that financial flows to LCCs through ODA will be of such magnitude as to meet the resources required for fully implementing the highly technological and resource-intensive EA model of the High Consumption Countries (HCCs). In other words, "squaring the hole" may not be affordable for LCCs in the foreseeable future.

Another determinant in shaping the EA model that eventually evolves in LCCs is the organizational strength of the movement for social change in these countries. There is no reason to believe that affected people will remain within the slots prescribed for them by governments.

The current developments in Thailand's Si Chang Island provides an excellent example. The interim Prime Minister recently visited the region as part of the government's public education program on the new legislation. He used the costly pollution clean-up in Pattaya and the controversy on Si Chang Island to highlight the need for a collective sense of responsibility and cooperation on environmental protection and management. Speaking in relation to the demands of the Si Chang Island residents the Prime Minister was reported to have said that "the Si Chang controversy should serve as a lesson that future development must be taken not only for economic gain, but also for social and environmental reasons." He underscored the need to consider the views of local people affected by development projects but reportedly added that the "views of local communities affected by the projects should be secondary to national benefits" (Bangkok Post 1992f).

The Nation (1992a) gave the following account of the villagers' response:

> A representative of the Si Chang residents said after the meeting with Anand yesterday that the islanders were not satisfied with the premier's unclear response to their demand for a complete stop to the rock blasting and the port project. Noi Saencharoensap said if the government fails to take any action in 10 days to end the quarrying and the planned port construction, the islanders will petition HRH Princess Maha Chakri Sirindhorn for help. Noi said the villagers did not want the port. Instead they want the whole island declared a national heritage.

Lessons for Donors and IFIs

The implementation of the EA process in LCCs will depend on several factors. First, donors and IFIs should review the concept of exclusion lists, for example, the Inter-American Development Bank's (IDB) Category I and II. As the Khor Jor Kor experience in Thailand unequivocally shows, even environmental rehabilitation projects (for example, park conservation schemes, reforestation programs) can have serious indirect environmental impacts. If project lists are used, then there should be explicit mechanisms for post-project impact monitoring and periodic review of the lists.

Second, if the interest of donors and IFIs in EA as a planning tool extends beyond meeting the demands of HCC-based constituencies, they should devote some resources to examining cost-effective ways of dealing with the environmental impacts of small industries. Small family-operations, such as metal-plating, metal-finishing, furniture-making, and piggeries, are a dominant and socio-economically important feature in LCCs. Most of these industries produce hazardous wastes and simply do not have the resources to manage them properly. None of these industries receive external funding; hence, none of the impacts will be linked to donors and IFIs and draw the attention of HCC-based environmental groups. But the serious environmental and human health impacts are well established and are neither prevented nor mitigated by simply undertaking an EA. The EA procedures need to be modified so that small industries do not clog up the EA system but are instead used to assist in adopting low-waste technologies, for example, water recirculation systems or source segregation and recovery systems for cyanide, heavy metals and solvents. Potential areas of assistance include downscaling available low-waste technologies, phasing out end-of-pipe technologies, and identifying appropriate policy instruments that would effectively bring about these technological changes.

Third, along the same lines, there is need to gather and analyze case experiences of EA methods that are truly cost-effective. If the institutionalization and implementation of EA in LCCs is to be sustained through indigenous resources, donors and IFIs should actively support experiments at developing less-costly but effective EA. The information and resource intensity that is typified by the EA process in Canada

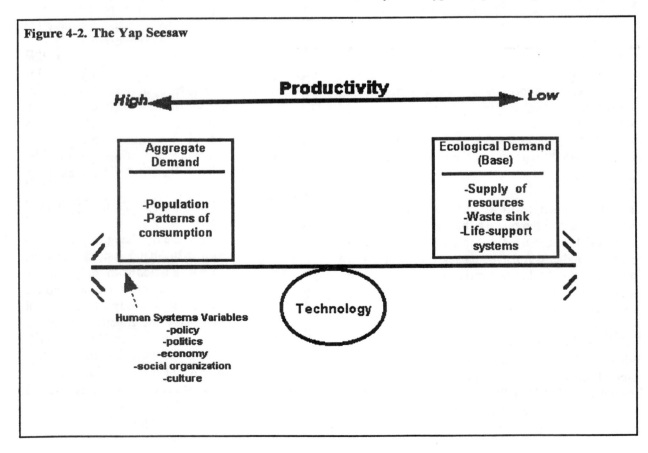

Figure 4-2. The Yap Seesaw

and the United States may be feasible for externally funded projects but is unrealistic for the majority of economic development activities that are being undertaken and will continue to be pursued in LCCs.

What are currently being passed off as cost-effective EAs are simple truncations of the U.S. or the Canadian model. They may cost less, but their effectiveness is debatable (Lohani 1988). Creative ways of using rapid appraisal and modified Delphi techniques to link up the EA process and indigenous technical knowledge systems should be explored.

Fourth, if indeed the objective of impact assessment is the promotion of sustainable development, bilateral donors and IFIs should shift from environmental assessment to technology assessment, formally recognizing that sustainability is determined not only by the biophysical but also by the social, economic, cultural and political environments (Lohani 1988; Yap 1990b; CIDA 1992). The impacts on these dimensions must all be included in the assessment.

All development interventions introduce some form of technology or induce some technological change. Technology is in fact *the* immediate *stressor*. If one pictures the pursuit of sustainable development as the struggle to balance the human demands against the ecological base or capital, as in a seesaw with technology as the *pivot* (since it mediates the interaction between the two) and the *plank* being policy, culture, social and economic organization, then one can see what a limited tool EA is (figure 4-2). In undertaking an EA, one is by definition examining the impacts on the ecological base that is only one side of the seesaw. Technology assessment, on the other hand, is not as delimited. It is in effect an assessment of the positive and negative impacts of the intervention. It may be visualized as an assessment of the effects that a change in the *pivot* has on the various elements of the seesaw—population, patterns of consumption, cultural practices, and social and economic organization, as well as the ecological functions. All of these contribute to the overall balance or imbalance—to the overall sustainability or lack thereof. All of the impacts of the intervention on these dimensions therefore must be included in the assessment.

An integral part of operationalizing impact assessment within a sustainable development framework is a recognition of the inadequacy of our knowledge and understanding of the thermodynamics and kinetics of biogeochemical processes and our limited understanding of the dynamics of sociopolitical change. If the goal is sustainability, then impact monitoring and management should be integrated *into* the assessment process.

Fifth, donors and IFIs need to accept the reality that the modalities of public participation in the EA process in LCCs may not be familiar ones, and the process may not be tidy. Educating the public in HCCs should be undertaken. Public interest groups in HCCs must be made to recognize that there is no one "correct" model of public participation and that it is counterproductive for environmental NGOs, donors and IFIs to "pigeonhole" LCC communities into one process. To rearticulate an earlier argument, the public participation process in HCCs did not evolve in a vacuum, rather it is a product of the western political, technical, and cultural tradition. As is clearly demonstrated by the developments in Thailand and the Philippines, LCC "publics" will develop and struggle through their own process. The role of environmental NGOs, donors and IFIs is to actively facilitate the evolution, not decide its direction.

Finally, if only for cost-effectiveness reasons, donors and IFIs should start differentiating the needs of LCCs with respect to EA. Certainly in Southeast Asia, countries are at different stages of need. Thailand's greatest need appears to be in developing environmental expertise. The Philippines, on the other hand, has a relatively high number of highly qualified, committed environmental experts in the public and private sectors and in nongovernmental and nonprofit organizations. What is seriously hampering the efforts of this pool of experts is the lack of facilities—pollution monitoring equipment, laboratories, computers, and even telephone lines.

Donors and IFIs must dare to be flexible and creative; they should have the courage to experiment with tools that would facilitate the evolution of a participation process appropriate to the indigenous cultural, social and political context. At the same time, they must be creative and develop reasonably clear but flexible lines of accountability.

Notes

1. On June 23, 1992, Bill C-13 became the Act to Establish a Federal Environmental Assessment Process, Statutes of Canada, chapter 37.

2. Interview with Vannasaeng, Office of Environmental Policy and Planning, July 1992.

3. For a more detailed review of the Canadian EA process, see Robinson (1991).

4. In addition, several thousand projects undergo environmental screening a year; some require an initial

environmental evaluation (telephone interview with Pat Le Blanc, Director of the Federal Environmental Assessment Review Office, November 25, 1993).

5. This resulted in some economic costs to project developers. The most famous example is the Nam Choan Dam, on the Khwae Yai River in Kanchanaburi, proposed in 1982 by the Electricity Generation of Thailand. It was abandoned following protests by university students. The dam proposal was revived in 1986 only to be shelved once again by an even broader coalition of pressure groups (Hirsch and Lohmann 1989). Other examples of abandoned projects include: Shell Thailand Reforestation Project in Chanthaburi, Suan Kitti's Reforestation Project in Chachoengsao and the Cable Car Project in Chiangmai. All encountered strong public opposition after the projects had been initiated.

6. Attempts by ONEB to add to the prescribed list of projects or activities requiring an EA have apparently been resisted by industry (Vannasaeng, personal communication).

7. Khor Jor Kor, also called "A Program on Land Resettlement for the Poor Living in the Forest Reserves," was established in 1985 with the Royal Military as the implementing agency. The idea was to identify parts of (Gazetted) park reserves degraded from encroachment by landless peasants, officially declare them as degraded, relocate the peasants with promise of title to land outside the reserve, and thus allow for reforestation of the degraded area, generally through private sector industrial tree plantation. For example the military's 5-year plan for the north and northeastern region is to make space for industrial tree plantations by relocating 50,000 families (2,500 villages) who have encroached on park reserves. Implementation of the program has been beset by several problems. A common problem reported has been that the resettlement sites are already occupied and therefore unable to fully accommodate the newcomers. This has led to hostilities in some sites. In two instances, specifically the Taplan National Park in Nakhon Ratchasima and Dongkwang forest in the Kut Bak District, vast tracks of forested land were put under the axe to resettle the displaced park encroachers. Other sources of frustration and conflict include: (a) the promise of land titles not being fulfilled; (b) the amount of land granted being much less than that promised; and (c) the land granted being unworkable.

8. The Parliamentary Committee on the Environment will supposedly assess the potential environmental impacts of policy related to development projects. However, the committee does not have a legal mandate.

9. "The Proposed Canadian Environmental Assessment Act. Implications for international Projects." A brief presented by Probe International to the Special Committee on Bill C-78. November 1990.

10. Bill C-13 allows the Canadian government to establish Joint Panels with foreign governments and with institutions of these governments for the review of ODA-funded projects.

11. For the arguments, see Yap 1990.

References

Act to Establish a Federal Environmental Assessment Process. 1992. Statutes of Canada, chapter 37 (June 23).

Bangkok Post. 1992a. "A Thai Dances with Wolves." June 23.

———. 1992b. "Dam Threatens Mae Yom Park." May 10.

———. 1992c. "Dongkwang Forest New Relocation Site." May 10.

———. 1992d. "Estate Developers Told to Detail Development Plans." June 20.

———. 1992e. "Panel Set Up to Probe Clash with Encroachers." June 20.

———. 1992f. "PM says Si Chang Must be Properly Developed." July 19.

———. 1992g. "This Land is Our Land." June 17.

Biswas, A.K. 1989. "Recommendations on Environmental Impact Analysis for Developing Countries." *Environmental Conservation* 61.

Canadian International Development Agency (CIDA). 1991. "Thai Environmental Policies and Regional Resources Exploitation." Discussion Paper, CIDA, Canada.

———. 1992. *CIDA's Policy for Environmental Sustainability.*

Chia, Lin Sien, ed. 1987. *Environmental Management in Southeast Asia.* Singapore.

Government of Thailand. 1992. Enhancement and Conservation of National Environmental Quality Act, (B.E. 2535). Bangkok, Thailand.

Hirsch, P. and L. Lohmann. 1989. "Contemporary Politics of Environment in Thailand." *Asian Survey* 29(4):439-51.

Lohani, B.N. 1988. "Environmental Assessment and Management in the Bank's Developing Member Countries." *Training Workshop on Environmental Impact Assessment and Evaluation.* Proceedings and Training Manual. Vol. 1, January 18-24. Lucknou, India.

The Nation. 1992a. "Anand Meeting Fails to Cheer Islanders." July 19.

———. 1992b. "Cabinet Suspends Resettlement Plan." June 24.

———. 1992c. "Si Chang's Changing Face." July 16.

Ouano, R. n.d. "Overview of Environmental Impact Assessment in the Asia-Pacific Region."

Prasith-rathsint, S., ed. 1991. *Thailand's National Development Policy: Issues and Challenges.* Bangkok: Thai University Research Association/CIDA.

Probe International. 1990a. "The Proposed Canadian Environmental Assessment Act. Implications for International Projects." A brief presented to the Special Committee on Bill C-78. Canada.

———. 1990b. "Review of the Inter-American Development Bank's New Procedures for Classifying and Evaluating Environmental Impacts of Bank Operations." Discussion paper, Probe International. Canada.

Redclift, M. 1991. "The Multiple Dimensions of

Sustainable Development." *Geography* 36-42.

———. 1992. "The Meaning of Sustainable Development." *Geoforum* 23(3):395-403.

Robinson, R. 1991. "New Developments in Federal Environmental Assessment." *Impact Assessment Bulletin* 9(4):57-68.

Sekitar, J.A. n.d. *A Handbook of Environmental Assessment Guidelines*. Department of Environment. Kuala Lumpur, Malaysia.

TURA-CIDA. 1991. "Thai Environmental Policies and Regional Resources Exploitation." TURA-CIDA Discussion Paper.

Yap, N.T. 1990a. "Round the Peg or Square the Hole? Populists, Technocrats and Environmental Assessment in Third World Countries." *Impact Assessment Bulletin* 8(1 and 2):69-84.

———. 1990b. "Sustainable Development. Exploring the Contradictions." *Current* January.

5

Managing Tropical Forest Development: Technology Transfer in Environmental Assessment

Wilson Eedy and Lars Hurlen

Environmental assessment and management requirements have evolved rapidly in Southeast Asia, especially in tropical forest development, where international environmental pressure greatly influences multinational developers, funding and markets. International development funding agencies such as the Asian Development Bank (AsDB) and the World Bank have recently prepared environmental assessment (EA) guidelines that rival the state of the art in North America (AsDB 1990; World Bank 1992). Government funding agencies have also supported the development of local environmental regulation protocol. Application experience to make these laws functional is now greatly needed.

Canada and the United States have developed and instituted EA requirements for some twenty years. Their procedures have evolved through the stages of pure inventory, impact prediction, and mitigation planning, to the more proactive approaches of cumulative assessment, sustainable development, and adaptive environmental management (Jacobs and Sadler 1990). These mature application methods should be transferred to developing countries to ensure that their new laws and guidelines are not just good theory, but demonstrate sound environmental management.

Environment and development is the topic of the decade. It is intimately linked with key issues such as sustainable development, ecosystem diversity, and global quality of life. Its popularity began to peak with the report of the Brundtland Commission (1987) and has continued through the United Nations Conference on Environment and Development ("Earth Summit") in Rio de Janeiro (1992). The essential need for linking environment and development is a principle we all agree on; it is required by most international lending agencies and enshrined in the legislation of almost every country. But discussion is no longer enough; it is time for action.

The principles on which our work and this chapter are based are universally applicable; we believe it is essential that EA be used more extensively in environmental planning worldwide. To illustrate these principles we will discuss the environmental assessment process in Indonesia, using as a case study a major forest development project that includes plans for EA technology transfer. The project will develop a 1,700-tons-per-day (tpd) pulp mill and 300,000 hectares (ha) of reforestation plantation in southern Sumatra. The environmental assessment follows the Environmental Management Development in Indonesia (EMDI) program and the Asian Development Bank's EA guidelines. An initial EA has been completed and more detailed environmental investigations are planned. The studies are being funded by Beak Consultants Limited (BEAK), the Canadian International Development Agency (CIDA) and the Barito Pacific Group.

The overall objectives of the study are to (a) apply state-of-the-art environmental assessment practices and management technology to ensure both environmental and economical viability, and (b) demonstrate the critical need for transfer of technology and experience in environmental assessment and management to developing countries. This will involve the following application techniques:

• sustainability assessment of forest plantation management, cultural assimilation of itinerant farmers, and reforestation of grasslands;

• cumulative impact assessment, including existing impacts from, for example, slash-and-burn agriculture, population transmigration, water and air pollution, and soil depletion;

• adaptive management, including the requirement for monitoring and appropriate feedback about the management of forest plantations, effluents, and local employment; and

• transfer of technology through association with

EMDI, the Indonesian government, and Indonesian engineering consultants.

This chapter demonstrates the critical need for transfer of application technology and experience in environmental assessment and management in developing nations.

Population Growth and Deforestation in Indonesia

Tropical forests, especially those in Indonesia, are valuable for a number of economic activities and ecological services: local labor and foreign exchange; ecological diversity; watershed protection; nutrient cycling; subsistence use (for firewood and food, for instance); habitat for flora and fauna; cultural and social values; and global carbon dioxide (CO_2) fixation (World Bank 1990; CIDA 1992). On the islands of Java and Sumatra, population settlements, stable and shifting agriculture, and forest or other resource harvesting have left a large part of the land in a heavily used or unproductive condition. Eighty-five percent of the land base in Java is now under intensive cultivation, with the size of the average family farm less than 0.5 ha (World Bank 1990). The increasing population has to look elsewhere for land. Transmigration policies that were implemented to resolve the population concentration on Java have resulted in major forest impacts elsewhere, for example, by encouraging slash-and-burn shifting cultivation, which often causes *Alang alang* grasslands that have little economic or environmental diversity value. If these issues are not resolved, the impacts will continue to spread through the less-developed parts of Indonesia as well. The World Bank (1990) estimated that the outer islands were experiencing natural and migrant population increases of 5 percent a year. Table 5-1 provides a summary of the development pressures on forests in Indonesia.

Indonesia has 2.5 times the forest area of all of western Europe. In 1982, 60 percent of the land base of Indonesia was forested (110 million ha). At that time 800,000 ha per year were being logged, more than in all the rest of southeast Asia combined. Current estimates indicate that primary forest areas in Indonesia are disappearing at about 1 million ha per year (World Bank 1990). Indonesia's large population is striving to meet the economic standards of northern hemisphere lifestyles and this presents the major problem to meeting the definition of environmental sustainability (see Goodland 1993).

Planning and implementation are essential to

Table 5-1. Population Growth and Deforestation Pressures in Indonesia

Indicator	Java	Sumatra	Other	Total
1988 population (millions)	106	36.2	33.7	175.9
Population density (number/km2)	788	74	n.a.	90
Population growth (% annual)	1.7	3.1	2.5	2.1
Protected forest (1,000 ha)	988	10,778	37,267	49,043
Total annual forest loss (1,000 ha)	n.a.	n.a.	n.a.	900
Loss to logging (1,000 ha)	n.a.	n.a.	n.a.	180
Loss to development projects (1,000 ha)	n.a.	n.a.	n.a.	250
Loss to smallholder conversion (1,000 ha)	n.a.	n.a.	n.a.	500

n.a. Data not available
Source: World Bank 1990.

sustainable development. Indonesia has had the institutional and legislative tools for environmental management for some time, partly because of the CIDA-funded EMDI program over the past decade. EMDI has also introduced EA as an essential planning tool. The Indonesian government has since embraced environmental management as a critical concept in its current 5-year plan (Repilita). In a recent issue the *Jakarta Times* quoted President Suharto as telling industrial leaders that "Indonesia has given you the resources to develop your industries; now you must repay us with environmental protection and quality of life."

Adopting the Canadian Model for EA

Environmental assessment is a legislative requirement in Indonesia. Much of the EA process, as it existed in Canada in the mid-1980s, was transferred directly into Indonesian legislation through the EMDI.[1]

Although the institutional requirements have been put in place, they continue to be the subject of funding initiatives by the World Bank and the Asian Development Bank.

The Indonesian EA process, AMDAL, is similar to the Federal Environmental Assessment and Review Process (EARP) in Canada (see table 5-2). Both countries' requirements include environmental screening, initial environmental evaluation (IEE), and comprehensive study stages. Although independent review agencies have been instituted in both countries, the Indonesian legislation has more formalized EA review guidelines. There has as yet been only limited public participation in the Indonesian EA process. Several development projects have gone through the IEE or project evaluation level (PEL) assessment; only a few have been assessed at the full EA or ANDAL level.

Environmental assessment in North America has evolved from a project justification exercise to an innovative planning tool. Its main value is to provide a framework for ensuring that all aspects of the proposed development are thought through carefully and are planned and implemented in an environmentally optimal manner. These objectives of the EA process are difficult to transfer through written guidelines or legislation only: they must be demonstrated through practice—the implementation procedures and institutional framework—to ensure that they work. This effective transfer is one objective of our ongoing EA work in Indonesia. Our plan is to involve local consultants, researchers and government agencies throughout the study to demonstrate the importance of the planning and management components of an EA (Stone and Eedy 1977).

Table 5-2. Comparisons of Candian EARP and Indonesian AMDAL Environmental Assessment Procedures

EA Process	Canadian	Indonesian
EA Requirement criteria	Federal money, land or regulatory responsibility.	Potentially all existing or planned development.
Screening level	Performed by initiating federal department.	Performed by BAPEDAL (a Crown corporation set up through EA legislation).
Project initial level (PIL) or initial evaluation level (IEE) of new plan	Initiating department regulates or proponent does EA.	BAPEDAL regulates or proponent does EA.
Project evaluation level (PEL) or initial evaluation of existing development	Not done.	As above.
Full EA or AMDAL (new proposed project)	Project-specific panel to set EA and review results.	BAPEDAL sets project-specific guidelines and reviews results.
SEL or full EA of existing development	Not done.	As above.
EA guidelines.	Specific guidelines only at EA-level (set by panel). Other levels have generic guidelines.	General guidelines in legislation. BAPEDAL to set specific guidelines through negotiations with government regulating departments and proponent (process yet to be implemented).
Impact evaluation weightings and project acceptability	A decision of the review department or panel; no written guidelines.	Regulations set 7 criteria with 5 levels of impacts in each; becomes the target of EA to justify project.
Public involvement.	High level required.	Recommended but not yet implemented.

Note: This comparison is of the Canadian process prior to the Canadian Environmental Assessment Act 1991.
Source: EMDI 1991

The Musi Pulp and Forest Plantation Project

The proposed development is an integrated forest plantation and pulp mill project that includes a 1,500-tpd bleached Kraft pulp mill and a 300,000-ha forest management area. Forest operations involve replanting 200,000 ha of grasslands or old rubber plantation into a plantation of *Acacia mangium*, mixed with eucalyptus and other species. The benefit of plantation forestry with these species is the small area required and the short turnaround time. These species also may fill at least part of the demand for native tropical species and save virgin forest areas. A pulp mill of similar size in boreal Canada requires about 1.4 million ha of forest, with species that need about 90 years to mature.

Initial Findings

Biodiversity was a significant issue in the initial EA feasibility study. Plantation forestry is sustainable by design (assuming appropriate research and management is incorporated), but it has been criticized as a rather ecologically sterile monoculture. Forest research and management are important parts of our EA; the initial study recommended preserving the remaining native forest areas of the forestry concession, including significant blocks of forest and corridors along drainage systems that greatly diversify the overall vegetation and wildlife habitat potential of the area. Agroforestry intercropping and mixing of the plantation species and ages have also increased biodiversity. Developing plantations on *Alang alang* grassland or former rubber plantation areas has improved the diversity and productivity of the areas from their prior degraded state. It is planned that the provision for local forestry jobs and agroforestry production will also reduce some of the incentives to practice shifting (slash-and-burn) agriculture in the area. The following common issues have to be dealt with throughout the EA process:

• *Sustainability.* Studies are needed to determine the long-term effects (such as on soils, nutrients, diseases and pests) of short-term forest rotation and agroforestry.

• *No net loss.* The basic concept of sustainability is that the long-term resource base will not be deleted. This has been a planning requirement for some time in various sectors in Canada.

• *Cumulative effects.* This is one of the important components of EA in North America. It is especially important in forestry in Sumatra where slash-and-burn agriculture blackens the skies for months,

industrial development already affects air quality, and various other social and ecological factors must be addressed to evaluate sustainability.

• *Greenhouse effects and acid deposition.* Both are research priorities in many industrial countries and findings must be applied to the global sustainability equation.

• *Indigenous peoples and their rights.* These are major issues in North American forest management and are quickly becoming important in Indonesia and other developing countries.

Technology Transfer in Project Planning and Design

Technology transfer in the EA planning process includes the evaluation of design and environmental regulation issues, and we have found there is a great deal to learn from our Indonesian colleagues in the area of forest management. Initially, best available technology (BAT) economically achievable was our starting point for environmental protection at the pulp mill. This required a review of the engineering design information in light of our experiences in the Canadian forest industry. But forest genetics taught us new parameters in Indonesia: the 8-year growth cycles in Sumatra allow testing procedures that are just not feasible with the 80–90 year cycles in northern Canada.

Site-specific studies are still being conducted to determine the potential for further forest management, socio-economic infrastructure development, waste treatment or other special requirements. These studies are based on site meteorology, hydrology, ecology, resource use, ambient quality, regional socio-economic and other considerations. The following are some of the BAT concepts that were recommended in our initial EA:

• *Low-chlorine bleaching.* This operation was relatively new to an area that is just beginning to consider water quality issues in general and has not yet reached the complicated world of low-concentration by high-risk chlorinated hydrocarbons, which has become an important consideration to the world marketability of the product.

• *Low water consumption and recycling.* This process can be important even in a rain forest area, especially during the dry seasons and when there are heavy downstream resource uses.

• *Secondary treatment of mill effluent.*

• *Modern air emission control.* Process (condensate-stripping and low-odor recovery boiler) and emission treatment (precipitators or scrubbers).

Based on the EA studies currently in progress, site-specific recommendations will be considered for tertiary effluent treatment, low-volume gas collection system, or special outfall design. EA studies to determine these requirements include meteorological monitoring, hydrological data collection, biological resource and resource use studies in the receiving environment, computer modelling, assimilative capacity analyses, and effect assessment. The theory for such studies is well documented in the literature. The application to the Sumatra site requires an innovative and cooperative combination of our North American team's experiences and local knowledge. The transfer of technology is essentially a two-way process. The successful operation of BAT, of course, will also depend on adequate technology transfer to the operators.

The traditional EA approach, which seems to be the state of the art in many developing countries, is one that responds to guidelines or legislation without the need for innovative assessment, cumulative EA analysis, and management planning. It is largely equivalent to the North American state of the art in the 1980s when many of these guidelines and legislative initiatives were transferred. This approach is one of inventory, that is, documenting all of the environmental and developmental components in isolation without necessarily linking the various elements of the development, the environment, and the overall management picture. Sustainable development—the development integration we are trying to attain in the present EA process—requires the ability to link all of these factors and their potential interactions. Emissions from the mill will interact with the forest plantation, and runoff from the forest will affect the seasonal water supply to the mill. Forest production is intimately linked with the culture and resource use of the people in the area, as is the water used by the mill. The project can in theory meet the general guidelines for environmental sustainability, as indicated below:

• In using the best available technology, the mill should operate easily within the assimilative capacity of the local environment, but further studies have been proposed to demonstrate this. Once the mill is operational, the theory will have to be put into practice by local operators, and this is where transfer of technology will be essential.

• With tropical hardwood species, the forest area should produce more than enough to meet the mill fiber needs. There is need for some further research, as proposed, to determine the micro-nutrient requirements for multiple-cycle harvesting.

In order to optimize these interactions and achieve a sustainable development scenario, one has to look at a much broader and longer-term perspective. In our study we are attempting to demonstrate and transfer to the local government and consulting groups, this ecosystem approach to EA and this understanding of the interrelationship of the EA to the planning, management and long-term success of the project.

Conclusions

At the time of updating this chapter [late 1993], political and economic issues have interrupted our plans to continue the EA process to meet all of the objectives disucssed. However, the recommendations have been reviewed and accepted, in principle, by the government, financial institutions and the client. We hope the study will be able to continue in the near future and will include the technology transfer approach proposed.

At the conclusion of the study, we will have demonstrated, through application in Indonesia, the utility and value of the EA approach to environmental management. We hope this demonstration will convince government regulators of the standards that must be met for future EAs. This application and regulation must go beyond paper guidelines. We feel we can convince our industrial clients of the long-term benefits of integrated environmental planning through the EA process. Not only does this lead to a more viable, long-term (sustainable) return for their investment, but it also provides for a better environment and quality of life for their people. We are also integrating our local and North American study team expertise to transfer ability in applying the EA process as a planning and management tool over the long term.

Notes

1. The EA process in Canada is continually evolving through the Canadian Environmental Assessment Research Council, the new Canadian Environmental Assessment Act, Provincial EA requirements, and the practical experiences of developers, regulators, consultants, and the public.

References

Asia Development Bank (AsDB). 1990. *Environmental Guidelines for Selected Industrial and Power*

Development Projects. Manila, Philippines: AsDB.

Beak Consultants Limited, Geomatics International Inc., and Wiratman Engineering Limited. 1991. "Musi Pulp and Forest Plantation Project: Environmental Feasibility Evaluation." A report for The Canadian International Development Agency and the Barito Pacific Group, Ontario, Canada.

Beak Consultants Limited (BEAK). 1980. *World Bank Environmental Considerations in the Pulp and Paper industry.* Ontario, Canada: BEAK.

Brundtland Commission. 1987. *Our common future.* New York: Oxford University Press.

Canadian International Development Agency (CIDA). 1992. "Environment and Development: The Crucial Decade." *Development* (Spring).

Commission on Developing Countries and Global Change. 1992. *For earth's sake.* Ottawa: International Development Research Centre.

Eedy, Wilson. 1990. "Background paper–water." *Focus/ Visions 2020*:13–20.

Environment Management Development Indonesia (EMDI). 1991. "Documents Relating to the Environmental Impact Analysis Process in Indonesia."

Unofficial Translation. Jakarta, Indonesia: EMDI.

Goodland, Robert. 1993. "Definition of Environmental Sustainability." *IAIA Newsletter* 5(2): 1–2.

Goodland, Robert, Herman Daly, and Salah El Serafy, eds. 1992. *Population, Technology, and Lifestyle: The Transition to Sustainability.* Washington, DC: Island Press.

Jacobs, P. and B. Sadler. 1990. *Sustainable Development and Environmental Assessment: Perspectives on Planning for a Common Future.* Hull, Quebec: Canadian Environmental Assessment Research Council (CEARC).

Stone, D., and W. Eedy. 1977. "The Role of the Consulting Firm in Environmental Impact Assessment." *Chemistry in Canada* (February).

World Bank. 1990. *Indonesia: Sustainable Development of Forests, Land, and Water.* Washington, DC.

——. 1992. *Environmental Assessment Sourcebook.* vol. 1 Policies, Procedures, and Cross-Sectoral Issues (Technical Paper 139). vol. 2 Sectoral Guidelines (Technical Paper 140). vol. 3 Guidelines for Environmental Assessment of Energy and Industry Projects (Technical Paper 154). Washington, DC.

6

Rapid Urban Environmental Assessment: First Step Toward Environmental Management in Developing Countries

Josef Leitmann

Overview

The World Bank Urban Management and the Environment Program (UMP/E) has broad research experience in the area of rapid urban environmental assessment. This chapter uses comparable case studies to broaden knowledge about environmental issues and options for urban areas of developing countries, all during a relatively short period of time.

The methodology that has been developed and tested consists of a three-step process: (a) completion of a data questionnaire on urban environmental indicators; (b) preparation of an urban environmental profile, using data from the questionnaire and research assistance from local investigators; and (c) discussion of the results through a series of consultations, culminating in a priority-focused public workshop. The assessment process is designed to better prepare investments and to develop policy changes for improving urban environmental quality. These objectives are achieved through the formulation of an environmental management strategy and action plan for cities; contents of the strategy and plan are briefly outlined here.

Urban Management and the Environment

The rapid urban environmental assessment approach has been developed by the Urban Management and Environment component of the Urban Management Program (UMP), which is run jointly by the United Nations Development Programme (UNDP), the World Bank, and the United Nations Centre for Human Settlements (UNCHS). The UMP is a major effort by UN organizations and external support agencies (ESAs) to strengthen the contribution that cities and towns in developing countries make toward economic growth, social development and the alleviation of poverty. In addition to its environmental focus, the program seeks to develop and promote appropriate policies and tools for land management, infrastructure management, and municipal finance and administration. Through regional programs, the UMP has set up partnerships with national, regional and global networks and ESAs in applied research, dissemination of information, and experiences of best practices and promising options.

The research summarized in this chapter has been used, with background studies and research, to develop an overall document on environmental strategies for cities. The profiles and environmental data have been used for international forums on cities and the environment, the UNCHS Sustainable Cities Programme, the World Bank's *World Development Report 1992*, and urban environmental projects. In turn, the results of these and other activities will be used to improve the assessment process over time.

In addition to city-based activities, the environmental component of the UMP has prepared background papers and research on such topics as urban waste management and pollution control, energy-environment linkages in the urban sector, regulatory and economic instruments for pollution control, the environmental dimensions of urban land use, and the urban environmental planning and management process. These studies are designed to identify key urban development-environment linkages and suggest an environmental management strategy for cities in developing countries. Finally, research reports are being prepared on (a) the health impacts of urban environmental problems; (b) the economic valuation of urban environmental problems; (c) urban environmental data collection; (d) the local management of hazardous wastes from small-scale and cottage industries; and (e) the application of remote sensing and geographic information systems to urban environmental planning. All of these are inputs to a final paper on environmental strategies for cities in developing countries.

Guidance from the Recent Past: Obstacles and Objectives

Very little information is readily available on environmental conditions, the interaction between urban development and ecosystems, or the managerial setting for responding to environmental problems in the cities of the developing world. Recent attempts to develop such information have been incomplete because they focused on a limited number of variables that present a very narrow and limited picture of key environmental issues in metropolitan areas;[1] took a narrow perspective by examining only one sector within the city;[2] required several years of intensive, multidisciplinary research and analysis;[3] or did not develop a set of urban environmental data that would allow for comparison across different types of cities.[4] As a result, much of this work has not been immediately relevant to those who must respond to the environmental consequences of urban development in the developing world because the information and analysis are incomplete, sector-based, or outdated. For comparative purposes, past investigations may suffer from these problems *and* not be generalizable to other cases.

To learn from this recent history and overcome past limitations, there appears to be a need for urban environmental research that is comprehensive, multisectoral, relatively short-term, and consistent between cities. Therefore, one objective of the case study work (reported here) was to use and test in different cities rapid evaluation methods that cut across sectors. In addition, the work sought to identify common constraints and standard analytical approaches to problems; outline approaches for setting relative priorities among urban environmental problems; and indicate options that could form part of environmental management strategies.

Rapid Urban Environmental Assessment

A three-step process was developed to rapidly assess the state of the urban environment. This process is based on the need for measurement, observation, and validation. To *measure* a consistent set of data, an urban environmental questionnaire is used. To *observe* the nature, trends and factors that influence environmental quality in the cities, a common framework for preparing an urban environmental profile has been developed. To partially *validate* the results from the questionnaire and profile, consultations were held with key actors in the cities.

These three steps and how they relate to one another are described below.

Urban Environmental Questionnaire

A common questionnaire has been used to generate a data base on a range of environmental indicators. The survey instrument was designed over a one-year period (October 1989–September 1990) by a technical working group on urban environmental indicators, consisting of representatives from the following international agencies and international institutes working in the field of urban environmental research and policy analysis: the UN Fund for Population Activities, Statistical Office, the Department of International Economic and Social Affairs, Environmental Programme, Development Programme, and Centre for Human Settlements; the World Health Organization; the Organization for Economic Cooperation and Development; the World Bank; the International Center for Urban Studies; the International Institute for Environment and Development; the World Resources Institute; the Stockholm Environment Institute; and the Network for Urban Research in the European Community.

In designing the questionnaire, the working group sought to identify a minimum set of key data that have a high probability of successful measurement in a large number of the cities in developing countries. A number of analytical approaches[5] and relevant survey instruments[6] were reviewed to learn from past experience and avoid redundant data collection. It was concluded that indicators needed to be collected in the following categories:

- Baseline social and economic statistics
- Baseline housing conditions
- Baseline health conditions
- Natural environment
- Land use
- Urban transport
- Urban energy use
- Air pollution
- Noise pollution
- Water resources, supply and sanitation
- Solid and hazardous wastes.

Core indicators were then developed for these categories, with a definition of statistical variables and units of measurement. For example, to describe the predominant ecosystems in and around cities, the Goodall classification of terrestrial and aquatic ecosystems (twenty-nine descriptors) was selected. Depending on availability, data were collected for three levels: the city proper, the metropolitan area, and the urban agglomeration. The *city proper* is defined as the principal political jurisdiction containing the historical city center. The *metropolitan area* is a politically defined urban area set up for planning and administrative purposes that may combine several jurisdictions (municipalities or cities). The *urban agglomeration* is the total contiguous built-up area that may spill over defined political boundaries.

The categories and indicators were assembled into a draft questionnaire by the UMP. The UMP then provided the resources to field test the questionnaire in each of the seven case study areas. A local consultant, firm or group of institutions was identified in each city to complete the questionnaire. They were selected on the basis of demonstrated experience in environmental or urban research; ability to access information from a variety of public and private sources; and communication skills in English. The questionnaire was filled out, transmitted to the UMP/E team at the World Bank, and reviewed to identify problems with consistency, misinterpretation, and missing information. Requests for additional information and validation of questionable data were then communicated to the local researchers and, based on their responses, a final questionnaire was completed. This process occurred between September 1990 and March 1992, depending on the city. On average, two staff-months were required to complete, review and finalize the questionnaire.

The Urban Environmental Profile

Although a questionnaire can provide useful baseline data, more description and explanation are required for a fuller understanding of environmental issues in cities. Therefore, an outline for a generic environmental profile was developed that covers: (a) general background information; (b) the status of the environment in the urban region; (c) development-environment interactions; and (d) the institutional setting for environmental management. This was reviewed and modified with suggestions from staff at UNCHS (Habitat). A copy of the final generic outline is provided in box 6-1.

The *background* section is intended to provide a historical, geophysical and socio-economic perspective on urban development for each city, and to briefly explain how developmental activities and the environment have interacted over time. The *status* section summarizes existing information on the

---

Box 6-1. Generic Outline for Urban Environmental Profile

I.   Introduction
   Background
   Geophysical and land use
   Socio-economic setting (demographics, economic
      structure, urban poverty)
   Environment-development linkages over time

II.   Status of the Environment in the Urban Region
   Natural resources
      Air quality
      Water quality (surface, ground, coastal, fisheries)
      Land (forests and natural vegetation; agricultural
         land; parks, recreation and open space; historical
         sites and cultural property)
   Environmental hazards
      Natural risks
      Human-induced risks

III. Development-Environment Interactions
   Water supply
   Sewerage and sanitation
   Flood control
   Solid waste management
   Industrial pollution control/hazardous waste
      management
   Transportation and telecommunications
   Energy and power generation
   Housing
   Health care
   Rural-urban linkages
   Other

IV.   The Setting for Environmental Management
   Key actors
      Government (central, regional, local)
      Private sector
      Popular sector (community groups, NGOs, media)
   Management Functions
      Instruments of intervention (legislative and
         regulatory; economic and fiscal; direct
         investment; planning and policy development;
         community organizations; education, training
         and research; promotion and protest)
      Environmental coordination and decisionmaking
         (mechanisms for public participation;
         intersectoral coordination; across levels of
         government; between public and private sector;
         intertemporal; information and technical
         expertise)
   Constraints on effective management
   Ongoing initiatives for institutional strengthening

References

Table 6-1. Analytical Techniqued an Applicationd

Technique	Example of application
Spatial analysis of land use, seismic and other maps	Assessment of open space availability, flood-prone and seismically active areas in Accra.
Review of survey data and institutional analysis	Evaluation of functioning of sewerage and sanitation services in Accra.
Overlay analysis of maps	Assocation between water-borne diseases and biochemical oxygen demand in Jakarta.
Preparation and analysis of energy balance	Sectoral concentration of polluting fuel usage in Jakarta; air pollution in Tunis.
Trend analysis	Growth and shift in peak hour transport modes in Jakarta.
Organizational analysis	Environmental authority by level of government in Sao Paulo and Tianjin.
Long-run marginal cost pricing	Evaluation of degree cost recovery in Sao Paulo's water and sewerage charges.
Flow chart	Ocucpational and environmental health data flows in Katowice.

Source: The author.

quality of various environmental media (air, water, land and cultural property), and briefly analyzes the key natural hazards (both geogenic and human-induced) that affect the urban area. The *development-environment* section describes how development-oriented activities and services in the public, private and informal sectors influence environmental quality, *and* how environmental factors constrain or promote development. The *setting* section identifies the key public and private actors that are engaged in environmental management that affects the city, the existing management functions (instruments of intervention that are used, and mechanisms for coordination and decisionmaking), constraints on effective management, and the initiatives that are being undertaken to improve environmental management.

The same researchers who prepared the questionnaire also prepared the initial profile in each city. First drafts were based on information from the questionnaire, interviews, existing reports, and other data. These drafts were completely rewritten, using a large amount of additional information not cited by the researchers. Then, second drafts were returned to the researchers for their comments and clarification of inconsistencies. In the case of four cities (Accra, Jakarta, Katowice and São Paulo), responses were used to prepare third drafts that were taken to an international conference, "World Cities and Their Environment" (Toronto, Canada, August 1991),

where delegates from each of the cities were present. These draft profiles were reviewed with each of the city delegations and corrections as well as new information were obtained. After review by UNCHS, the World Bank and two external reviewers, a final environmental profile for each city was then prepared by the UMP/E World Bank team.

Several different analytical tools were used to interpret the information from the case studies, according to the issue that was being assessed as well as the quality and format of the data. The key techniques and examples of their application are presented in table 6-1.

Environmental Consultations

In four of the cities (Accra, Jakarta, Katowice, and São Paulo), a series of consultations with key individuals and organizations (culminating in a town meeting) were held to discuss urban environmental problems, priorities and possible solutions. This process served to obtain feedback on the draft profiles and questionnaires from interested citizens in the cities; acquire additional information from the organizations and individuals that participated in the meetings; and conduct an *ex post* comparison between the priorities that emerged from the data and profiles and those that were perceived by the key actors.

The consultations and town meetings were organized by the "Five Cities Consultation Project" (the fifth city being Toronto) through the University of Toronto's Centre for Urban and Community Studies. This effort was funded by the Canadian International Development Agency, the Department of External Affairs, the Mortgage Housing Corporation, the Federation of Canadian Municipalities, and UMP. In each city, a firm or local coordinators were hired to organize individual interviews and/or small roundtables with municipal politicians, local government planners, environmentalists, regional/national officials, community groups, universities, nongovernmental organizations (NGOs), and private industry; and to bring these actors together in a final forum to discuss their perspectives and determine whether there was a consensus on metropolitan environmental priorities. The format for the consultations and town meetings was determined by the organizers in order to accommodate local cultural practices and group dynamics.[7] However, the consultations all covered a minimum common set of issues: water resources, supply and sanitation/sewerage, land use, urban transport, energy use, solid and hazardous wastes, air pollution, and the natural environment. The town meetings were organized under the auspices of the top local official (mayor or governor)(McCarney 1991).

Successful meetings were held in each of the cities, concluding in town forums that took place in May and June of 1991. The dates and details for each forum are summarized in table 6-2 below.

After the consultations, an effort should be made to rank urban environmental problems by combining results of the public discussions with information contained in the questionnaire and profile. The following criteria can be used to rank the relative importance of these problems:

• The magnitude of health impacts associated with the problem.

• The size of urban productivity losses caused by the problem.

• The relative impact of the problem suffered by the urban poor.

• The degree to which the problem results in or is caused by unsustainable consumption of resources.

• Whether or not the problem leads to an irreversible outcome.

• The extent to which political support or a constituency exists to support resolution of the problem.

To apply the first five criteria may require that information be further developed during preparation of the environmental management strategy (see below). The results of the consultations can be a useful guide for applying the final criterion.

Rapid Assessment: A Step Toward Urban Environmental Management

Rapid assessment is the first phase of an approach that will enable urban managers to tackle priority environmental problems in their cities. Subsequent steps include: formulation of an environmental management strategy, development of an environmental action plan at the urban level, and sustained investments for environmental improvement. These steps are illustrated in figure 6-1 and briefly described in the next section.

Environmental Management Strategy

The process of rapid urban environmental assessment (data collection, profile, and consultations) is designed to provide an informational and consensual basis for

Table 6-2. Environmental Town Meetings

City	Date	Number and types of participants
Accra	5/15/91	50; local and national government, NGOs, donors, industries, community organizations, environmental consultants.
Jakarta	6/12/91	40; provincial and national governmetn, research/academia, donors, industries, community organizations.
Katowice	5/17/91	25; municipal politicians, city and regional officials, state industries, research institutes, academia, community groups, NGOs, private sector.
Sao Paulo	5/31/91	120; city and state government, NGOs, research institutes, academia, professional organizations, media.

Source: The author.

Figure 6-1. Flow Chart of Environmental Management Process

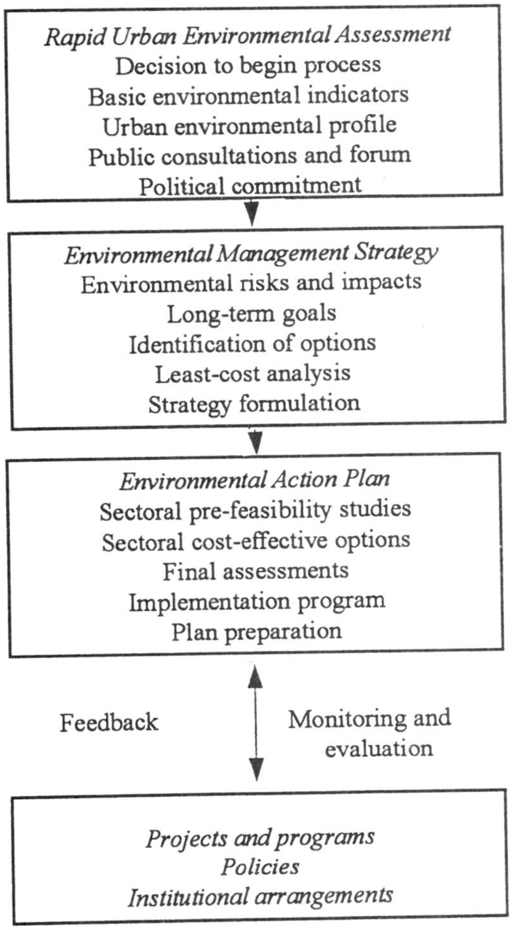

Rapid Urban Environmental Assessment
Decision to begin process
Basic environmental indicators
Urban environmental profile
Public consultations and forum
Political commitment

▼

Environmental Management Strategy
Environmental risks and impacts
Long-term goals
Identification of options
Least-cost analysis
Strategy formulation

▼

Environmental Action Plan
Sectoral pre-feasibility studies
Sectoral cost-effective options
Final assessments
Implementation program
Plan preparation

Feedback | Monitoring and evaluation

Projects and programs
Policies
Institutional arrangements

preparing an urban environmental management strategy (EMS). The goal of the EMS is to accelerate the improvement of environmental conditions in cities, especially by integrating key aspects of urban policy and environmental management. The objectives are to establish long-term environmental goals for the urban region; set interim environmental goals and objectives; rank pollution control and other measures to improve environmental quality; identify priority sectors for channeling investments; and recommend policy reforms, instruments, and institutional arrangements needed to implement the EMS. The EMS process builds on existing sector and project work but emphasizes continuity in decisionmaking to implement agreed policies and approaches. It should provide a decisionmaking framework for public and private investments, while recognizing that the investments will be primarily

private (by households and firms). It therefore requires a participatory process among decisionmakers in government and the private sector, often using working groups of officials in consultation with technical specialists and key private/informal sector actors, to commit themselves to act, and agree on the policies and strategies they themselves will define.

In general, the EMS is developed by the following steps:
• Overcoming information gaps identified in the rapid assessment by intensive data collection and analysis.
• Preparing a detailed diagnosis of the present state of environmental infrastructure and services, existing urban development and sector plans, related environmental risks and impacts, and possible interventions.
• Carrying out a diagnosis of institutions with urban environmental management authority, including policies, regulations, and capacities.
• Using a cost-benefit or cost-effectiveness framework to establish first-order estimates of the costs of environmental interventions and corresponding impact reductions.
• Formulating a strategy that includes socially acceptable, long-term environmental quality goals; identification and phasing of priority sectoral actions to achieve the long-term goals; and needed policies, instruments and institutional development.

Broad-based acceptance of the resulting strategy requires participation of all stakeholders in this process, including mechanisms for negotiation and conflict resolution. A suggested approach is to name an EMS manager to be charged with day-to-day supervision of the effort, supported by a steering committee, a public advisory committee and technical working groups. Strategy development should require between nine and twelve months.

Urban Environmental Action Plan

The EMS provides the framework for integration and coordination to ensure consistency across environmental media and across sectoral strategies. Within this framework, sectoral action plans need to be formulated to implement the EMS. These plans consist of both a sectoral development strategy and a set of short and medium term environmental interventions, both corrective and preventive, for implementing the sectoral strategy. Then, an urban-wide environmental action plan (EAP) can be formulated that combines needed actions in the various critical sectors to achieve the objectives set forth in the EMS.

The EAP should be developed using the same participatory process for preparing the EMS. It would consist of the following elements:

• *Status of the urban environment*. A description of the existing quality of environmental media, the risk of environmental hazards, key environment-development interactions, and the setting for environmental management.

• *Optimal environmental quality*. A summary of long-term urban environmental objectives, and interim targets to be achieved.

• *Possible scenarios*. A presentation of the health impacts, productivity effects and ecological consequences associated with different levels of environmental degradation. This could include a business-as-usual case, a scenario based on interim objectives, and a long-term/best-case situation.

• *The least-cost approach*. A series of pre-feasibility studies that develop the alternatives that comprise the least-cost strategy in greater detail.

• *Economic and financial analysis*. An assessment of the projected economic and financial costs and benefits of least-cost strategy. The strategy could be assessed as one single project, or as a set of separate but linked activities.

• *Institutional analysis*. An assessment of the managerial improvements, organizational arrangements, jurisdictional changes, training requirements, and so forth that would be necessary in order to implement the strategy.

• *Implementation program*. The costed, scheduled and coordinated core of the action plan that covers issues such as financing, institutional responsibility, timing of investments and policy changes, monitoring, evaluation, and public participation. Preparation, review and completion of this plan would take between one and two years.

Sustained Investment Program

The EMS/EAP process results in priorities for investments in pollution control and other measures to improve urban environmental quality, which are in turn incorporated in a multiyear economic plan. Implementation of a sector investment package must be supported by the corresponding policy reforms and institutional, legal and fiscal programs resulting from the EAP. Depending on budget constraints and current environmental conditions, a succession of staged investments spread over fifteen to twenty years will be needed to reach the EMS environmental quality goals. Success will depend on sustaining both investments and institutional development programs over the long-term. Procedures for long-term monitoring and evaluation are needed, as are feedback mechanisms into an iterative EMS/EAP process.

Case Studies for Applying the Methodology

The case study approach was selected as the means of testing the methodology partially by default and partly because of the advantages it brings to helping identify appropriate urban environmental interventions. There is no unified theory for explaining and predicting the dynamics of the urban environment. Consequently, there is no rigorous, theory-driven methodology for conducting analysis in this field. Still, there is a need to collect information, describe observations, and suggest explanations for phenomena in an attempt to establish a pre-theoretical cause-effect framework. Though second-best in comparison with the more replicable and generalizable techniques of theory-based inquiry, the case study method is a valid research tool in the absence of theoretical guidance.

This argument aside, preparing and comparing cases is a worthwhile approach to problem evaluation for several reasons. To begin, cases that focus on previously underexplored territory collect knowledge that is based on experience; as lessons from practice are accumulated and assessed, a base of data becomes available for developing theories. Next, cases allow for observation of a wide range of variables, their interactions, and the outcomes of this interplay. Third, they provide an opportunity to test hypotheses in a number of different settings. Finally, case studies have a non-academic value: because cases are derived from experience, they are more readily understood by practitioners who are responsible for shaping policy, prioritizing problems, and implementing solutions.[8]

Criteria for Selection

If the case study method is to be used, then how should one select the individual cases? Criteria for selecting the cities were derived from several simple assumptions:

• Transnational generalizations will require evidence from diverse geographical, political, and economic settings.

• Urban environmental problems vary according to the level and distribution of a city's wealth.

• These problems also vary depending on the structure and location of a city's economic base.

• Megacities have different and more complex systems for managing environmental problems than smaller ones.

• Rapid data collection and analysis are more readily achieved in cities where work of a related nature is already taking place.

The following criteria flow from these assumptions: (a) the cities should be selected from different continents, cultures and political systems; (b) they should reflect different levels of per capita income, with varying degrees of poverty; (c) they should be characterized by different stages and types of industrialization; (d) both large and smaller cities should be included in the sample; and (e) baseline data should be available from ongoing activities in the cities so that primary research can be minimized.

The Case Studies Chosen

These criteria were combined with a resource limitation to select six cities and one urbanizing area: *Accra* (Ghana), *Jakarta* (Indonesia), *Katowice* (Poland), *São Paulo* (Brazil), *Tianjin* (China), *Tunis* (Tunisia), and the *Singrauli* region (India). Though Singrauli is not a city, it was selected for two reasons: first, it is a good example of the urban environmental shadow that cities cast on the hinterland (in this case, environmental degradation from urban demand for electricity and, secondarily, coal); and second, it is a rapidly urbanizing region that has a special set of environmental problems. Table 6-3 presents information on these seven areas, organized according to the selection criteria presented above (a-e).

The ability to tie into related work was crucial for the process in each city. For *Accra*, environmental information had been developed from the UNCHS

Table 6-3. City Characteristics by Criteria

Criteria	Accra	Jakarta	Katowice	Sao Paulo	Singrauli	Tianjin	Tunis
Diverse geography	Africa	SE Asia	Europe	S. America	S. Asia	NE Asia	N. Africa
Diverse political/ economic systems	Military/ dereg. to market economy	1-party/ dereg. to market economy	Democracy/ former socialist economy	Democracy/ market economy	Democracy/ regulated market economy	1-party/ socialist economy	Multi-party/ market economy
Diverse income level (US$ per capita)	350	850	4,475	2,540	340+	380	1,260
Diverse income level (percentage in poverty)	48	17	2	37	47	6	18
Diverse industrial level/base	Low/ agric. products	Medium/ manufact.	High/ heavy industry	High/ wide-range	High/ mining and energy	High/ wide-range	Medium/ manufact.
Diverse city size (metro. pop. '000)	1,565	16,828	2,180	16,938	696	8,660	1,558
Related work	UNCHS Structure Plan; SEI; NEAP; IBRD Urban I & II	MEIP city; SEI; IBRD Jabotabek I-III	Local research institutes; IBRD Env. mgmt. loan	CETESB; NGO work; SEI; IBRD loans	EdF EIS; TCP study; IBRD review	IBRD loans	UNDP/WB EPM; NEAP; IBRD loans

Source: The author.

(Habitat)-supported structure planning process, known as the Accra Planning and Development Programme, preparation of Ghana's national environmental action plan, the Stockholm Environment Institute (SEI) urban household environment study, and through the World Bank's first urban project in Ghana (completed in 1991) and second urban loan (initiated in 1991). For *Jakarta*, related work included activities of the UNDP/World Bank Metropolitan Environmental Improvement Program (MEIP), the SEI study, and the World Bank's First (1988), Second (May 1990) and Third (June 1990) Jabotabek Urban Development Projects. For *Katowice*, environmental data had been collected by a number of national and local research institutes in Poland, and the World Bank's environmental management project (1990). For *São Paulo*, urban environmental work had been conducted by the São Paulo state environmental company (CETESB), nongovernmental research organizations and the city government, the SEI study, and a number of World Bank sector loans over a fifteen-year period (industry, pollution control, water supply, sanitation). For *Singrauli*, environmental information had been developed through a number of studies in the region: an environmental impact assessment prepared by Electricité de France; an environmental review by the Indian Town and Country Planning Department; and an ongoing World Bank environmental planning study. In *Tianjin*, environmental and background information had been developed as part of the World Bank Light Industry Project and the Urban Development and Environment Project. Finally, in *Tunis*, the assessment could draw on work of the UN/World Bank Environmental Program for the Mediterranean, the national environmental action plan, and a range of World Bank lending operations for urban development, water supply, sewerage, flood protection, and transportation.

Lessons for Future Research

The research described in this chapter yielded observations on process as well as substance. This information can be divided into two categories: (a) the utility of the research methodology, and (b) areas that would benefit from further inquiry or different research approaches.

Advantages and Limits of the Methodology

The benefits and disadvantages of the overall methodology will be reviewed first, followed by comments on each of the three components (questionnaire, profile and consultations). Briefly, the advantages of the general approach are that it is rapid, costs relatively little, centralizes diverse information, and benefits from local access to information. On average, the three-step rapid assessment required six person-months of efforts over a period of five to nine months. The local costs for research, writing, and organization of the consultations ranged between $16,000 (Accra) and $27,000 (Jakarta) per city. The research and public discussions led to the centralization of a wide range of environmental information in one place for the first time in each city. Involving local researchers and institutions facilitated access to information and decisionmakers for a variety of reasons (knowledge of the local language(s) and cultural practices, past experience with the subject matter, relevant organizations and individuals, and established reputation in the field).

On the other hand, the general methodology also had a number of disadvantages. The first limitation stems from an intrinsic part of the process: the methodology generates purely descriptive information. It provides some guidance as to what might be a priority problem but little to no indication as to what might constitute the range of possible solutions. Second, the approach relies on existing sources of information. By using secondary data, results (numbers, analyses and discussions) are confined by the range and quality of work that has already been done. However, the methodology identifies gaps in knowledge. Third, results cannot always be used for comparison between cities because the information applies to different time periods, was derived in a different manner, or is based on a different sample.

Narrowing the critique to each step of the process, the benefits of the questionnaire are that it is a straightforward guide to gathering a comprehensive set of data on a particular city or metropolitan area; brings together data from many different sources and allows for intra- and intersectoral comparisons that are often not possible from a single source of information; and can serve several useful purposes, for example, generating information for preparing the profile, the consultations, and inter-city comparisons. On the negative side, some of the questions were subject to misinterpretation. A good deal of effort went into correcting these errors and/or explaining the meaning and means of answering particular questions. Also, in each city, certain data were simply not available from secondary sources. This meant that the question or table was left blank, that conversion factors from other cities were used to calculate values (with uncertain degrees of error), or that primary data should have been collected (unfortunately, funds were not available for this option).

The benefits of preparing the profile were that it summarized information on causal relationships between environmental quality and development activities and on the institutional dimension of urban environmental issues that were not collected in the questionnaire; brought together conclusions from reports developed in different sectors or over time that referred to a common problem; and served as a useful background document for the consultations, government agencies, NGOs, donors, and others. The principal drawback of the profile is that it is a static document. Each will have a relatively short lifespan as no provisions were made to institutionalize the updating of the profile. There were also a set of practical problems, similar to those for the questionnaire, concerning preparation of the document: information was missing; key reports were not available in the city or were not used by the local researcher(s); significant amounts of time and effort were required to explain particular sections and review the draft information; and the quality of the writing itself was often poor. In most cases, the revised version of the profile bore little resemblance to the locally-prepared research.

The consultations and town meetings had the advantage of being flexible instruments for involving a broad spectrum of concerned publics. Because they were organized locally according to local traditions, they generated meaningful discussion for the participants and allowed them to reach a consensus in each case. However, since the method for arriving at a consensus differed in each case (from subtle negotiation and polite acquiescence in Jakarta to a formal parliamentary-style session in São Paulo), the ability to compare results is limited. More importantly, the consultation process ended with the final forum. The consensus was not linked to any formal planning or decisionmaking process (though the mayor's or governor's office was centrally involved in each of the town meetings). Thus, whatever momentum that was built up did not have anywhere to go; in many ways, the consultation process was a lost opportunity. This will not occur when the rapid assessment is linked to the development of an urban environmental management strategy.

Directions for Future Research

The following topics are fruitful areas for future research (presented in no particular order of priority):

• *Linking Health Effects with Environmental Conditions.* In all of the cities except Katowice, there was relatively little information on the cause-effect relationships between environmental problems and their human health consequences. Useful epidemiological and other analytical work could be done on the emissions-dispersion-exposure-health impact pathway.

• *Valuing the Economic Costs and Benefits of Urban Environmental Activities.* Reliable values for the productivity, amenity and other losses and gains associated with environmental conditions and hazards were not available in all of the cities. There are many techniques for calculating the monetary value of these impacts; they could be tested to determine which are most appropriate for different types of problems and levels of available information.

• *Alternative Methods of Assessing Public Priorities.* Consensus-oriented discussion is only one of several techniques for developing a sense of what people think is important. Other approaches include: revealed preference, contingent valuation and willingness to pay,[9] classic public opinion survey research (see Beatty 1991; Egunjobi 1989), and special models for discerning public preferences.[10] These could be tried in the same cities and compared with consultation results, or used in conjunction with consultations in other cities.

• *Matching Jurisdictions with Ecological Boundaries.* More information is needed about the results, limitations and opportunities for creating or modifying institutions so that their area of responsibility corresponds with the ecosystems that affected them. Research could be done on authorities in cities of developing countries that are organized around water basins, airsheds, waste management areas, agricultural zones, sites of historic or cultural value, and so on.

• *Comparing Policy Instruments for Environmental Management.* Cities often adopt similar or different policies to deal with the same type of environmental problem. Why do the same or different approaches succeed or fail? For example, both Jakarta and São Paulo are faced with degradation of their main watershed. Guided land and infrastructure development was a fairly successful protection policy in Jakarta. Regulation and enforcement of zoning have been near-complete failures in São Paulo. What factors were behind these experiences?

Notes

1. An example of this is the Population Crisis Committee's analysis of environmental quality in the world's 100 largest metropolitan areas. An "urban living standard score" is developed for each city by combining scores on indicators of public safety, food costs, living space, housing, communications, education, public health, peace and quiet, traffic flow, and clean air. This approach forces the often arbitrary selection of one value to represent a complex indicator, for example, public health is assessed on the basis of infant mortality per 1000 live births, which excludes consideration of the status of adult mortality and morbidity. A second methodological problem is that different data are used for different cities to rank the same indicator, for example, air quality is measured on the basis of ozone, sulfur dioxide, suspended particulate matter, or nitrogen oxides. Third, in order to develop a table and rankings without missing variables, the number of indicators was limited to those mentioned above, resulting in the exclusion of important areas such as water quality, open/green space, sanitation and industrial pollution (see Population Crisis 1990).

2. For example, studies have been done on the linkages between environment and health in particular cities. Some representative titles include: Radhika Ramasubban and Nigel Crook "Mortality Toll of Cities: Emerging Patterns of Disease in Bombay," *Economic and Political Weekly*, Vol. XX, No. 23, 1985; C. Hertzman "Poland: Health and Environment in the Context of Socioeconomic Decline," Health Policy Research Unit Report No. 90:2D, Vancouver; University of British Columbia, January 1990; Pedro Jacobi "Habitat and Health in the Municipality of São Paulo," *Environment and Development*, Vol. 2, No. 2, October 1990; and Office of Housing and Urban Programs "Ranking Environmental Health Risks in Bangkok, Thailand," Washington, DC; USAID, December 1990.

3. One of the first efforts in this area, the Hong Kong Human Ecology Programme, is a good example of this limitation. It was initiated in 1972, field work was completed in 1975, analysis was completed in 1980, and the results were published in 1981 (see Boyden and others 1981).

4. For example, the United Nations has collected a set of data for over 100 cities internationally. (United Nations Population Fund. 1988. *Cities: Statistical, Administrative and Graphical Information on the Major Urban Areas of the World*. Barcelona; Institut d'Estudis Metropolitans de Barcelona, 1988). However, most of the data are quite general and do not allow for any detailed environmental analysis. The "Ecoville" project (University of Toronto) generated a number of environmental reports on cities in the developing world during the mid-1980s, but the content and quality of these documents varied greatly, limiting their comparability.

5. These included: UN Statistical Office "Concepts and Methods of Environment and Human Settlements Statistics—A Technical Report," 1988; European Economic Community "Green Paper on the Urban Environment," draft, 1990; World Bank "Survey of Resource and Environmental Accounting in Industrialized Countries," 1990; and UNEP/UNCHS "Urban and Regional Environmental Planning and Management Guidelines," 1987.

6. These included the questionnaire on "The State of the Environment" used by the OECD/EUROSTAT; the "City Date Framework" used by UNCHS; the ECE's "Experimental Compendium on Environmental Statistics in Europe and North America"; the questionnaire for NUREC's *International Statistical Yearbook of Large Cities;* and the draft UNEP/IEO questionnaire to evaluate national hazardous waste situations.

7. For example, three roundtables (on water resource problems and priorities, air pollution, and housing and the natural environment) and two seminars (on hazardous waste and industrial development) were organized to accommodate the large number of actors and to avoid duplication of previous consultations. In São Paulo, institutions and key individuals were contacted separately, through both interviews and questionnaires.

8. Recently, these and other reasons provided the justification for a case-study approach to evaluating environment-development linkages in rural Africa (see Blackwell, Goodwillie and Webb 1991).

9. This approach is being used by the Stockholm Environment Institute's household environment survey teams in Accra, Jakarta, and São Paulo.

10. Several of these exist. A recent application, based on weighting and ranking the discussions and responses of concerned publics, focuses on public priorities as they relate to equity and efficiency in air quality (Davos 1991).

References

Amuzu, A.T. and J. Leitmann. 1991. "Environmental Profile of Accra." Draft. Urban Management Program. Washington, DC.

Bartone, Carl, Janis D. Bernstein, and J. Leitmann. 1992. "Environmental Strategies for Cities: A Framework for Urban Environmental Management in Developing Countries." Draft. Urban Management Program. Washington, DC.

Beatty, Kathleen. 1991. "Public Opinion Data for Environmental Decisionmaking: The Case of Colorado Springs." *Environmental Impact Assessment Review* 11:29-51.

Blackwell, Jonathan, Roger Goodwillie, and Richard Webb. 1991. *Environment and Development in Africa: Selected Case Studies*. Economic Development Institute Analytical Case Study 6. Washington, DC: The World Bank.

Borkiewicz, Jerzy. 1991. "Environmental Profile of Katowice." Draft. Urban Management Program. Washington, DC.

Boyden, S., S. Millar, K. Newcombe, and B. O'Neill. 1981. *The Ecology of a City and Its People: The Case of Hong Kong*. Canberra: Australian National University Press.

Davos, Climis. 1991. "Public Priorities for Evaluating Air Quality Management Measures." *Journal of Environmental Management* 33: 205-267

Egunjobi, Layi. 1989. "Perception of Urban Environmental Problems: A Pilot Study of the City of Ibadan, Nigeria." *African Urban Quarterly* Vol. 4, 1 and 2 (February, May).

Hadiwinoto, Suhadi, G. Clarke, and Josef Leitmann. 1991. "Environmental Profile of Jakarta." Draft. Urban Management Program, Washington, DC.

Leitmann, Josef. 1992. "Environmental Management and Urban Development in the Third World." PhD Dissertation. Berkeley: University of California.

———. 1991a. "Environmental Profile of São Paulo." Draft. Urban Management Program. Washington, DC.

———. 1991b. "Environmental Profile of Tianjin." Draft.

Urban Management Program. Washington, DC.

McCarney, Patricia. 1991. "Draft Terms of Reference for Local Consultants Working on 'World Cities and Environment: A Five City Consultation Process.'" Centre for Urban and Community Studies, University of Toronto, Canada.

McNeil, Mary. 1991. "Local Concerns Voiced on Urban Environment." *The Urban Edge* 15(6).

Nirody, Anita. 1992. "Environmental Profile of the Singrauli Region of India." Draft. Urban Management Program. Washington, DC.

Population Crisis Committee. 1990. "Cities: Life in the World's 100 Largest Metropolitan Areas." Washington, DC: Population Crisis Committee.

Société d'Ingénierie pour le Développement Economique et Social. 1992. "Profil environnemental de Tunis." Draft. Urban Management Program. Washington, DC.

Urban Management Program. 1992. "Urban Environmental Indicators Questionnaire." Washington, DC: Urban Management Program.

World Bank. 1991. *Urban Policy and Economic Development: An Agenda for the 1990s*. A World Bank Policy Paper. Washington, DC.

7

Applying Proven GIS Technique in a New Setting: GAP Analysis in Costa Rica

Basil G. Savitsky, Thomas E. Lacher, Jr., G. Wesley Burnett, Jorge Fallas, and
Christopher Vaughan

Overview

The biological resource base in Costa Rica and other developing countries is changing rapidly. There is a critical need for timely information about the status of wildlife species and their distribution within changing ecosystems. This problem is exacerbated by the transnational migratory behavior of wildlife and by the differences between nations in environmental policy and in environmental data.

Costa Rica was selected for this project because it is well-studied, has an excellent system of parks, and has the appropriate level of data and experience in the fields of remote sensing and Geographic Information Systems (GIS).[1] GIS is a mature technology consisting of computer hardware and computer mapping software that is becoming more affordable, available and powerful. The implementation of a national biological resources GIS for Costa Rica will provide capacity to analyze pertinent considerations in habitat mapping, assessment, and conservation, such as site selection, minimum size or shape requirements, and connectivity. By establishing priorities for conservation areas, GIS can be used to incorporate existing digital geographic data from various sources at variable scales. GIS also provides rapid analysis of numerous spatial parameters concurrently and is easier to use for map updating of dynamic data.

GIS

GIS has emerged as a promising tool for environmental planning and has attracted growing attention. A broad understanding of GIS is critical to the successful implementation of a system, particularly since it offers great potential for natural resource management and therefore runs the risk of raising inflated expectations. These differing expectations are reflected in the numerous definitions of GIS (see Maquire 1992). Some stress the *geography* within GIS, relating issues such as geographically referenced data, spatially indexed data (Hassan and Hutchinson 1992), and integration of data on features such as points, lines and polygons. Others emphasize the *information* within GIS, addressing the computer processes of data entry, storage, retrieval, analysis and display. A few definitions have evolved to describe the *system* within GIS—that is, the modeling or decision-support role of the system. For example, Carter (1989) defines a system as "an institutional entity, reflecting an organizational structure that integrates technology with a database, expertise, and continuing financial support over time."

In order to have appropriate expectations from an investment made in GIS, it is essential to understand the three GIS components described by Dickinson and Calkins (1988): technology (hardware and software), data, and infrastructure (staff). Walklet (1991) estimates that data costs consume 80 percent of the GIS bill. If data already exist in digital format, then this cost may be reduced for some applications. However, this is rarely the case, particularly in international applications. In most cases, effort must be allocated for data collection and verification. Where mapped data exists in cartographic format, it must be converted to digital format—either manually traced or automatically scanned and interactively edited. Two other data sources used in this project are satellite data and field data collected using Global Positioning System (GPS) receivers. GIS is also a useful tool for integrating all of these data sources and for reaching new levels of analytical capabilities. Further, GIS can be useful in catalyzing avenues of interagency cooperation.

Sometimes, the process of automation is more significant than the final product. In order to produce maps for decisionmakers that are meaningful and reliable, agencies are forced to develop standards, decide which data are truly worth automating, and prioritize funding for future data improvements. This level of communication and cooperation can extend much further than simple data sharing.

Gap Analysis

Gap analysis is a GIS technique that correlates species distributions with boundaries of ecosystems and protected areas to identify efficient linkages in the conservation network. Gap analysis provides a method for assessing present measures to protect biological diversity and for identifying focus areas for optimal conservation efforts (Scott and others 1987). Gap analysis is defined by Davis and others (1990) as a search process for biotic communities and species in need of preservation management. GIS is used to overlay maps or layers that are geographically referenced to each other and to create new information through the combination of those map files. The various data layers include information on the distribution of features across a broad spectrum of disciplines: biology, physical geography, resource management, and rural sociology. Thus, gap analysis is a tool that forces standardization and communication between scientists of various disciplines—a concept which is gaining popularity in the environmental management dialogue between scientists and policy analysts.

Although there is currently little published on gap analysis, it is receiving a high level of attention from conservation agencies and organizations. It is considered politically attractive for several reasons. Gap analysis is an effective tool for decisionmakers and policy analysts because it clearly maps out conservation priorities and the path used to reach those priorities. Gap analysis results can be combined with economic development needs as constraints or opportunities in geographic selection of sustainable development projects. In addition, gap analysis has a good track record. It is being utilized in the United States in Idaho, California, Oregon, Utah, and Hawaii; and GIS operations are being supported by the National Ecology Research Center of the U.S. Fish and Wildlife Service (Scott and others 1990). Davis and others (1990) describe proposed U.S. legislation (H.R. 1268) that would establish a National Center for Biological Diversity and Environmental Research. A major aspect of the proposed legislation is the synthesis of a variety of data sources of varying scales in GIS format to perform gap analysis. Thus, gap analysis is likely to be a focal technique in biodiversity and sustainable development research in the future. However, gap analysis has been demonstrated only in the United States, where data is readily available. The technique remains untested where different data availability conditions prevail.

Gap Analysis in Costa Rica

Costa Rica is one of the most data-rich among the developing countries and should serve as a meaningful case in the international implementation of gap analysis. More significantly, other countries in Central America are comparatively data-poor, and the extension of the gap analysis model to a regional framework could enhance databases for regional and global studies.

This project is testing the hypothesis that a gap analysis model at the national level for Costa Rica, using available digital and cartographic holdings and satellite imagery, provides new insights into the development of national priorities for biodiversity conservation. In order to test the hypothesis, GIS will be implemented for an analysis of biological resources data in Costa Rica. The evaluation of available data sources will facilitate the establishment of data requirements for the international application of gap analysis. The research objectives in this project are: to identify and place in digital format existing data on geographic distributions of selected important wildlife species; to generate land cover and vegetation maps using satellite imagery at three levels of spatial resolution—30 meters (m), 80 m, and 1 kilometer (km); to combine the wildlife distribution data with the vegetation/cover data and with digital maps of public protected areas to identify gaps in the conservation network; and to develop an automated decision framework for prioritizing land areas for conservation and sustainable development.

Wildlife Data

The amount of available baseline data is small compared to the number of species that remain unidentified or poorly studied. However, it is beyond the scope of the study to utilize all the data published for Costa Rica. The purpose of the project is to identify those species that can be utilized effectively in gap analysis. The combination of wildlife distribution data layers with other data layers forms the basis of the gap analysis model.

The extent and quality of species distribution maps are highly variable. Range data are more readily available for mammals, such as primates or species of birds, having special interest groups such as parrots. Reptile, fish, insect, and plant range data are not as well documented. Studies performed on the scarlet macaw (Vaughan, McCoy and Liske 1991), and on the collared peccary (McCoy, Vaughan, Rodriguez and Kitchen 1990) indicate the level of effort required to provide good data on individual species.

The entry of available biodiversity data into a GIS format will be based upon previously collected vertebrate range data and existing data on endangered species. Species data maps prepared by the Universidad Nacional on nineteen species (Vaughan 1983) are being updated through field visits and interviews. Distribution data for game species and select endangered species are being added through the combination of field interview data with the digital data available from the Instituto Nacional de Biodiversidad (INBIO) in Costa Rica. Maps for each of the species are being generated at a scale of 1:200,000 for their distribution throughout Costa Rica.

Image Analysis

Remotely sensed data provide an operational GIS with timely and synoptic data. Remotely sensed data are vital to the project because they provide a means for updating existing vegetation maps and performing regional vegetation mapping.

Three types of satellite data are being utilized: Landsat Thematic Mapper (TM), Landsat Multispectral Scanner (MSS), and Advanced Very High Radiometric Resolution (AVHRR). Although each of the sensors vary in spectral resolution (number of bands) and in temporal resolution, the primary difference in their utility in vegetation and land cover mapping lies in their spatial resolutions. The TM has a spatial resolution of 30 m, while the MSS has a resolution of 80 m. Spatial resolution of the AVHRR is 1 km. Each of the three types of maps generated through the image classifications require different levels of ground truthing and verification. If calibration between the various stages is achieved, then a finer database can be used, in part, to train and verify the coarser level. The calibration of coarse resolution data to data of higher spatial resolution should enhance the level of information extraction from the coarse resolution data. Thus, the application of satellite imagery will be improved through the implementation of a method and data source that is more rapid, lower in storage and processing requirements, and more cost-effective.

Vegetation mapping is commonly performed utilizing satellite imagery analysis techniques. Although the use of remotely sensed data is becoming more widely practiced, it is an expensive technique because of the cost of satellite imagery. Staff specialists and image interpretation software and hardware are required. As a result, very few areas within Central America have existing satellite classification maps. Landsat scenes have been analyzed in the Yucatan (Green and others 1987) and the U.S. National Aeronautics and Space Administration (NASA) has done extensive analysis in Costa Rica (Sader and Joyce 1988), but most of Central America remains unmapped.

In order to provide a comprehensive vegetation map at a meaningful scale and data volume, AVHRR satellite data are being analyzed. Although AVHRR provides a spatial resolution of 1 km, Kerber and Schutt (1986) report that in a Level 1 land cover study (of forests and agriculture and urban areas) performed for the Chesapeake Bay area, classification accuracies were increased by only 5 percent when the 80-meter MSS data classification was compared to the AVHRR classification. Successes in vegetation mapping of the Nile Delta (Tucker, Gatlin, Schneider and Ruchinos 1982) and in land cover mapping for Africa (Tucker, Townshend and Goff 1985; Justice, Holben and Gwynne 1986) indicate that AVHRR classification should provide a meaningful vegetation map for Costa Rica. A country the size of Costa Rica (51,100 km^2) would populate a vegetation database with approximately 50,000 points. AVHRR is a good medium-resolution alternative to MSS, particularly if the techniques in this project are extended to the remainder of Central America or to other regions, because the size of the AVHRR dataset is approximately 1 percent as large as an MSS dataset for the same area (Hastings, Matson and Horbitz 1989).

In assessing the utility of coarse resolution satellite data, Roller and Colwell (1986) list several benefits of synoptic sensors such as AVHRR and Coastal Zone Color Scanner (CZCS). These benefits have immediate savings for the global modeling community if certain compromises in spatial resolution can be accepted. The acquisition of a single database acquired at one time eliminates the need to merge and edgematch numerous adjacent images. It is often easier to obtain cloud-free or cloud-reduced imagery with the higher temporal repetition available with coarse resolution sensors. It is possible that multi-temporal analysis can compensate for some of the information loss associated with decreased spatial resolution.

Roller and Colwell (1986) cite two cases in the United States where resource inventories have been shown to be effective using a combination of stratification and calibration techniques. Regional trends were depicted in Wisconsin surface water mapping using CZCS, while select areas were calibrated using Landsat MSS data. Extrapolating the data to the state of Wisconsin resulted in totals comparable to aerial photo interpretation techniques (within 7 percent). In an inventory of irrigated agricultural land in Nebraska, AVHRR data were used successfully in conjunction with MSS photographic prints.

A major focal point in the assessment of international data sources is an evaluation of the three distinct image sources for vegetation mapping. It is hoped that the integration of two or more of the sources will provide a meaningful and cost-effective mechanism to perform regional analyses of vegetation. There are various trade-offs in relying on any one of the three data sources, and it is not known to what degree the three can be used synergistically.

The most obvious factor in weighing the trade-offs among TM, MSS, and AVHRR data is cost. The higher spatial resolution TM data are much more expensive, currently US$4,400 per scene. Historical MSS scenes (older than two years) are available for $200, and AVHRR data costs $80 per scene. It also requires more TM scenes than MSS or AVHRR scenes to cover the same geographic region. Thus, coverage for Costa Rica using AVHRR costs $80, while MSS costs $1,200, and TM costs $27,600.

In contrast, the better spectral resolution of TM makes it more attractive, because classification maps produced from analysis of TM imagery yield a higher number of classes than either MSS or AVHRR analysis can produce. Ongoing TM imagery analysis at the Universidad Nacional for the Guanacaste region is generating approximately thirty-two vegetation and land cover classes. A comparable analysis applying MSS or AVHRR data is expected to produce only six classes. The degree to which gap analysis can be performed using fewer classes than is possible with TM data will be assessed.

One problem with most imagery in the tropics is limited data availability due to extensive cloud cover. In order to build a national coverage of Costa Rica using adjacent MSS scenes, it will be necessary to acquire three different dates of one of the scenes to overcome the problem of cloud cover in different parts of the scene. It is not yet certain that a national composite map can be generated using AVHRR, because of the high cloud cover at the time of day of the satellite overpass. In contrast, forty-four TM scenes were identified as having 20 percent cloud cover or less.

If it is possible to integrate the three different satellite sources, a stratified approach may be employed in regional mapping. This approach would utilize the higher spatial and spectral resolution data to increase the efficacy of the lower resolution data. Likewise, the more expensive data would have to be acquired for those areas where gaps in the lower resolution data occur.

Identifying Protected Areas Using Gap Analysis

The GIS overlay process identifies the gaps in the conservation network by adding the map layers on wildlife distribution to map layers on vegetation derived from image analysis and boundaries of protected areas. The term protected area includes a full range of types of geographic entities set aside for various purposes. The quality of individual conservation areas will vary according to the type of protected area (national park versus forest reserve), the funding allocated for management of the reserve, and the conservation ethic and development pressures associated with the local and national political geography. The International Union for Conservation of Nature and Natural Resources (IUCN) 1982 list for Costa Rica includes two international biosphere reserves (728,955 hectares [ha]), thirteen national parks, four biological reserves, a national reserve, a wildlife sanctuary (317,113 ha), twenty-four anthropological reserves (295,338 ha), and seventeen forest reserves (335,273 ha).

To assess the functional linkages between the biosphere reserves and the other protected areas, classification criteria are being established and employed in the gap analysis for Costa Rica. The criteria will result in a ranking of protected areas as well as an identification of economic and political realities which can be contradictory to the mission of the park.

It is not sufficient to merely identify the boundary of a protected area in digital format without an assessment of the condition of the boundary. Edges can be frontier, fenced, or an imaginary line heeded only on paper. Schonewald-Cox (1988) makes a case for the condition of the boundary of a preserve as indicative of the health of the entire preserve, analogous to the condition of the skin of an organism. Clarifying the boundary health of a reserve would enhance the gap analysis model significantly, but more realistically, such a value is not readily available and is more likely to be a result of the overlay of the protected areas layer with data from the demographic layers.

Baseline data on protected areas are presently being placed in digital format as part of the Food and Agriculture Organization of the United Nations' (FAO) Tropical Forests Resource Assessment. Additional digital data will be acquired from the United Nations Environment Programme (UNEP) Global Environment Monitoring System (GEMS) Global Resource Information Database (GRID) (Croze and Gwynne 1988), and from the IUCN Conservation Monitoring Centre (Pellew and Harrison 1988). Boundaries of protected areas are being labeled according to unit name and function (park, forest, or wildlife sanctuary).

During the implementation of the gap analysis model at the national level for Costa Rica, only that portion of the nation covered in the TM image analysis is being utilized in the first iteration of the model. Understanding of geographic phenomenon is strongest at the highest spatial resolution. In addition, a portion of the country is intentionally being left for later examination at the national scale, so that an unbiased evaluation of the model's performance at the national scale can be made. There are numerous geographic issues that will be assessed at this phase. For example, does the model identify the gaps in the conservation network that the Costa Rican team members know exist? Are new areas identified? Are the new areas valid? How well does the model handle distributions of riverine species, such as crocodilians? How does the number of areas identified in the model vary as spatial resolution (vegetation layer used) is changed from 30 m to 80 m to 1 km? How does the absolute geographic dimension of specific areas identified vary when using the three pixel sizes?

Implementing GIS in Costa Rica

Turning the GIS into an automated decision framework moves the gap analysis model from the theoretical mode to implementation in a resource management environment. The decision framework is the computer programming associated with replicating the various steps in the gap analysis in a "user-friendly" manner. Documentation of the data flow between various programs in the model is necessary in order to change variables or weights in the gap analysis model and to use the model in an operational setting.

The significance of the project extends beyond environmental benefits because the GIS in this project provides a framework that includes both ecosystem and land use data. It is an ideal technique for strengthening understanding of the interrelated processes of conservation and sustainable development. Not only are areas of habitat conservation identified and ranked, but also potential locations for sustainable development projects are identified. By relating the output from the gap analysis model to other data and to the related issue of sustainable development, an information system process allows concurrent examination of the issues linking environmental and developmental modeling.

Physical and demographic map layers are two categories of data used to enhance the gap analysis model and to apply the model in identifying sustainable development project areas. The physical database includes climate, elevation, soils, and hydrological data. These data are typically available in digital format at extremely general scales for regional studies (1:10,000,000). Most of the data in these data layers are being transferred from traditional cartographic products and placed in digital format (digitized). This is a time-consuming process and is slowed further by the need to collect maps of different national publication sources of varying qualities and scales. Soils maps exist for Costa Rica at a scale of 1:100,000 and slope and geological maps are available at a scale of 1:200,000.

The demographic database is designed to identify general human impacts on the ecosystem. It is composed of the locations of urban areas, smaller human settlements, and transportation infrastructure. Data on the locations of indigenous populations are being included because that information is particularly significant in the identification of sustainable development projects, the preservation of buffer areas around wildlife sanctuaries, and the assessment of human disturbance to reserves. Costa Rican map coverage of the road system and of human populations are available at 1:200,000 and 1:50,000. One project performed by Environmental Systems Research Institute, Inc. (ESRI) for the Defense Mapping Agency (DMA) provides digital data useful for the human geography data layers at the scale of 1:1,000,000. The Digital Chart of the World (DCW) project is based on 270 map sheets providing global coverage of the DMA Operational Navigational Charts (ONC) series commonly used by airplane pilots (ESRI 1989). The DCW data provides a good framework for the regional database as well as for transportation and human settlement systems. General land use trends will be generated from the combination of the DCW data with the AVHRR vegetation/land cover data.

We expect that a strong spatial correlation will be indicated between the physical data collected in this task and the output from the gap analysis model. Consideration will be given to whether these data should be included in the gap analysis model to enhance its accuracy or improve its efficiency. The availability of the physical data will be weighed against the difficulty of achieving accurate vegetation mapping in order to assess whether the physical data can be used instead of the vegetation data in special cases. The identification of sustainable development project locations is a process that begins by masking out all geographic areas that are urbanized. Then an assessment is made of the role of the various types of roads in the transportation network in economic development. Buffers are drawn around areas that are impacted by negatively scoring highways. Mining developments are considered in a similar fashion. The areas not suitable to sustainable development are subtracted using standard GIS techniques. Areas around indigenous population centers and communities having appropriate population densities are added to a map generated by creating a buffer around protected areas (excluding the protected areas themselves). The intersection of the two maps contains areas worthy of examination for sustainable development projects associated with human-biosphere edges and interactions.

Conclusions

Gap analysis is a technique that is timely for policy development in conservation geography. The prospect for the international application of gap analysis appears good since it is technically feasible. Examination of data sources by the four major categories (wildlife, vegetation from satellite imagery, protected areas, and physical/demographic) indicates that much information is currently being placed in digital format or is available in traditional cartographic media.

The satellite-derived vegetation map should serve to integrate a variety of data sources and data layers. We will determine which sensor system affords the most meaningful and cost-effective scale for that integration. Available species distribution data used to generate the gap analysis study for Costa Rica should facilitate the identification of geographic areas and specific species that warrant additional research.

The results of the gap analysis also should provide the scientific community with conservation data that are helpful in bridging the continuum between environmental science and environmental policy and law. Increased understanding of regional database construction and data quality is vital to better modeling of regional and global change and impact assessment.

Notes

1. This research was supported under grant No. HRN-5600-G-00-2008-00, Program in Science and Technology Cooperation, Office of the Science Advisor, United States Agency for International Development.

References

Carter, J.R. 1989. "On Defining the Geographic Information System." In W. Ripple, ed., *Fundamentals of Geographic Information Systems: A Compendium*. Falls Church, VA (USA): American Society of Photogrammetry and Remote Sensing.

Croze, H., and M.D. Gwynne. 1988. "The GEMS/GRID Toolbox." In V. Martin, ed., *For the Conservation of Earth*, Proceedings, 4th World Wilderness Congress, Denver, Colorado.

Davis, F.W., D.M. Stoms, J.E. Estes, J. Scepan, and J.M. Scott. 1990. "An Information Systems Approach to the Preservation of Biological Diversity." *International Journal of Geographical Information Systems* 4(1):55-78.

Dickinson, H., and H.W. Calkins. 1988. "The Economic Evaluation of Implementing a GIS." *International Journal of Geographic Information Systems* 2:307-327.

Environmental Systems Research Institute (ESRI). 1989. "ESRI Awarded DMA Contract for Digital World Database Project." *ARC News* 11(4):1-2.

Green, K.M., J.F. Lynch, J. Sircar, and L.S.Z. Greenberg. 1987. "Landsat Remote Sensing to Assess Habitat for Migratory Birds in the Yucatan Peninsuls, Mexico." *Vida Silvestre Neotropical* 1(2):27-38.

Hassan, Hassan M., and Charles Hutchinson, eds. 1992. *Natural Resource and Environmental Information for Decisionmaking*. Washington, DC: World Bank.

Hastings, D., M. Matson, and A.H. Horbitz. 1989. "AVHRR." *Photogrammetric Engineering and Remote Sensing* 55(2):168-169.

International Union for Conservation of Nature and Natural Resources (IUCN). 1982. *IUCN Directory of Neotropical Protected Areas*. IUCN Commission on National Parks and Protected Areas. Dublin: Tycooly International Publications, Limited.

Justice, C.O., B.N. Holben, and M.D. Gwynne. 1986. "Monitoring East African Vegetation Using AVHRR Data." *International Journal of Remote Sensing* 7(11):1453-1474.

Kerber, A.G., and J.B. Schutt. 1986. "Utility of AVHRR Channels 3 and 4 in Land-Cover Mapping." *Photogrammetric Engineering and Remote Sensing* 52(12):1827-1833.

Maguire, D.J. 1992. "An Overview and Definition of GIS." In D.J. Maguire, M.F. Goodchils, and D.W. Rhind, eds., *Geographical Information Systems: Principles and Applications*. Essex: Longman Group United Kingdom

Limited.

McCoy, M.B., C.S. Vaughan, M.A. Rodriguez, and D. Kitchen. 1990. "Seasonal Movement, Home Range, Activity and Diet of Collared Peccaries (Tayassu tajacu) in Costa Rican Dry Forest." *Vida Silvestre Neotropical* 2(2):6-20.

Pellew, R.A., and J.D. Harrison. 1988. "A Global Database on the Status of Biological Diversity: The IUCN Perspective." In H. Mousey, ed., *Building Databases for Global Science*. Philadelphia, PA: Taylor and Francis.

Roller, N.E.G., and J.E. Colwell. 1986. "Coarse-Resolution Satellite Data for Ecological Surveys." *BioScience* 36(7):468-475.

Sader, S.A., and A.T. Joyce. 1988. "Deforestation Rates and Trends in Costa Rica, 1940 to 1983." *Biotropica* 20(1):11-19.

Schonewald-Cox, C.M. 1988. "Boundaries in the Protection of Nature Reserves: Translating Multidisciplinary Knowledge into Practical Conservation." *BioScience* 38(7):480-486.

Scott, J.M., B. Csuti, J.D. Jacobi, and J.E. Estes. 1987. "Species Richness: A Geographic Approach to Protecting Future Biological Diversity." *BioScience* 37(11):782-788.

Scott, J.M., F. Davis, B. Csuti, B. Butterfield, R. Noss, S. Caicco, H. Anderson, J. Ulliman, F. D'Erchia, and C. Groves. 1990. *Gap Analysis: Protecting Biodiversity Using Geographic Information Systems*. Workshop Handbook, University of Idaho, October 29-31.

Tucker, C.J., J.A. Gatlin, S.R. Schneider, and M.A. Ruchinos. 1982. "Monitoring Vegetation in the Nile Delta with NOAA-6 and NOAA-7 AVHRR Imagery." *Proceedings*. International Symposium of Remote Sensing of the Environment. Cairo, Egypt, January 19-25.

Tucker, C.J., J.R.G. Townshend, and T.E. Goff. 1985. "African Land-Cover Classification Using Satellite Data." *Science* 227(4685): 369-375.

Vaughan, C. 1983. *A Report on Dense Forest Habitat for Endangered Species in Costa Rica*. Editorial Department. Universidad Nacional, Costa Rica.

Vaughan, C., M. McCoy, and J. Liske. 1991. "Scarlet Macaw (Ara macao) Ecology and Management Perspectives in Carara Biological Reserve, Costa Rica." *Proceedings*, I Mesoamerican Workshop on Conservation and Management of Macaws of the Genus Ara, Tegucigalpa, Honduras, January 4-7.

Walklet, Donn C. 1991. "The Economics of GIS: Understanding the Economic Motivation and Requirements which Justify the Use of GIS as a Practical Solution for Environmental and Resource Planners." *Proceedings*, GIS/LIS '91, Atlanta, Georgia.

Part III
Sectoral and Social Issues in Environmental Assessment

8

Impact Assessment of Dams and Reservoirs: The Work of the International Commission on Large Dams

Jan A. Veltrop

Life on earth, as we know it, is impossible without water. A reliable source of water for domestic use and irrigation has been provided by dams for well over 5,000 years. Civilizations have risen when water supplies were assured and have fallen when knowledge and experience to maintain and repair dams was lost. Hydroelectric power has been developed only during the past 100 years, although water turbines have been around for 2,000 years.

Today, there are 37,000 dams in the world over 15 meters (m) high; nearly 80 percent of these dams are lower than 30 m (figure 8-1). The dams serve many purposes, but more than 85 percent have been constructed since mid-century to satisfy the increasing demands for water and energy (figure 8-2). Soaring populations and expectations for improved living conditions are escalating the requirement for food production, industrialization, and economic growth. More dams, of whatever size, are needed to regulate the hydrological cycle and to provide a reliable source of water supply, especially in the developing countries (figure 8-3). Without dams people would be faced with years of hunger, alternating with years of flooding.

The creation of reservoirs, however, has a profound impact on the environment, ecosystems, and flora and fauna upstream and downstream of the dam, as well as on the human inhabitants of the affected area. Some fifty years ago the environmental, social and cultural impacts of reservoirs were not very well understood and were often overlooked. Yet in 1556, the German scholar Agricola wrote in *De Re Metallica* that several centuries of gold and silver mining in Saxonia and Bohemia had "devastated the fields, because water used to wash the ores poisoned the brooks and streams and destroyed the fish or drove them away. As a result, the inhabitants of these regions on account of the devastation of their fields, woods, groves, brooks and rivers, find great difficulty in procuring the necessities of life, and by reason of the destruction of the timber they are forced to greater

expense in erecting buildings." He then noted "it is clear to all that there is greater detriment from mining than the value of the metal which the mining produces." Today, there is still evidence of neglect to balance the allocation of benefits and costs among the various social groups.

Many lessons have been learned from oversights and neglects. As a result, environmental impacts now form an inherent part of project evaluation and acceptance in many countries throughout the world. A multitude of effects are analyzed and incorporated in the design of dams, such as hydrologic regime, water quality, underground seepage, water tables, seismicity, as well as effects on climate. Illustration of lessons learned is one of the keystones of the work of the International Commission on Large Dam (ICOLD) and should be used in developing guidelines and legislation for future projects.

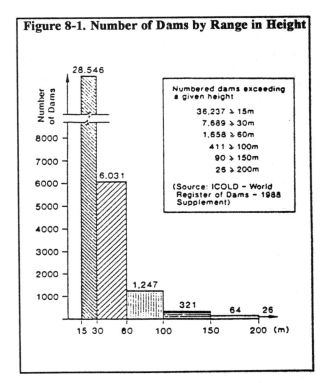

Figure 8-1. Number of Dams by Range in Height

Number of Dams

Numbered dams exceeding a given height

36.237 ≥ 15m
7.689 ≥ 30m
1.658 ≥ 60m
411 ≥ 100m
90 ≥ 150m
26 ≥ 200m

(Source: ICOLD – World Register of Dams – 1988 Supplement)

28.546
6.031
1,247
321
64
26

15 30   60   100   150   200 (m)

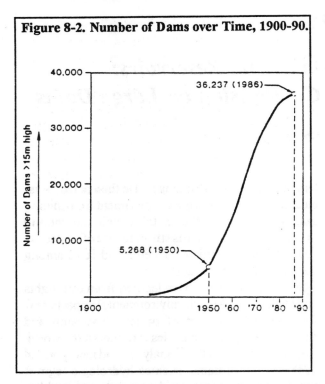

Figure 8-2. Number of Dams over Time, 1900-90.

recent decades construction of new dams has frequently become controversial. Comprehensive studies of the impacts of dam projects would include biological, geophysical, political, social, economic, and financial evaluations.

Environmental Impacts and the Role of ICOLD

Impacts of dams and reservoirs are both direct and indirect. Direct impacts occur on soils, vegetation, wildlife, wetlands, fisheries, and climate in the watersheds upstream and downstream of the dam. Downstream impacts include migratory fish, water logging, spread of diseases, and saltwater intrusion. Alteration of river flow downstream may also have major affects on ecosystems and human activities. Reservoir impoundment submerges agriculture and forest lands and affects human populations directly.

Indirect impacts are due also to construction work and other induced developments. During construction, new access roads and construction camps will be built, as well as transmission lines. Dams may induce agricultural, industrial and municipal development activities.

On the other hand, reservoirs themselves are affected by the development of land and water resources in the catchment area above dams. Examples are agriculture, population resettlement and forest

With increased density of population, evident limitations on availability of new lands for agriculture, the presence of chemical poisoning of the environment, and, most of all, with the recognition that man may be affecting his environment in a detrimental and possibly irreversible way, it is no wonder that in

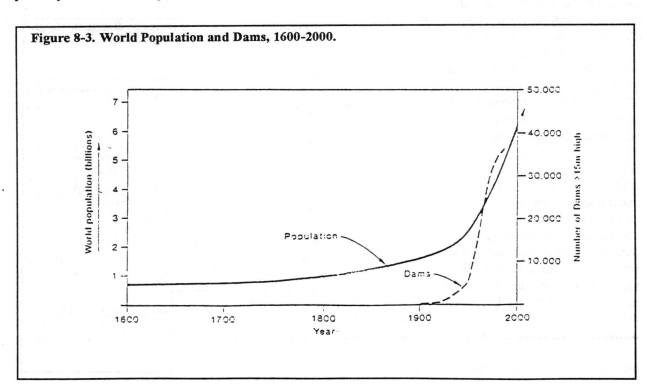

Figure 8-3. World Population and Dams, 1600-2000.

clearing, which cause increased siltation and changes of water quality.

The thrust of this chapter is to point out many successful ways in which designers, engineers and scientists can plan dam projects to prevent or ameliorate their adverse effects. Major effects do preserve the ecosystems of entire watersheds. These activities are addressed in papers and during discussions at the triennial Congresses of ICOLD and are highlighted in the technical bulletins produced by the ICOLD Committee on the Environment.

ICOLD promotes the advancement of dam engineering by providing its 5,000 members with a forum for discussion and exchange of knowledge and experience. Its principal objective is to ensure that dams are built safely, economically and with respect for the environment. ICOLD plays an important role in expanding on the knowledge and the ability of engineers and planners to properly incorporate environmental factors in the planning, design, construction and operation of large dam projects. Effective implementation of such knowledge and the experience of project planners and designers is usually in the hands of owners, legislators, local and national governments, as well as financial institutions such as the World Bank.

Before presenting some examples of ICOLD's work, it is important to point out that construction of new dams has not been stopped. On the contrary, the current survey by ICOLD among its 79 member countries and 15 others, shows that more than 2,000 dams over 15 m high were under construction in 1991. These include 71 very large projects, defined as having a dam over 150 m high, or a volume of over 15 million cubic meters (m^3), or a reservoir capacity of over 25 cubic kilometers (km^3) or a power station of over 1,000 megawatts (MW) installed capacity. There were 271 such projects in operation worldwide during 1990 and 86 more were being planned.

The environmental impacts of dams and reservoir construction have been reviewed in more than 250 papers submitted to ICOLD Congresses between 1973 and 1991 (see appendix 8-1). These include not only planning and design, but also management and monitoring of impacts during construction and subsequent operation.

The six bulletins published by ICOLD (see appendix 8-2) cover examples of successful mitigation and the influence of regional climates (temperate, tropical, subtropical, arid and severe winter). The first bulletin also provides a matrix for listing and evaluating the impact of individual dams and related construction work on specific aspects of the environment. The bulletin on "Dams and the Environment—Notes on Regional Influences" describes the history of five projects in different climatic areas in Austria, Finland, Mali, Sweden, and the United States. Another bulletin describes in detail the effects of the closure in 1932 of the Zuiderzee in The Netherlands, and the measures taken during development of the four polders to accommodate the drastic change from a marine-brackish estuary with two tidal movements a day to an eutrophic freshwater system with a fixed water level.

Management of Environmental Impacts

Management Plans

Management plans to achieve environmental and sociological goals and to monitor progress and success frequently cover a single project and sometimes an entire river basin. The Mount Elbert Pumped Storage Project in Colorado (United States) is an example of the former, and the Delta Works in the Netherlands of the latter. The Three-Gorges Project in China offers an example of the use of existing methods to assess the basin-wide impact of a huge project.

THE MOUNT ELBERT PROJECT (TWIN LAKES, COLORADO). The Twin Lakes have been subjected to ecological changes ever since humans settled in the area over one hundred years ago. Being oligotrophic (nutrient poor) the lakes have always been known for their quality cold-water fishing, even though the lakes were converted into irrigation storage reservoirs in 1901. The original fauna was replaced with lake and rainbow trout and freshwater mysis shrimp. Development of roads, transmountain diversions and mining activity in the area increased heavy metal deposition in the lakes. At the same time, population settlement changed the chemical limnology of the lakes due to the addition of plant nutrients, such as phosphorus.

Development of the power project included the purchase of all the land surrounding the lakes and its conversion to public recreation areas. Historical buildings were protected and restored. Most of the power plant structures, all water conveyance tunnels and the power lines were placed underground. These measures vastly improved the aesthetic appearance of the area. The area remains a valuable fishery resource and provides peaking power and water to thousands of people. The positive and negative impacts of the power plant on the lakes' ecology were evaluated after construction. Positive effects are: aeration of the lower lake during winter stagnation; increased reservoir habitat for shrimp and plankton production; increased supply of planktonic food for fish, especially in the area of the power plant tailrace; and increased contribution, circulation, and production of nutrients to the euphoric zone.

Negative impacts include: some mortality of game fish; the transfer of mysis shrimp from the lower lake, where they are most needed, to the forebay where they are least needed; a slight increase in turbidity due to turbulence in the lakes; and an increase in the fluctuation of lake levels making it more difficult for ice fishermen to use the lakes.

The engineering of this water resource project has been carefully blended with environmental protection and development values.

THE DELTA WORKS PROJECT (THE NETHERLANDS). The management of the Eastern Scheldt barrier as part of the Delta works, demonstrates the far-reaching influence of environmental interests and the fishing industry on the design and operational procedures for managing the barrier. The twofold objective of the dam was to safeguard the region against flooding and to preserve the unique saltwater tidal environment.

Studies covered the physical situation expected after construction, the most suitable form of management, and use of the barrier during closure of secondary dams. Operational policies will be evaluated after five years, and, if necessary, will be modified. Safety evaluation will be concerned with the strength of the barrier and the dikes. The development of the ecosystem toward a new equilibrium will be carefully monitored to verify earlier forecasts and to modify and adapt the models that have been developed previously. Opportunities for further development of the area will be studied, including reduction of flow rates, changes in level of salting and extension of fishing and recreational activities without risking the natural environment.

THE THREE-GORGES PROJECT (CHINA). The comprehensive assessment of the huge Three-Gorges project on the Yangtze River utilized the ICOLD matrix presented in Bulletin 35, as well as methods proposed by UNESCO and UNEP. Project benefits include flood control, power generation, and improved irrigation. Environmental impacts on the entire river basin include: climate, water quality and temperature,

thermal stratification, aquatics, fish, fauna and flora, sedimentation, geology, induced seismicity, soil, public health, inundation, and resettlement, as well as effects on the downstream river and on the estuary. The loss of land and the relocation of some 300,000–800,000 people are extremely important issues. It was concluded from these studies that proper planning and non-engineering measures can mitigate undesirable impacts.

Application of Regulations

Environmental regulations often have a profound effect on project planning, design, construction, and operation. New procedures for project planning have resulted in new engineering designs, such as multi-level outlet structures to optimize downstream water quality and temperature for fish protection; in-reservoir and/or downstream oxygen injection to provide dissolved oxygen for fish; clearing of vegetation to avoid water quality problems, maximize biological habitat diversity, and provide for safe recreation; provisions for fish screens, fish ladders, fish lifts, and bypass structures to assist migratory fish; implementing reservoir operational rules for downstream flows at critical times to protect reproductive habitat, migratory routes, recreation use, and water quality; reservoir shoreline development to provide biologically productive wetland habitat; completion of extensive pre-impoundment cultural, sociological, and economic studies and subsequent development of appropriate resettlement programs. Much of this new technology is being applied to existing projects as well, thereby improving the environment of established reservoirs.

Regulations originate, first, from government laws; second, from organizational policies; and third, from the requirements of financial institutions such as The World Bank. Selected examples from these categories are presented below.

• *Regulated Flows (France).* An agreement between the Ministry of the Environment and Electricité de France (EDF) has fixed the targets for downstream regulated flows, fish migration and reservoir drainage.

• *European Economic Community (EEC) Guidelines (Italy).* The development of criteria for selecting potential reservoir sites for a water resources master plan in Sardinia, Italy, required preparation of environmental impact assessments of twelve alternative dam sites using the policy guidelines of the EEC and the ICOLD matrix of Bulletin 35.

• *Environmental Assessment (Poland).* An EA of the effects of hydraulic structures on the environment before and after construction is obligatory in Poland. This includes: climate changes, groundwater levels, reservoir slopes, water quality, floods, biological changes along the reservoir rims, and regional management.

• *Environmental Impact Studies (Spain).* Environmental impact studies are required in Spain. Detailed studies of the watershed processes have been carried out leading to successful implementation of such beneficial alteration methods as reforestation, increased infiltration, reduced soil loss, and control of drainage system channels.

• *Federal Law (Switzerland).* The new Federal law on Protection of the Environment was enacted in 1985. It addresses the development of natural resources while protecting the environment. It protects persons, animals, plants and their biological communities and habitats against harmful effects or nuisances, and maintains the fertility of the soil. It minimizes the impact of any installation which may appreciably affect the environment, including hydroplants with an installed capacity over 0.3 MW. A recent EA report for a new project in a pristine, isolated valley addresses the landscape of the valley, vegetation, and the protection of nature, fauna, fisheries and alpine pastures.

• *Regulatory Agency (Thailand).* The National Environment Board (NEB) in Thailand, which is the regulatory agency on environmental policy, has prepared ten categories of the types and sizes of projects that require an environmental impact report, aimed at allocating water resources to the various users (municipal, industrial, irrigation and environment). One of these deals with dam and reservoir projects with a volume of 100 hm^3, or a reservoir area over 15 km^2, and another with irrigation projects larger than 12,800 hectares. For the Chiew Larn Multipurpose Project environmental issues were effectively integrated early in the project planning stage. These included resettlement of 400 families, timber logging, clearing forest areas, partial inundation of a wildlife sanctuary, reforestation, excavation of archeological artifacts, preventive measures against waterborne diseases, construction of new fishery stations and studies to improve saline soils in downstream irrigable areas. The total cost of this environmental mitigation program was reported to be less than 4 percent of the project cost.

• *Environmental Laws (United States).* The civil works program of the Corps of Engineers must comply with thirty-five environmental laws, which present environmental requirements and needs along with other water resource development and management considerations and responsibilities.

• *Legislation (former USSR).* Design, construction and operation of reservoirs in the former USSR are controlled by the principles of land and water legislation and similar acts on, for example, woodlands, soils, wildlife, and protection of historical and cultural monuments. The law on "Environmental Protection and Rational Utilization of Natural Resources" became effective in 1975. Following their introduction, proposals for several hydroelectric projects on rivers in Siberia were rejected because large areas of arable land would be flooded.

• *Policy (World Bank).* One of the major concerns of the World Bank is that the sociological and environmental concerns of dam projects are addressed at the earliest possible stage of project planning and that actions are carried out throughout project construction and into operations. World Bank policies cover indigenous people, wildlands, and cultural properties.[1] The most important issue for the Bank is to decide whether a dam should be built or not. This decision is usually based on an economic analysis, which includes sociological and environmental factors.

Control of Water Quality

Water quality in rivers and reservoirs is profoundly affected by the construction of a dam. Physical, chemical and biological processes in the reservoir affect the quality of the water released from the reservoir to the river. Climate, reservoir shape, quantity and quality of inflow, upstream water use, land productivity, industrial activity and structural features of the dam and outlet works, as well as project operation affect the limnological processes in the reservoir and the quality of water in the river downstream.

Mathematical and physical modeling has greatly improved the understanding of the causes of poor water quality, as well as the development of mitigating measures. Decomposition of organic matter, thermal stratification and production of organic matter by phytoplankton and aquatic weeds all have negative effects on water quality.

Eutrophication of lakes and reservoirs as a result of excessive nutrients is undesirable and must be averted. The process of eutrophication takes quite a long time in nature and depends on the climate and local conditions, but it can be greatly accelerated by human actions. It is a highly complicated phenomenon that depends on the hydrodynamical, chemical, physical, biological and geographical characteristics of the reservoir. Measures to counter eutrophication have been carried out at many reservoirs, for example, water is released over the spillway in Ireland and bottom outlets are being tried in Morocco to evacuate nutrients and weaken stratification, while activities in the watershed are being controlled. Selected examples worldwide are described below to illutsrate various responses for water quality problems.

• *Groundwater (Austria).* Groundwater studies near the Vienna-Danube channel indicated the effectiveness of a system of pairs of large diameter vertical filtering wells, as part of the construction of the Vienna - Freudenau hydro power plant to simulate the original interaction of the Danube River with the surrounding areas.

• *Water Quality (Brazil).* Application of models to water quality problems in reservoirs in Brazil demonstrated the importance of residence time, the presence of vegetation, and upstream pollution. For example, due to the very short residence time, good water quality developed in the Tucurui reservoir, despite the decomposition of large amounts of organic matter from drowned vegetation. The Balbina reservoir, also in Brazil, shows the opposite because of long residence time.

• *Downstream Releases (Czechoslovakia).* Frequently water quality is controlled by downstream releases. Frequency and volume depend on the purpose and function of the reservoir, its storage capacity, the demand of the users and the type of releases. In Czechoslovakia the negative influence of increased fluctuation and a decrease of minimum discharges due to power operation of reservoirs was minimized by construction of a re-regulating reservoir downstream.

• *Multipurpose Reservoirs (Czechoslovakia).* Multipurpose use of reservoirs can easily affect water quality. In Czechoslovakia, 150 reservoirs were analyzed by means of physical and mathematical methods. It was concluded that the use of drinking water reservoirs for sports and recreation should not be forbidden a priori; instead, each case should be analyzed separately.

• *Oxygenation (Czechoslovakia).* Ecological balance was restored in the downstream section of a river through aerial oxygenation by using Howell Bunger outlet values.

• *Conflicting Water Use (France).* Multiple and often conflicting uses of water are addressed by planners and operators through drawing up comprehensive plans for alternative uses of water; implementing delayed socioeconomic structures around new projects; conserving water quality; and pooling skills and funding sources.

• *Aeration Measures (Germany).* In the heavily populated Ruhr River Basin, careful planning and management of a reservoir demonstrated that intensive recreation can be balanced to protect and enhance the natural environment. Water quality improved after construction of a dam and was maintained by aeration measures to prevent stratification and eutrophication. Silt was removed from the reservoirs without seriously impacting on water quality.

• *Ecological Model (Germany).* In Germany dams supply about 20 percent of the total consumption of industry, agriculture and population. Increasingly, water purity is affected by exploitation of the catchment areas by man, which leads to pollution and eutrophication. Methods to limit the inflow of nutrients into the water were found to be more successful than the application of in-reservoir techniques. An ecological model was developed to predict water quality in the reservoirs and lakes, and to provide a basis for decision making.

• *Eutrophication Control (Japan).* In Japan aeration and circulation have been used in four reservoirs to counter eutrophication. Lowering the water intake from 1.5 m to 10 m was effective in combatting eutrophication, hydrogen sulfide, and offensive odors and taste. In another case, a movable fountain was developed to pump colder water and precipitate it onto the water surface to reduce the phytoplankton breeding environment. Water quality was controlled for another reservoir in Japan by manipulation of the vertical stratification using a multilevel outlet works.

• *Regulating Ponds (Republic of Korea).* It is common practice to use regulating ponds downstream of large dams to allow the temperature of the released water to increase by exposure to the atmosphere.

• *Ozonization (Spain).* Two-phase ozonization has been studied successfully in a pilot plant for a reservoir in Spain to replace the oxygen in this typical hot lake with its single stratification in the summer.

• *Tidal Barrage (United Kingdom).* Construction of a tidal barrage across the Severn Estuary would greatly effect the existing highly stressed ecosystem.

Mathematical models of water movement and physical processes, involved with the sedimentary processes, have provided an initial assessment of the changes the barrage would cause to the sediment regime. The results of these studies will be made widely available to the public and encourage consultation and comments.

• *Reaeration (United States).* Surface-fed reaeration was successful in eliminating anaerobic conditions in southern California. Results were diminished alga blooms and creation of a year-round cold water fishery.

• *Water Temperature Control (United States).* The temperature of the water released from the Lost Creek dam on the Rogue River is critical for the breeding of anadromous fish. The study indicated improved temperatures during fall releases by accepting warmer-than-desired releases in the spring and summer.

Countermeasures to Sedimentation

Because dams and reservoirs are among the largest artificial structures on earth, they can be expected to affect the environment. Sedimentation is of great concern because it reduces reservoir capacity. Long-term operation of reservoirs should be controlled by the lifetime of the civil works, not by sedimentation. Reservoirs should last 250–300 years; and in cases of large, known sediment inflows, "reserve" capacity should be available for 100–150 years, or even 200. Large reservoirs behind the Glenn Canyon and Hoover Dams in the United States and the Aswan Dam in Egypt meet these criteria.

Potential losses of reservoir capacity can be countered by soil conservation measures in the catchment area, interception of sediments in the upper regions, flushing of sediments through bottom outlets, venting of density currents and by dredging. The main disadvantage of flushing of sediments is the waste of water. The water-detritus ratio varies from the 20–50 range to a maximum of 100. This amount of water can be reduced significantly when flushing is carried out together with suction dredging or venting by density current.

Adverse effects of sedimentation are not limited to the loss of reservoir storage space. In addition, there is contamination of the environment due to absorption of chemicals on the surface of sedimentary particles; physical damage to the turbines; ecological effects on the growth of fish because of changes in the dissolved oxygen content; and adverse effects on tourism by making the delta too shallow for boating.

Other beneficial and negative effects occur downstream, including: stabilization of the river regime by reducing the tendency to wander; decrease in water temperature fluctuation; undermining of bridge piers; continuing erosion of river banks; aggradation of the riverbed; loss of nutrients; and detention of plankton in the reservoir. Long-term erosion effects have been studied with computer models for both the Rhine and the Rhone rivers.

Rapid population growth and increased human activities are increasing soil erosion problems, (for example, in Indonesia). While soil conservation measures in the catchment area are the best cure, such practices have been successful mainly in relatively small watersheds. The following selected examples show various responses to sedimentation problems.

• *Sediment Flushing (Algeria).* Flushing of sediment is done by reservoir emptying at the end of the irrigation season. In the Fergoug reservoir, 90 percent of the sediments have been sluiced out in this manner.

• *Density Current (China).* Venting of the density current has become an art and a science in China. Certain conditions have to be met in order to assure that the density current entering the reservoir reaches the dam and the sluice. Knowing the incoming flow, the hydrographs, the reservoir characteristics and the size and elevation of the bottom outlets, it is then possible to predict the amount of sediment sluiced out through the density current.

• *Reservoir Emptying (France).* Of 450 dams, 15 reservoirs were emptied about once a year, as reported to ICOLD in 1988. Advancements in instrumentation and the development of mathematical models have enabled the judicious operation of various outlets in the dams to control the impact on fish life.

• *Sediment Removal (Republic of Korea).* Methods used at the Palding dam reservoir in Korea included a silt protector at the intakes and the use of a hydro-clone, an oil fence and a suction dredger.

• *Sediment Outflow (Morocco).* Submerged guide embankments were constructed in the Oued Neckor Reservoir to lead the suspended sediment flows over the spillway.

• *Sediment Transportation (Switzerland).* Good agreement on quantities of transported sediments was obtained between actual operations and model tests for the Gebidem Reservoir in Switzerland.

• *Flushing (Yugoslavia)*. Favorable results were obtained by flushing smaller reservoirs through bottom outlets resulting in no further build-up of sediments in front of the dam and no significant consequences in the river downstream. Sediment inflow into the reservoirs was reduced by constructing small sediment retention dams and through the application of biological measures. The cost of these works exceeded the original cost of the dam by a few percent. For larger dams, considerable effects of sediment concentrations were observed on the ecology of the river downstream.

• *Mechanical dredging*. This method has been employed successfully to remove course deposits in Austria, China, Japan and the Netherlands. Dredged materials are often transported through pipes over long distances (16–18 km). There are wide differences in the world concerning preference for sediment disposal. For example, in Japan fine materials are left in front of the dam to be carried downstream by floods, but in China these fine particles are used for irrigation fields and land reclamation.

Conclusions

The principal question facing society is whether a future dam will be useful or detrimental, whether such a dam will improve the environment as a whole as well as the wellbeing of humans—or whether the particular dam will spoil these. And if a dam is to be built, according to what characteristics and criteria should it be built?

Those who see the need for more dams and at the same time are concerned about possible adverse impacts of the dam face two formidable challenges: to inform the public of the beneficial effects of dams and to convince owners, financiers and governments of the necessity to remedy the drawbacks of dams.

Appendix 8-1: Environments Topics Discussed at ICOLD Congresses, as Published in the Proceedings.

1973 Eleventh Congress (Madrid)

Question 40 The Consequences on the Environment of Building Dams: (a) physical effects (for example, sedimentation, erosion, water regimes, water quality; (b) biological effects (for example, fish, eutrophication, deformation; (c) influence on humans (pollution, displacement and resettlement of population); and (d) evaluation of beneficial and detrimental effects of damming.

1976 Twelfth Congress (Mexico)

Question 47 The Effects on Dams and Reservoir of Some Environments Factors: (a) problems of floating material, sedimentation, salination (excluding eutrophication); methods for forecasting and remedial measures; (b) special design and construction considerations in regions subject to extremes of temperature and precipitation; and (c) economic evaluation of these environmental factors.

1982 Fourteenth Congress (Rio de Janeiro)

Question 54 Reservoir Sedimentation and Slope Stability—Technical and Environmental Effects: (a) sedimentation (estimation of sediment load and silting, control and release of sediments, and downstream effects); and (b) stability of reservoir slopes (geotechnical, hydraulic aspects, and other aspects).

1988 Sixteenth Congress (San Francisco)

Question 60 Reservoirs and the Environment— Experience in Management and Monitoring: (a) environmental regulations and impacts on promotion, construction and operation; (b) effectiveness of environmental protection measures, including water quality; (c) Costs of environmental protection measures; (d) benefits to the environment; and (e) management plans, monitoring and comparison with predictions.

1991 Seventeenth Congress (Vienna)

Question 64 Environmental Issues in Dam Projects: (a) contributions of dam projects to human and environmental needs; (b) environmental evaluations (biological, geophysical, political, social, economic, and financial, etc.), and water quality; (c) operational appraisal (case histories and comparison with original objectives); and (d) public awareness.

Appendix 8-2: ICOLD Bulletins Related to Environmental Effects

Bulletin 35 (1980) Dams and the Environment
Bulletin 37 (1981) Dam Projects and Environmental Success
Bulletin 50 (1985) Dams and the Environment– Notes on Regional Influences
Bulletin 65 (1988) Dams and Environment–Case Histories
Bulletin 66 (1989) Dams and Environment– Zuiderzee Damming

Bulletin 86 (1992) Dams and Environment–Socio-economic Impacts

A series of state-of-the-art papers on geophysical, water quality, flora and fauna aspects and another bulletin on case histories are under preparation.

Notes

1. For a summary of the Operational Directives (ODs) and policies on environmental and social issues related to Bank-financed projects, see the fourth annual report on the environment (World Bank 1993).

References

Goodland, Robert. 1989. *The World Bank's New Policy on the Environmental Aspects of Dams and Reservoir Projects*. World Bank Series 458, Washington, DC.

International Commission on Large Dams (ICOLD). 1973. "The Consequences on the Environment of Building Dams." Transactions of the Eleventh Congress, Madrid. Vol. 1, Question 40. Paris: ICOLD.

———. 1976. "The Effects on Dams and Reservoirs: Some Environmental Factors." Transactions of the Twelfth Congress, Mexico City. Vol. IV, Question 47. Paris: ICOLD.

———. 1982. "Reservoir Sedimentation and Slope Stability: Techinical and Environmental Effects." Transactions of the Fourteenth Congress, Rio de Janiero. Vol. III, Question 54. Paris: ICOLD.

———. 1988a. "Reservoirs and Environment: Experience in Management and Monitoring." Transactions of the Sixteenth Congress, San Francisco. Vol. I, Question 60. Paris, ICOLD.

———. 1988b. World Register of Dams.

———. 1991. "Environmental Issues in Dam Projects." Transactions of the Seventeenth Congress, Vienna. Vol. I, Question 40. Paris: ICOLD.

World Bank. 1993. *The World Bank and the Environment: Fiscal 1993*. Washington, DC.

9

Public Participation in Environmental Assessments in Africa

Cynthia C. Cook and Paula Donnelly-Roark

The involvement of an informed public and the participation of affected groups in project planning are critical to the success of development projects, in Africa as elsewhere. The World Bank recently introduced environmental assessments (EAs) for its projects that include consultation with local groups and nongovernmental organizations (NGOs). The purpose of these procedures is to ensure that the views of such groups are fully taken into account in project design and implementation in order to improve project viability and sustainability.

This chapter reports the results of a review of the first generation of EAs undertaken for Bank-financed projects in Sub-Saharan Africa. The purpose of the review was to: (a) identify the range of approaches used to secure public participation; (b) evaluate the effectiveness of these approaches in achieving the objectives of different groups; and (c) recommend ways to improve the effectiveness of public participation in future EAs of projects in the Bank's Africa Region.

World Bank Experience with Participation

The World Bank began to recognize the importance of popular participation in development projects as evaluation evidence began to link project success and sustainability with beneficiary participation.[1] World Bank sociologists took the lead in bringing this relationship to the attention of Bank management (Cernea 1985). A review of Bank-financed projects carried out in the mid-1980s showed that failure to attend to social variables in project design and implementation often led to failure to attain project objectives (Kottak 1985). Another chapter in this collection pointed out several ways in which beneficiary participation could lead to project success (Uphoff 1985). Bank-sponsored evaluation research on selected urban projects, based on the participant-observer approach, developed into the methodology of beneficiary assessment (Salmen 1987).

In 1987, fifty projects in urban housing, population, health and nutrition, and irrigation were reviewed to assess the lessons of Bank experience with community participation. This review defined participation as "an active process by which beneficiary/client groups influence the direction and execution of a development project with a view to enhancing their well being" (Paul 1987). It identified the potential objectives of participation as (a) empowerment, (b) capacity building, (c) increased project effectiveness, (d) increased project efficiency, and (e) cost sharing. It pointed out that Bank policies tend to encourage participation in relation to project effectiveness, efficiency, and cost sharing; capacity building and empowerment are not often seen as Bank objectives. It also pointed out the lack of operational guidelines for Bank staff and the fact that appropriate participation techniques are likely to vary by country, sector, and stage in the project cycle.

A subsequent review of Bank projects involving participation found that, although there was substantial literature on participation within the Bank, individual Bank staff had made few attempts to involve beneficiaries in project design and implementation. The review also noted that the link between participation, project success, and sustainability seemed to have been clearly demonstrated but that Bank policy and practice did not yet fully support this approach (Nagle and Ghose 1990). Partly in response to this finding, the World Bank has recently undertaken an extensive Learning Process on Participation, based on an in-depth study of twenty Bank-supported operations that are considered to be especially participatory. The process defines popular participation as "a process by which people, especially disadvantaged people, *influence* decisions which affect them" (World Bank 1991a, emphasis added). In defining disadvantaged people, the process refers not only to the absolute poor, but to a broader range of people who are disadvantaged in terms of poverty, illiteracy, ethnicity, or gender. It further specifies that "influence" means more than simply involvement in project implementation or sharing in project benefits.

World Bank Policy on Environmental Assessment

In October 1989, the World Bank issued its first Operational Directive on environmental assessment (OD 4.00, Annex A). This directive called for the involvement of affected groups and local NGOs in project design and implementation, particularly in the preparation of EAs.[2] To supplement the operational directive (OD), a chapter in the Bank's *Environmental Assessment Sourcebook* (1991b) was devoted to "Community Involvement and the Role of Nongovernmental Organizations in Environmental Assessment." This chapter defines the roles and responsibilities of Bank staff, EA team members (implementing agency staff and consultants), affected groups and local NGOs; describes the public consultation process at national and local levels; and provides checklists to help Bank task managers and others carry out the process. The guidance provided in this chapter is necessarily general, as it must apply to all parts of the developing world.

The main responsibility for assisting Bank task managers in implementing the operational directive falls upon the Regional Environmental Divisions (REDs). In turn, it is the task managers' responsibility to assist the borrowers who are responsible for preparing EAs. Task managers usually work with borrowers at a very high level of responsibility; thus, part of their task is to enable their counterparts in government to work with field staff and local authorities to ensure that EA participation requirements are met. Borrowers in countries that do not have a high degree of environmental management capacity in government for preparing EAs often call upon consultants, either international or local, for assistance. EA consultants also have an important role to play in the process of local participation.

In October 1991, the World Bank issued a revised version of the EA OD as Operational Directive 4.01. With respect to participation, the new OD further interpreted the requirements set forth in the original version:

> Consultations *do not reduce the decision authority of the borrower*, but are a valuable way to improve decision making, to obtain feedback...and to increase community

cooperation in implementing the recommendations of the EA (para 19, emphasis added). Such consultations should occur at least at the following two stages of the EA process: (a) shortly after the EA category has been assigned, and (b) once a draft EA has been prepared (para 20).

The new OD also elaborated on the requirements for information disclosure:

> In order for meaningful consultations to take place ... it is necessary that the borrower provide relevant information prior to consultations ... in a timely manner and in a form that is meaningful for, and accessible to, the groups being consulted.... In addition, the borrower should make the EA report available at some public place accessible to affected groups and local NGOs for their review and comment (para 21).

The African Context

Governments in Sub-Saharan Africa were poorly prepared to meet the Bank's new requirements for environmental assessment, particularly with regard to their provisions for public participation. After two to three decades of development experience, African countries entered the 1990s almost as poor as they were at the end of the colonial period (World Bank 1989).

Analyzing development failure

The manifest failure of the World Bank and other donors to find ways of assisting African countries to embark on sustained growth caused much soul searching within the donor community and led to a more open dialogue with African decisionmakers. One of the main conclusions of this dialogue has been that development efforts in Africa have failed because of the inappropriate behavior of governments:

> The post-independence development efforts failed because the strategy was misconceived. Governments made a dash for "modernization," copying, but not adapting, Western models. The result was poorly designed public investments in industry; too little attention to peasant agriculture; too much intervention in areas in which the state lacked managerial, technical, and entrepreneurial skills; and too little effort to foster grassroots development. This top-down approach demotivated ordinary people, whose energies most need to be mobilized in the development effort (World Bank 1989).

An analyst of development administration in Africa points out the paradox in regimes that came to power on a wave of popular participation in the struggle for independence feeling forced to move in the direction of single-party systems and increasingly centralized control (Hyden 1983). The power of political leaders is rooted in personal charisma and clan allegiances rather than in legitimacy derived from an accepted political system. Consequently, they are vulnerable to attack and prone to construe any disagreement as a political challenge. Few African countries offer the protections for human rights that would permit and encourage individuals to speak out against official decisions. Thus the "enabling environment" for popular participation in development is far from favorable.

Other factors, too, make it difficult for most Africans to participate effectively in public decisionmaking. Poverty, of course, is the major disabling factor; when people's energies are concentrated on day-to-day survival, they cannot give high priority to participating in decisions relating to a distant future. Rurality creates additional obstacles to participation because of the relatively high cost of reaching small, scattered groups of people and the high opportunity costs borne by those who do participate. Illiteracy and the proliferation of local languages are further barriers to participation. Social and cultural patterns constrain the participation of women, young people, and certain ethnic groups. Finally, there may be conflicts between customary law and modern legal systems, particularly concerning rights and responsibilities, with respect to local resources that can complicate the participation process.

Nevertheless, there is in Africa a resurgence of popular participation in development, largely expressed through NGOs rather than through participation in the bureaucratic processes of governments. These local NGOs and their national and international networks have often been more effective in bringing about positive change than governments have been. An NGO initiative at the U.N. General Assembly in 1988 led to the organization of an International Conference on Popular Participation in the Recovery and Development Process in Africa, held in Arusha, Tanzania, in 1990. The agencies, governments, and NGOs at the conference adopted an "African Charter for Popular Participation in Development and Transformation," also known as the Arusha Declaration. The Charter calls upon African governments to establish a new partnership with the people, ensuring the involvement of women at all levels of decisionmaking, and extending and protecting people's basic human rights. It calls for an end to internal armed conflicts and the redirection of national resources to productive activities and social services. Finally, it urges that national development programs be planned and implemented in the framework of a participatory political process and that strategies for economic growth be based on the concepts of self-reliance and sustainability.

Popular Participation and Environmental Assessment in Africa

With regard to environmental assessment, no Sub-Saharan African country has yet established formal requirements, although in some countries such requirements may be implicit in legislation and regulations pertaining to mining, construction, and industrial development (World Bank 1991c). Countries that have prepared National Environmental Action Plans (NEAPs) with the World Bank and other donor assistance agencies (Madagascar, Mauritius, Lesotho, Ghana, Rwanda, Burkina Faso, and the Seychelles) have all placed the passage of EA legislation high on their policy agendas. Without such a legislative framework, there can be no domestic policy on public participation in environmental assessment. Countries needing to meet World Bank requirements for environmental assessment have had to develop participation procedures on a project-specific, ad hoc basis.

Soon after the World Bank's EA policy was first issued, the Bank's Regional Environmental Division for Africa (AFTEN) organized a consultation meeting with leading African experts from governments, grassroots institutions and NGOs, to explore the concerns and the constraints experienced by affected groups and local NGOs participating in project activities in Africa (Kamugasha 1990). The purpose of this workshop was to explore ways and means through which African borrowers could implement the Bank OD requirements for local participation in environmental assessments. The workshop explored the roles of international, national and local NGOs and the meaning of "community involvement." The workshop strongly recommended that approaches to local participation in Africa be grounded in the use of traditional institutions, still perceived as the most legitimate source of decisionmaking authority at the local level.

In 1991, AFTEN issued guidance to task managers based partly on the learnings from this workshop. It defines "local participation" to include the participation of public agencies, private interest groups, and national NGOs, at one level; and the participation of people directly affected by the project, at another level. With regard to affected groups, it says:

> This includes, but is not limited to, the intended beneficiaries. Other groups, particularly those that also make use of the local resources on which a project may depend, will also be affected by a project. They have a right to be informed about it and to make their views known to project planners. All of the groups that will be directly affected by a project should have an opportunity to *influence* the decision to go ahead with a project and the choice among different design options, as well as the detailed design of a project and the inclusion of components to reduce, or compensate for, costs that will be borne by local people. (World Bank 1991d, emphasis added)

Methods and Analysis

This study evaluates World Bank experience with local participation in the first generation of EAs undertaken for Bank-financed projects in Africa over the last five years. It is a first attempt to document and analyze how successful the Bank's EA requirements for its projects—that now include consultation with affected groups and local NGOs—have been in promoting local participation. The primary objectives of this review were to explore and analyze how local participation has been addressed in EAs carried out in the Africa Region and to develop recommendations to assist task managers and, indirectly, borrowers to improve the effectiveness of local participation in future EA efforts. The method used to achieve this operational level of analysis is based upon an analytical framework that, by utilizing preferred levels of sustainability, defines strategy distinctions and options within the participatory process (Donnelly-Roark 1992).

Methodology

EA DATABASE. A total of thirty-five EAs were available for preliminary review. Three of these EAs were executed before the Bank had any formal environmental assessment requirements. Twenty-seven EAs, a majority of the sample, concerned projects whose preparations were well advanced

when the EA policy was first issued and to which the provisions of this policy technically did not apply. In connection with these projects, regional staff were instructed to make a "best effort" to comply with OD 4.00 requirements, consistent with project processing schedules. The third category included five EAs for projects whose preparation began after the OD guidelines were implemented. For these projects, full efforts should have been made to include local participation. Ongoing EAs that did not have at least a completed draft by June 1992 were not included in the review.

The EAs were undertaken in twenty-five countries, or more than half of all the countries in Sub-Saharan Africa. The majority of countries included had only one EA completed or in progress. Two EAs each were done in Ghana, Madagascar, Malawi, Mozambique, and Senegal; three EAs have been carried out in Kenya, and five in Nigeria. The EAs reviewed are also representative of the three main sectors subject to EA work: nine were for agriculture projects (three in area development, three in forestry/environment, one livestock, one irrigation, one fisheries); fifteen in infrastructure (six water supply, seven transport, and two urban); and eleven in energy and industry (seven energy/hydropower, two petroleum, one mining, one industrial zone) (see box 9-1).

After the preliminary review assessed the range of approaches used to secure local participation in the thirty-five EAs and defined the primary issues relating to its effectiveness, fifteen EAs representing the range of issues identified were then analyzed in greater detail. The countries represented in this subsample include Benin, Chad, Gabon, Ghana, Lesotho, Malawi, Mali, Mauritius, Mozambique, Nigeria, Seychelles, Tanzania, Uganda, and Zaire. The EAs cover projects in agriculture (area development, forestry, and irrigation), infrastructure (transport and water supply), and energy (power). Ten were selected from the twenty-seven "best effort" projects, and all five "full effort" projects were included (see box 9-2).

The analysis of documentary materials for this subsample was expanded through personal or telephone interviews with task managers, EA consultants, and other involved country department, central policy, and AFTEN staff. A series of telephone interviews with national experts and NGOs involved with EA report meetings in selected countries was also completed so as to move beyond internal Bank perspectives. All interviews attempted to document

Box 9-1. Environmental Assessment Reports Reviewed

EAs completed before October 15, 1989

Botswana: Tuli Block Roads
Central African Republic: Boda-Bambio Road
Rwanda: Gitirama-Kibuye Highway

Best Effort (EAs for projects initiated before October 15, 1989)

Benin: Power Rehabilitation
Chad: Petroleum and Power
Djibouti: Urban II
Ghana: Feeder Roads
Ghana: Livestock
Guinea-Bissau: Energy
Kenya: Export Promotion (industrial zone)
Kenya: Olkaria Geothermal Energy
Lesotho: Highlands Water
Madagascar: Tana Plain Development (urban)
Madagascar: Ilmenite Minit
Malawi: Fisheries
Mali: Agricultural Sector Adjustment
Mauritania: Water Supply
Mozambique: Agricultural Services
Mozambique: Rural Rehabilitation
Niger: Transport II
Nigeria: Oso Condensate (offshore oil)
Nigeria: Multi-state Roads
Nigeria: Multi-state Water (Funtua Dam)
Nigeria: Multi-state Water (Zonkwa Dam)
Senegal: Water III
Senegal: Dialakoto-Kedougou Road
Seychelles: Infrastructure/Environment
Tanzania: Forest Resource Management
Uganda: Power III
Zaire: Forestry/Environment

both the experience and the perspective of the individual interviewed concerning the issues discussed in this report and other areas of importance identified by the person interviewed, that were not originally anticipated by the interviewer.

DEFINITION OF PARTICIPATION. The review required specification of a working definition for local participation in EA processes. The Bank's OD 4.01 description of the expected process was the primary reference.

> The Bank expects the borrower to take the views of affected groups and local NGOs fully into account in project design and implementation, and in particular in the preparation of EAs. This process is important in order to understand both the nature and extent of any social or environmental impact and the acceptability of proposed mitigatory measures, particularly to affected groups....Such consultations should occur at least at the following two stages of the EA process: (a) shortly after the EA has been assigned, and (b) once a draft EA has been prepared. (OD 4.01, paras 19-20)

In describing the public consultation process in developing countries, the Bank's *Environmental Assessment Sourcebook* notes a premise essential to EA success in Africa when it observes that EAs for developing countries "cannot function in the reactive, responsive stance suitable to industrial countries, but must take a proactive, initiatory approach to encourage and promote citizen participation" (World Bank 1991b).

ANALYTICAL FRAMEWORK. Starting in the early 1980s, the notion of sustainability, adapted from the environmental disciplines, has become one of the criteria by which project success is defined and evaluated. Sustainability is linked to local ownership of projects, acquired through participation:

> Participation [is] a way of factoring local behavior and beneficiary assessments of risks, costs and benefits into project design....While those assessments consist of rational economic decisions in the context of the socio-economic/cultural environment, they are inclined to be

Box 9-2. EA Reports Selected for Detailed Analysis.

Best Effort EAs

Benin Power Rehabilitation
Chad Petroeum and Power
Ghana Feeder Roads
Lesotho Highlands Water
Mali Agricultural Sector Adjustment
Mozambique Agricultural Services
Seychelles Infrastructure/Environment
Tanzania Forest Resource Management
Uganda Power III
Zaire Forestry/Environment

Full EAs

Gabon Forestry/Environment
Malawi Power V
Mauritius Sugar Energy (Bagasse)
Nigeria Fadama Irrigation
Tanzania Power VI

misunderstood by, or to seem illogical to, the project designer....Beneficiary participation in a project would also serve to align project objectives and activities with local needs and aspirations. Alignment appears necessary for project success and ultimately for sustainability....Alignment would also seem to promote community involvement and grassroots institutional development, as beneficiary groups will be more inclined to organize around problems and opportunities they regard as important (World Bank 1985).

The growing concern for sustainability has effectively supported the case for including both local participation and environmental assessment in projects. These two aspects of project design are mutually reinforcing. Requirements for participation in environmental assessments implicitly recognizes both people's rights to participate in decisions that will affect their ecological systems, and the value of their information and analysis in defining options and making decisions. At the same time, the relevance of indigenous peoples' knowledge systems and management practices is increasingly recognized as the environmental disciplines signal the importance of these systems and practices for successful conservation (McNeely and others 1990).

Because the purpose of EA within the Bank is "to ensure that development options under consideration are environmentally sound and sustainable," it makes sense to evaluate the success of EA local participation strategies in terms of sustainability objectives.

One of the most useful typologies classifies participation approaches currently used by international donor organizations into four categories: mobilization, community development, organizing, and empowerment (Oakley and Marsden 1984). Each of these categories is defined in terms of the intent to share power and the types of organizations involved. Briefly, the *mobilization strategy* assumes that the basic decisions underlying a proposed action are taken at a national level and then invites identified beneficiaries to endorse and collaborate with decisions taken. The *community development strategy* organizes meetings to better understand community perceptions about a pre-identified constraint to development and involves the affected people in the design and maintenance of project initiatives to solve the problem. The *organizing strategy* facilitates group efforts to increase their influence on areas of decisionmaking that affect them. Finally, the

empowerment strategy initiates a group analysis and learning process that allows specific groups to initiate action to bring about structural change (Oakley and Hardssen 1984).

These four participation strategies, as defined in the typology, differ substantively in terms of intent, and not unexpectedly, the results are also quite different. Key to the differentiation is the level of power sharing and control taking place within each category. It has been observed that these participatory categories become differentiated strategies that are increasingly complex but more directly able to attain the objective of locally sustainable development as participant responsibility and control are increased. Using this observation, an analytical framework emphasizing the critical relationship between participant control over project processes and realistic expectations for project sustainability has been developed. It is therefore utilized in this study to further demystify the concept of participation and make it more accessible to operational initiatives (Donnelly-Roark 1992).

The participatory strategy of mobilization *consults* internal participants but keeps the control solely in the hands of external initiators, and is therefore easy to initiate and manage. Because it has no internally engendered control, it has a minimal chance of creating a sustainable base among the local actor/participants. Actions to sustain must therefore continue to rest with the external agents. Different from mobilization, but similar to each other, the participatory community development/organizing strategies are at the same level of power-sharing.[3] These two categories *negotiate* the type, level, and timing of control with local participants and are therefore capable of generating adequate levels of sustainability if the project output meets a strongly felt community need. Finally, the most complex strategy of participation— empowerment—encourages participants to *create* autonomous realities, thereby placing the highest level of control and responsibility in their hands, with consequent high levels of sustainability (Donnelly-Roark 1992).

Based upon the Bank's definition of local participation in environmental assessments, it appears that the "consultation/mobilization" strategy has been selected for implementation. In the EA process, the consultation/mobilization strategy can fulfill two different participation objectives: (a) it can *inform* people about the project and project planners about people's views and concerns, and (b) it can create opportunities for people to *influence* program design and implementation, *without* giving them the power to take decisions. Both of these objectives are covered by the Bank definition of desired EA outcomes. These two substrategies, although both are within the consultation/mobilization category, use different techniques to promote the two-way information exchange necessary for all participation strategies and can be expected therefore to have very different impacts on project sustainability.

The EA "inform strategy," useful primarily in industrial country environmental assessments, assumes that the people understand the issues involved and have the ability, the willingness, and the resources to be competitive and confrontational in promoting their perspectives with the institutional initiators of the proposed programs. This confrontational approach allows for a two-way exchange of information, effectively releasing the informing organization from any further obligation or responsibility to the involved groups.

The EA "influence strategy," on the other hand, must operate differently to achieve its objectives. The "influence strategy" is based on an assumption of cooperation, which requires that the initiating institution recognize its responsibility to be responsive to the ideas and concerns of local groups. Therefore, it cannot depend upon the implicitly confrontational nature of "inform strategies" to create a two-way dialogue. Rather, proactive initiatives are necessary to create situations whereby involved groups and local people may influence proposed programs and decisions.

DEFINITION OF SUCCESS. When the Bank limited its definition of participation in environmental assessment to the consultation/mobilization strategy, without negotiation or real power-sharing, such participation could not be expected to make a major contribution to project sustainability. Within this strategy, however, two substrategies have been identified that are likely to have different results. Limiting participation to an exchange of information between the implementing agency and other groups will do little to enhance local commitment and improve project performance. In contrast, the "influence" strategy is likely to be more effective in establishing a dialogue that both contributes to beneficiary willingness to be involved and promotes a more meaningful information exchange that can contribute to project effectiveness. Thus, the use of consultation strategies that create the required "space" for local people to influence EA and project outcomes is defined as the criterion for successful local participation in this study.

Findings

The preliminary review of the thirty-five EAs identified ten techniques used to focus on local people's concerns. The identified techniques and the number of EAs using them are presented in table 9-1. An unexpected finding of the preliminary analysis was the very limited range of participatory approaches implemented in the EAs reviewed.

The first five techniques listed in table 9-1 (socio-economic document review, institutional interviews, prior survey results, field interviews, and field survey) are not participatory. They are information-gathering techniques used in social science analyses. Twenty-three of the thirty-five EAs reviewed used one of these five techniques as their most participatory effort. Thus, in two-thirds of the cases, real local participation did not happen at all.

The sixth category includes projects that used field survey techniques to gather information, in which some participatory methods may have been used. However, such efforts were not adequately documented. Four of the EAs used this approach as their most participatory effort. The techniques described in levels seven through ten (consultation/scoping meetings held in the capital city, meetings to present the draft EA, scoping and review meetings, and scoping meetings in the capital combined with consultation at the local level) are more participatory, but only the last one fully meets the OD requirements. A total of ten EAs were placed in the participatory categories, but only four EAs, or 11 percent of the sample, met all OD requirements for local participation.

None of the three EAs conducted before the Bank had put its EA policy in place involved any public participation. In the "best effort" category, thirteen of twenty-three also relied exclusively on surveys or other information-gathering techniques, one may have used undocumented participation methods, and seven did make a serious effort to comply with the EA policy, including three that fully met the requirements. However, among projects approved since the EA policy came into effect, only one fully met the requirements, two used surveys and may have used nondocumented participatory techniques, and two

Table 9-1. Participation Strategies Used in EAs

Technique	EA Category		
	Completed	Best Effort	Full EA
Non-participatory (n=22)			
1. Socio-economic document review	0	2	0
2. Institutional interviews	0	4	0
3. Citation of prior survey results	0	0	0
4. Field interviews	3	12	0
5. EA field survey	0	1	0
Undocumented (n=3)			
6. EA field survey indicating probable use of non-documented participatory techniques	0	1	2
Participatory (n=10)			
7. Consultation/ scoping meeting	0	3	2
8. Meeting to present draft EA	0	1	0
9. Consultation/ scoping meeting and meeting to present draft EA	0	3	1
10. Consultation/ scoping meeting in capital and consultation at the local level	0	3	1
Totals	3	27	5

Note: Each EA was categorized based upon the most participatory strategy used. For example, an EA categorized at level 5 has most likely undertaken some of the activities listed in categories 1 through 4, but has not utilized any strategies in categories 6 through 10.

conducted only scoping meetings in capital cities to secure NGO input.

Analysis of differences among the twenty-three nonparticipatory EAs and the ten EAs that had identified participation initiatives is instructive. There was no significant variation in terms of project sector, country cultural background (anglophone/ francophone), or geographical origin (East/West

Africa). Both the Uganda Power III resettlement plan and the Gabon Forestry/Environment EA were rated as fulfilling all OD requirements, though they are very different in terms of sector, region, and linguistic and cultural background.

Interesting patterns do develop, however, when the type of consultant used and the amount of time allowed are factored in. For example, three of the four EAs that fulfilled OD requirements had social scientists on their teams, in two instances professionals from the countries themselves. One task manager noted that he was offered knowledge and guidance from a national environmental NGO and that the participatory aspects of the EA were undertaken by a social scientist from the local university. Although it was impossible to ascertain definitively, because in many cases the expertise of EA team members was not identified, it seemed that only one, or possibly two, of the twenty-two EAs classified in the nonparticipatory categories (one through five) in table 9-1 had social scientists working with the EA team.

Participation inputs for most of the reviewed EAs were undertaken at the latter stages of project identification, during project preparation, and before project appraisal. Both technical EA findings and participation inputs often seem to have had little influence on the proposed project's direction. It was not clear whether EA consultants understood that local groups were to be given the opportunity to influence project decisions, as opposed to only informing them of project plans. For instance, while a number of EA reports called for people's participation in the project itself, the EA consultants did not seem to feel that they could open up the discussion on project alternatives with local people during the EA process. These findings raised several important concerns.

Concerns

NONPARTICIPATORY APPROACHES. The first five techniques listed in table 9-1, classified as nonparticipatory, were selected by 66 percent of the EAs to meet participation requirements. For instance, interviews at the institutional level or at the field level were often assumed to fill the requirements by EA consultants and in a few instances were explicitly classified as a method of participation by team members. But because the primary objective of an interview is to gain information, it does not qualify as a participation strategy. In the interview process one may inform the other of one's purpose, but the main focus is on meeting the informational needs of the interviewer. The interviewee understands this as part of the unspoken rules of the interview and therefore will not press for information.

Within the field interview technique such as that in the twelve EAs in the "best effort" category, some of the consultants did extensive one-on-one field interviews. Not all of the consultants claimed that this fulfilled EA requirements, but this was the implicit effect since it was their most "participatory" effort. In the institutional interviews, on the other hand, several consultants defined normal working interviews with various institutions as fulfilling their local participation obligations. Field surveys were also used to fulfill the local participation requirement. But the field survey, as normally implemented in standard social science practice, also does not qualify as a participation action for reasons similar to the field interview. Standard practice for surveys is for the consultant to define questions, select sample populations, administer the survey, and analyze responses—actions all based upon the gathering of information.

The field interviews, although not fully participatory, seemed to be legitimate first efforts using techniques that were known to the consultants. To some extent, it seemed as though any research technique normally used by sociologists or anthropologists was deemed to be adequately participatory. The use of agency interviews to fulfill local participation obligations seems, on the other hand, to be more of an end-run around organizationally imposed obligations that were not appreciated or understood by the borrowers or the consultant EA teams.

LACK OF DOCUMENTATION OF PARTICIPATORY APPROACHES. Some participatory activities undertaken were not adequately documented. These were most often found in the case of national consulting sociologists. Three field surveys, presented in the accepted field survey format in EA reports, probably undertook substantial participatory consultation during field survey efforts. This became apparent during the review because despite the lack of documentation, the information gathered and discussed was not of the type that one can gather in the regular type of field survey. This participatory orientation was documented in one instance through an interview.

This lack of documentation appears, at first glance,

to be easily rectified. But it should be noted that local social scientists may have good reasons for failing to document these methodologies. First and foremost are the anticipated attitudes of donor agencies who may label techniques such as surveys and field interviews "subjective and anecdotal" and therefore of marginal value. Many social scientists, even though they use participatory techniques in their work, believe that it is necessary to overlay this technique with an objective survey in order for the final report to be taken seriously by the funding donor. A second reason for lack of documentation may be that the survey-reporting format places a third person between the local person and the reader. Because many social scientists do not wish to place community informants under undue pressure, this is a convenient way to depersonalize the reporting.

MEETING THE OD REQUIREMENTS. Only four of the thirty-five EAs (11 percent) were found to meet the operational directive requirements for local participation, another six were identified as using some documented participatory initiative, and another three as perhaps having involved some undocumented participation. Of course, a large majority (thirty) of the EAs reviewed were carried out before the Bank's OD requirements came into force. However, it is interesting to note, that there was not a large increase in the share of fully satisfactory EAs between "best effort" (3 of 27, or 11 percent) and "full effort" (1 of 5, or 20 percent). This finding indicates that the introduction of a formal requirement for public participation is not sufficient for its successful implementation. Furthermore, this evaluation makes no distinction between the "inform" and "influence" sub-categories of consultative participation. When "influence" is defined as the objective of EA participation, only two (6 percent) of the EAs reviewed meet this criterion.

In concluding this comparative assessment, it appears that two factors primarily contributed to the extensive use of nonparticipatory approaches in the reviewed EAs. First, there was a lack of EA team knowledge or expertise about what constitutes adequate public participation, and how to go about it; and second, a lack of EA team expertise on how to document participatory activities. For those ten EAs that used demonstrable levels of participation, one primary factor in their success was EA consultants who were knowledgeable about participatory techniques.

Critical Issues

This section considers three categories of issues that became apparent during this assessment of EA participation activities. The first category includes current organizational strategy issues and their likely relationship to long-term effectiveness. The second category analyzes implementation issues from the viewpoint of a participation practitioner. The third category includes the operational perspectives of task managers and EA consultants.

Strategic Issues

This review indicates that further clarification is needed by task managers and governments about which methods to use and what participatory objective to pursue. The results also suggest that a sectoral approach to participation strategy selection may be most effective.

PARTICIPATION OBJECTIVES. Only two of the EAs used an "influence" strategy. However, project documentation and interviews with task managers and consultants indicate that more positive results were achieved in the case of the two EAs that focused on "influence," as compared to the eight that attempted only "inform" procedures (see table 9-2). For instance, in the Gabon Forestry/Environment and possibly to a lesser extent in the Tanzania Forestry/Environment EAs—both of which fulfilled OD requirements—local groups were seen to have positively influenced the shape of the resulting project. Thus, it is likely that both EAs left the participants feeling that it was worth the effort to get involved. On the other hand, there are several projects classified as participatory that did generate involvement and did "inform," but because of their unwillingness or inability to respond or be "influenced" by local concerns, are likely to have generated feelings of skepticism. The Mozambique Agricultural Services EA discussed later in this sections falls in this category.

This differentiation between the "influence" and "inform" processes points to a critical anomaly in present Bank participation procedures, in that the OD-stipulated meeting requirements only achieve the sub-optimal "information objectives" within the consultation strategy of participation. And achievement of this minimal level may not be adequate in terms of the EAs' overall intent. Other parts of the same OD require, for instance, the EA initiator to allow consulted parties to exercise influence without the decisionmaker giving away the right to decide. In

Table 9-2. EAs Meeting Participation Objectives (percentage)

Objective	All EAs (n=35)	Participatory EAs (n-10)
No participation	63	n.a.
To inform affected and interested groups	23	80
To enable influence by affected and interested groups	6	20

n.a. Not applicable.
Source: The authors.

the Bank documents cited earlier, and in other high-level internal discussions, the phrase "take the views of [the groups concerned] fully into account" is interpreted to mean provision of adequate opportunity for consulted parties to express their views, and be taken seriously, rather than to be involved in a *pro forma* exercise. Although still within the most minimal participation range of consultation, reorienting these consultative strategies to the "influence" rather than the "inform" objective—by reformulating the stipulated meeting procedures—is of particular importance because it offers more substantive and sustainable results.

PROJECT SECTOR FACTORS. The reviewed EAs did not adjust participation approaches for project sector, intent and impact. However, the analysis clarified how sectoral differences may affect the outcome of the EA participation process. For instance, a project such as Lesotho Highlands Water, which primarily benefits the national government while causing direct harm to some individuals or groups, is quite different from Mozambique's Rural Rehabilitation project that was designed to benefit the participants. Despite these obvious differences, both EAs used similar participation approaches.

Of the ten EAs using participatory techniques, eight used, as an informal model, the OD prescribed consultation and scoping meetings in the capital city and, to a lesser extent, direct consultation with affected groups in local areas. Results of these efforts varied according to sector. This orientation worked well for EAs in the energy sector where resettlement or mitigation was required. For instance, both Lesotho Highlands Water Supply and Uganda Power III fulfilled OD requirements and defined substantive mitigation plans. The fit between energy sector projects and present OD consultation requirements is further illustrated by the fact that six of the ten EAs rated at level seven or above are from the energy sector.

The other four projects that were rated at level seven or above were all in the agricultural sector. Because agricultural projects depend on and are expected to benefit local people, there was a good fit between this sector and the participation process. This sector-oriented fit was borne out in interviews with the task managers who indicated they made greater efforts to promote local participation when it seemed relevant to the EA process and to the project itself. Where participatory efforts seemed inappropriate or peripheral, as for example in infrastructure projects, reliance on nonparticipatory strategies was, in essence, the default selection.

Energy EAs that had few mitigation or resettlement problems found the prescribed model redundant; with no immediate impact on local people, there was little reason to involve them. For example, the Chad Petroleum and Power Project had no resettlement problems related to the placement of the pumping station and the pipeline. The possibility of the local people near Lake Chad being able to "influence" national level decisions concerning the project seemed remote to the implementing agency and the task manager. Nigeria's Oso Condensate Project (offshore oil) found itself in a similar situation where there was no immediate impact requiring resettlement or compensation. It was clear that the small fishing communities surrounding the designated ocean bay were not in a position to influence Nigeria's energy policy. Both EAs therefore used nonparticipatory techniques that gathered information on possible impact but did not share information with the local communities.

However, using these nonparticipatory methodologies left substantive issues aside that could have been of critical importance to local people. For instance, in the Nigeria Oso Condensate EA, the possibility of leaks slowly diminishing the productivity of shrimp fields, although of clear concern to local people who depended on these fields for their income, was not discussed because the EA was nonparticipatory. Agency officials and task managers are aware that in large national energy or infrastructure initiatives where there are few mitigation alternatives, there is realistically little chance of local groups influencing the government. And if the views of local people are of no account, requirements for local participation are likely to be

seen as essentially a *pro forma* exercise.

Sectoral considerations are also relevant to the use of "influence" rather than "inform" substrategies. For instance, several energy sector projects were able to fulfill OD requirements using a participation strategy based on "informing" affected groups and subsequently involving them in mitigation discussions. Although it could be argued that these discussions involved an element of influence, these local discussions concerning mitigation had little to do with influencing the choice or design of a project but rather with diminishing the most negative affects of a *fait accompli*. Thus, although this "inform" process met the OD requirements, the majority of task managers involved in energy EAs made it clear that they doubted the borrower would comply with the terms of agreed mitigation or compensation plans if the Bank did not monitor them.

In comparison, the agricultural sector EAs often opted for the "influence" process. For instance, in the Gabon Forestry/Environment EA (see box 9-2), the task manager initially assumed that the EA local participation requirement meant "inform" only. However, as the process began to take form in the country through a series of meetings with local groups, it created a situation such that local people's perceptions clearly influenced the project in terms of an increased focus on agro-forestry in the final plan. This orientation to the "influence" sub-strategy can also be seen in Tanzania's Forest Resource Management EA, and to some extent, in Nigeria's Fadama Irrigation EA, among others.

Implementation Issues

The second level of analysis concerns itself with implementation issues, from the viewpoint of the participation practitioner, that could impede effective local participation in EAs. The five issues discussed here are illustrated by particular EAs but are relevant to all EAs whose objective is to promote local participation that can influence project decisions.

TWO-WAY COMMUNICATION CAPACITY. Successful participation initiatives are built upon effective two-way communication systems. In the preliminary review, two substantial obstacles to communication were found in most EAs. The first obstacle involved the difficulty experienced by task managers and implementing agency staff in identifying legitimate local groups that could effectively link EA participatory initiatives with traditional community institutions to facilitate substantive communication and participation.

Identification of local groups is related to the problem of establishing adequate communication with groups that represent various perceptions, including women and poor people who are marginalized in their access to both information and ability to be heard. Contacts with indigenous councils may be criticized for being all male or elite, while contacts through government-formed groups such as cooperatives may lack legitimacy with local people. However, two groups of projects found some workable solutions. For instance, the Gabon Forestry and Tanzania Forestry EA teams contacted diverse groups through initial contact with local authorities and subsequent use of radio to announce open meetings. This method, which must include return visits and be tailored to the individual situation, is one that is used throughout Africa. It gets the information out and the discussion going. With variations, it can be used also in capital cities. Another method that can be used successfully is that of a seminar of one to three days with interested NGOs and agencies, as illustrated by the Mozambique Rural Rehabilitation EA and the Malawi Power V EA.

The second obstacle to effective two-way communication is failure to provide adequate information to local people so that they can develop the capacity to influence or take decisions. Here the problems experienced revolved around the code of confidentiality, especially concerning budget information or expected negative impacts. For example, in the Tanzania Forest Resource Management EA, the EA team did not have the necessary project budget information to answer questions raised at community meetings. In the Mauritius Bagasse meeting with NGOs, the written information provided with the invitation addressed the issues only in a very general way, effectively obscuring issues that could be debated.

GENDER AND POVERTY ISSUE. Only two of the EA reports made any mention of efforts to secure the participation of women, while none made mention of specific efforts to include poor people. Nigeria's Fadama Irrigation EA mentioned that women's views were not included because of the difficulty of talking with women in a Muslim culture. The Ghana Feeder Roads Project EA made mention of women's planned involvement in the proposed project.

Even when strong participatory efforts were made,

gender inclusion was minimal. For instance, in the Tanzania Forest Resource Management EA, six participatory meetings were held with a total attendance of eighty-nine people, only five of whom were women. The Gabon Forestry project, although not well documented, made better efforts to involve women, perhaps because the person in charge of initiating local participation was a woman. Overall, however, there was a gap between stated Bank policy and operational performance in this area.

INFORMATION NEEDS. The EA, with its challenge to confidentiality requirements and mandate for local participation, requires a rethinking of how information can be more effectively shared. There are often large amounts of important information in reports prepared for the Bank, but this information is rarely shared with local people. Since Bank reports have not adequately documented local people's perceptions as to project impact and problems, the validity of local community information may not be recognized by government or Bank officers. For instance, the Fisheries Project EA done for Malawi had no input from local people. However, it is a well-done and informative study that could have benefited from local people's knowledge. Just as importantly, involved communities could have benefited from having this analysis presented to them so as to better inform their own decisions.

EXPERT DECISIONS. A number of reports reviewed make it clear that in discussions with NGOs or other groups, strong fears or criticisms concerning the expected impact of a project are often voiced by the participants. In some cases, the reports indicate that the EA team dismissed these objections as not probable, or, that in the team's view, there was insufficient evidence to give them further consideration.

For instance, the Mozambique Agricultural Services EA reports that NGOs were extremely concerned that most of the fertile land in the project area would be used for cotton crops rather than food crops. The EA team did not agree with this assessment and responded with a five-page analysis of the relationship between food and cotton production. However, this type of response did nothing to allay the real and valid concerns raised by the NGOs. Instead, it denied the validity of their locally based views in comparison to those of the expert who may or may not be able to predict the outcome more successfully. This expert orientation works against participatory inputs, undermines local authority, and diminishes local knowledge systems. Such attitudes pose major obstacles to developing community capacity for self-reliant, self-sustained development.

FOLLOW-THROUGH. The question of follow-through is essential if local people are to see that their participation in EAs has any impact. A large number of EA reports make suggestions—both environmental and participatory—concerning issues that need to be addressed for long-term, sustainable success.

Actions to address local concerns need to be included in the mitigation plans recommended by EAs and adopted by governments in agreement with the Bank at negotiations. Although it seems to many that the Bank should have sufficient administrative and monitoring procedures to follow through on the agreements made and assurances provided at negotiations, only conditionality associated with the loan or credit agreement is really enforceable.

One of the critical issues for local participation is making the draft EA available to interested groups, as provided for in the OD. Except for the EAs that held seminars such as Malawi Power V, there is little information as to where and how this information has been made available. Other issues concern the execution of agreed programs, such as compensation for property taken by a project. For instance, although much time (and money) has been spent defining compensation for affected groups in the Uganda Power III and Lesotho Highlands Water Projects, the proper execution of these programs will require continuous monitoring. The EA for the Mauritius Sugar Energy Project suggests both air quality and worker health monitoring. According to the task manager, Mali's Agricultural Sector Adjustment Loan (SECAL) seems to have supported a systematic follow-up on most of the issues identified in the EA.

Ensuring effective follow-through on recommendations from participatory consultations is critical for long-term success, as effective participation is always based upon expansion of trust. An illustrative case is the Tanzania Forest Management EA that strongly recommended and emphasized the need for local groups to participate in preparation of Forest Reserves Management Plans. When these types of actions are discussed at length with local groups, effective follow-up is critical to the long-term success of the project. Because Bank endeavors to support effective participation are often regarded with skepticism by local people and outside groups, inadequate follow-through on issues that are important to local communities will only confirm such skepticism.

Operational Issues

This third level of analysis briefly documents task managers' perspectives on operational issues and discusses them in terms of effective program implementation. Interviews indicate that several of the operational issues seen from the task manager perspective are similar to implementation issues as seen from the participation practitioner perspective. Interview results also indicate a strong concern among task managers about the sustainability of the EA local participation process, given the resources allocated for its support.

Issues of operational concern were similar among the fourteen task managers interviewed. All mentioned *timing* as a primary concern. The majority mentioned both *funding* and organizational *incentives* as extremely important to the success of EA local participation initiatives. A majority also indicated interest in systemization of local participation processes and expanded *training* for task managers.

TIMING. The inadequacy of the time allocated to facilitate or initiate successful local participation was the primary concern of all task managers. All but one felt that the time allocated to them was not sufficient to ensure success. For instance, several task managers had made no country trip related to EA local participation during planning or implementation. It is interesting to note that the one task manager who felt he did have sufficient time pointed out that he was able to make three trips to the country during the EA process, and that the local participation phase had actually taken about nine months. He attributes the EA's substantial success primarily to the involvement of groups at all levels, which also took substantial amounts of his and their time.

Task managers who were the most sanguine about time issues had been able to work with strong national institutions and pass the responsibility to them. Examples of this type of situation include Uganda Power III and Nigeria Multi-State Water. For the majority who used international consultants, finding and organizing funding for EA local participation initiatives was also a time-consuming task. Several task managers pointed out the difficulty of attempting to facilitate participation planning during regular project preparation missions. They felt that it needed someone that could stay involved and come and go every several months. Most thought the minimum process time would be approximately nine months. One task manager suggested that for the countries she worked in, an ideal situation would be to use a regional consultant from a neighboring country.

FUNDING. A majority of task managers pointed to inadequate funding for local participation efforts as an obstacle, while others felt that there was always funding available somewhere, but once again it took *time* to find adequate and appropriate sources of support. The use of Bank trust funds ruling out use of national consultants was also seen as a problem by some task managers. Others pointed out the negative impact of having no funding to continue participation processes if the project appraisal is delayed for unrelated reasons.

Where governments funded the EA, task managers were forthright in stating that the borrowers carried out EAs and included local participation only because they were required to do so by Bank policy. This perspective is most commonly reported in connection with energy projects, such as Uganda Power III, that were primarily concerned with impact mitigation. However, in agricultural sector projects, such as Gabon Forestry/Environment and Mali Agricultural SECAL, task managers reported an increasing concern and involvement among government agencies. This was also reported of Malawi Power V, which was more concerned with environmental management than mitigation.

INCENTIVES. All task managers were clear and articulate about the *lack* of Bank organizational and career development incentives to promote local participation processes in EAs. There was a clear belief and consensus that EA local participation policies were initiated due to outside pressure and that internally the organization would continue to reward its more product-oriented, time-sensitive, top-down managers and staff. Many of these same task managers said they spend more time on these issues than warranted by the present incentive structure of the Bank. They thought the situation would not really change, however, until senior management provided adequate resources of time and funding to accomplish these tasks and rewarded staff for taking these initiatives.

TRAINING. Most Bank task managers are not well prepared to assist borrowers in designing and carrying out public participation processes in connection with EAs. While the long-term regional strategy is to strengthen in-country EA processes and institutions through the implementation of NEAPs, this process will take a long time. In the meantime, task managers and their counterparts in project implementing agencies need to gain a more precise understanding of what is expected of them and to acquire process skills in order to demonstrate and model the use of participatory methods in project planning and implementation.

Implications and Conclusions

The World Bank strengthened its EA policy with the incorporation of requirements for local participation. However, this study indicates that the policy decision was the first and easiest step. Successful implementation will require substantive, long-term organizational commitment. The study indicates that public participation in EAs can have definitive positive impacts on both the EA process and the proposed project. However, and more importantly, the report indicates that this is not presently the case for the large majority of EAs assessed. More than half of the EAs reviewed were found not to have used any discernible participation initiative whatsoever, and only four of the thirty-five EAs fully met the OD requirements. Finally, the preceding analysis indicates three areas where recommendations can be made to improve the process of local participation in project environmental assessments in Africa.

Organizational Changes

Participation processes are unique in terms of organizational initiatives to promote change. The results of participation endeavors are never neutral— they always have a felt impact, whether positive or negative. Unsuccessful or perfunctory, *pro forma* participation initiatives can create problems rather than contributing to project success. Often, however, negative impacts are not immediately experienced by the organization itself but rather by participants involved with the institution in its participatory endeavors. Consequently, organizations may be slow to make the necessary adjustments. However, negative impacts can be diminished if organizations are aware of the potential problems and take prompt and appropriate action.

The findings reported in this paper suggest that an array of sustained organizational initiatives will be needed in order for the Bank to successfully promote public participation in EAs in Africa even at the minimum level of participation presently being promoted. The analysis indicates that participatory initiatives should emphasize consultation strategies that permit and encourage local groups to "influence" proposed projects, if they are to generate some level of trust and commitment—always needed for participatory processes—among the participants. Implementation and operational analysis indicate that if EA local participation processes are to be effectively supported by the Bank, a number of long-standing organizational practices will need to be changed. And finally, overall results of the review indicate that the responsibility for the EA process itself needs reconsideration.

Implication for Sustainability

In participation endeavors, dynamic processes build trust and energy for mutual action, while perfunctory processes build cynicism and feed negative conflict. One task manager illustrated the Bank's difficult situation—in terms of sustainability for EAs—when he pointed out that while he was strongly in support of participation efforts, he found the present situation and policy both "very useful and very dangerous." This task manager believed that much of the work being undertaken under the participation rubric was "totally misconceived rubbish and the whole approach will fall into disrespect if standards are not met."

He has a point. While the very nature of participation eludes the structure of guidelines, it is enhanced when expectation and standards are made explicit. When standards are not made explicit, participatory rhetoric tends to confuse the issue and the end result is destabilization of process and product. This means that potential dynamic participatory processes will become perfunctory conditionalities where Bank and borrower staffs spend the minimal time required for superficial compliance. Internally, voices will begin to complain that participation does not work; externally, borrowers will make fewer efforts to comply with what they perceive as "green conditionalities" imposed on them by the Bank in the name of environment and participation.

Defining participatory standards is therefore essential for successful and sustainable implementation. The first step in the specification of participatory standards is the matching of objectives with a preferred participation strategy. Here it is of critical importance not to confuse overly optimistic expectation or rhetoric with what the participatory

strategy can actually accomplish. Using the analytical framework briefly described in this chapter, the World Bank OD, with its specification of "consultation" strategies, has chosen to utilize the minimal level of participatory dialogue, which either "informs" or invites "influence" but does not share or negotiate decisionmaking. A case can be made for selection of this minimal standard, because it is the borrowers (governments) who will, in the long term, be responsible for these initiatives, and the identification of this particular participation strategy provides a base for a definition of standards that can, most likely, be mutually adopted.

However, while the Bank, as a development assistance agency, can do its best to help borrowers develop their capacity to carry out this responsibility, among many others associated with economic and financial management, it cannot, and does not, control this process. For sustainable follow-through to emerge at the borrower level, the Bank will therefore necessarily be obliged to change its present way of implementing policy and begin to utilize specified participatory strategies with each government. The important point here is understanding the implications of where sustainability rests during the long term rather than just during initiation activities. Key sustainability decisions are always taken by those with the responsibility for program maintenance as opposed to only program initiation. This is true whether it is a project interacting with community people or a donor interacting with a government.

In conclusion, participatory strategies that expect to build sustainability must move away from the compliance posture to mutual definitions of problems and actions. Mixing expectations of sustainability with participation based on compliance requirements is a formula for failure. Thus, expecting governments to take responsibility for a process implemented between the Bank and government by using conditionalities or, at best, consultation strategies, places the long-term intent and sustainability of the environmental assessment program at risk. These issues need to be considered if EAs and local participation endeavors are to become successfully institutionalized in donor and government agencies.

Notes

1. The philosophy that participation would make for better projects and programs made its way into international development assistance thinking during the late 1960s and early 1970s. Several studies (Paddock and Paddock 1973;

Huntington and Nelson 1976; Honadle and Klauss 1979; Bryant and White 1982; Johnson and Clark 1982; and Chambers 1983) evaluated the failure of the first two decades of international development assistance to eliminate world poverty, suggesting that the mere transfer of Western models might not respond very well to the realities of life in the developing world. Participation in project planning was seen as a way of ensuring that projects served the needs and priorities of the beneficiaries and would be appropriate to the political and socio-cultural context. It was expected that participation in planning would lead to more effective mobilization of resources for project implementation and increased sustainability of development programs after initial projects were completed. Reviews of experience with poverty-oriented development assistance programs from the early 1970s stressed the apparent relationship between participatory design and program success (Lele 1975; World Bank 1988).

2. When the United Nations Environment Programme (UNEP) first prepared EA guidelines for developing countries, its treatment of "public information" was circumspect. While commending the notion of "scoping" as a way of incorporation "local values" in the decisionmaking process, UNEP proposed that public review and comment be deferred until much of the technical work was done (Ahmad and Sammy 1985). This recommendation was based on the belief that "the public is better able to grasp and react to clear predictions rather than nebulous concepts" and "there is a tendency to lose interest in an issue over time." The purpose of public review procedures is described as being to ensure that affected parties will not seek redress through unacceptable actions such as demonstration or lawsuits—in other words, co-option. The UNEP guidelines explicitly rejected the public hearing approach used in the United States, suggesting that informal meetings or other methods may be more effective in developing countries.

3. Arnstein (1969) distinguished eight levels in a "ladder" of public participation, ranked according to the degree of citizen control over planning decisions. The first two levels, "co-opting" and "therapy," she describes as non-participatory; they involve manipulating public opinion to gain consent for the project, rather than paying attention to the views of the people. The middle steps, "information" (informing people about the project), "consultation" (obtaining people's views about the project), and "placation" (modifying the project to make it more acceptable to the people), she describes as tokenism. Only the upper part of the ladder, involving "partnership," "delegated power," and "community control," can be seen as enabling citizens to participate in the decisionmaking process.

References

Ahmad, Yusuf J. and George K. Sammy. 1985. *Guidelines to Environmental Impact Assessment in Developing Countries*. Sponsored by UNEP. London: Hodder and Stoughton.

Arnstein, Sherry R. 1969. "A Ladder of Citizen Participation." *Journal of the American Institute of Planners* 35(7): 216-224.

Bryant, Coralie and Louise G. White. 1982. *Managing Development in the Third World*. Boulder, Colorado: Westview Press.

Cernea, Michael M., ed. 1985. *Putting People First: Sociological Variables in Rural Development*. 2d ed. 1991. New York: Oxford University Press.

Chambers, Robert. 1974. *Managing Rural Development: Ideas and Experiences from East Africa*. Uppsala: Scandinavian Institute of African Studies.

———. 1983. *Rural Development: Putting the Last First*. London: Longman.

Donnelly-Roark, Paula. 1992. "Effective Support of Grassroots Participation Within Large Donor Organizations." UNDP Briefing Paper. New York: BPPE.

Honadle, George and Rudi Klauss, eds. 1979. *International Development Administration: Implementation Analysis for Development Projects*. New York: Praeger.

Huntington, Samuel P., and Joan M. Nelson. 1976. *No Easy Choice: Political Participation in Developing Countries*. Cambridge: Harvard University Press.

Hyden, Goran. 1983. *No Shortcuts to Progress: African Development Management in Perspective*. Berkeley: University of California Press.

Johnston, Bruce, and William C. Clark. 1982. *Redesigning Rural Development: A Strategic Perspective*. Baltimore: Johns Hopkins University Press.

Kamugasha, B.B. Nganwa. 1990. "Local Participation in Environmental Assessments in Africa." Environment Division Technical Note 10, Africa Region, World Bank, Washington, DC.

Kottak, Conrad. 1985. "When People Don't Come First: Some Sociological Lessons from Completed Projects." In Michael M. Cernea, ed., *Putting People First: Sociological Variables in Rural Development*, 2d ed., 1991. New York: Oxford University Press.

Lele, Uma. 1975. *The Design of Rural Development: Lessons of Experience*. Baltimore: Johns Hopkins University Press.

McNeely, J.A., K.R. Miller, W.V.C. Reid, R.A Mittermeier, and T.B. Werner. 1990. *Conserving the World's Biological Diversity*. Washington, DC: International Union for the Conservation of Nature, World Resources Institute, World Bank, World Wildlife Fund, and Conservation International.

Morss, Elliott R. 1976. *Strategies for Small Farmer Development: An Empirical Study of Rural Development Projects*. Boulder, Colorado: Westview Press.

Moynihan, Daniel P. 1969. *Maximum Feasible Misunderstanding*. New York: Free Press.

Nagle, William J., and Sanjoy Ghose. 1990. "Community

Participation in World Bank Supported Projects." Strategic Planning and Review Discussion Paper 8. Washington, DC: World Bank.

Oakley, Peter, and David Marsden. 1984. "Approaches to Participation in Rural Development." Geneva: ILO.

Owens, Edgar, and Robert Shaw. 1972. *Development Reconsidered: Bridging the Gap between Government and People*. Lexington, Mass.: Heath.

Ortolano, Leonard. 1984. *Environmental Planning and Decision Making*. New York: John Wiley and Sons.

Paddock, William, and Elizabeth Paddock. 1984. *We Don't Know How: An Independent Audit of What They Call Success in Foreign Assistance*. Ames, Iowa: Iowa State University Press.

Paul, Samuel. 1987. *Community Participation in Development Projects: The World Bank Experience*. World Bank Discussion Paper 6. Washington, DC: World Bank.

Ranney, David C. 1969. *Planning and Politics in the Metropolis*. Columbus, Ohio: Merrill.

Salmen, Lawrence E. 1987. *Listen to the People: Participant-Observer Evaluation of Development Projects*. New York: Oxford University Press.

Uphoff, Norman. 1985. "Fitting Projects to People." In Michael M. Cernea, ed., *Putting People First: Sociological Variables in Rural Development*, 2d ed.,

1991. New York: Oxford University Press.

World Bank. 1985. *Sustainability of Projects: First Review of Experience*. Operations Evaluation Department Report 5718. Washington, DC.

———. 1988. *Rural Development: World Bank Experience, 1965-86*. Operations Evaluation Department. Washington, DC.

———. 1989. *Sub-Saharan Africa: From Crisis to Sustainable Growth*. A Long-Term Perspective Study. Washington, DC.

———. 1991a. "A Common Vocabulary: Popular Participation Learning Group." Unpublished paper, External Relations Department. Washington, DC.

———. 1991b. *Environmental Assessment Sourcebook*. Vol. 1 Policies, Procedures and Cross-sectoral Issues. Technical Paper 139. Vol. 2. Sectoral Guidelines. Technical Paper 140. Vol. 3. Guidelines for Environmental Assessment of Energy and Industry Projects. Technical Paper 154. Washington, DC.

———. 1991c. "Country Capacity to Conduct Environmental Assessments in Sub-Saharan." Africa Region, Environment Division Working Paper 1. Washington, DC.

———. 1991d. "Local Participation in Environmental Assessments." Africa Region, Environment Division Working Paper 2. Washington, DC.

10

Flood Prevention and Mitigation in Bangladesh: The Need for Sustainable Floodplain Development

C. Emdad Haque

In recent years, many scholars have vigorously debated the question of whether flood prevention should depend mainly on *structural* (macro-engineering) measures to confine floodwater in the river channels or whether there should be a much greater emphasis on the development and implementation of *non-structural* measures to mitigate the impacts of floods. The preliminary findings from three years of feasibility studies have influenced the World Bank and other donor agencies to move away from a sole emphasis on structural-engineering schemes toward more non-structural measures. At the time this chapter was written, the Government of Bangladesh still favored large-scale engineering intervention for flood control and mitigation. Consequently, the debate on *structural* versus *non-structural* measures has recently moved to a different level—that is, from an academic discussion to the domain of actual decisionmaking process involving both the Bangladesh national government and other international agencies.

The principal objective of this chapter is to critically assess some of the key elements of the above stated debate, within the context of the 1988 catastrophic flood, and to determine the major limitations and potentials offered by the two paradigms. In order to shed light on some of the alternatives to implementing *"la grande"* engineering schemes, an attempt is made here to outline the nature and potentials of indigenous adjustment and coping strategies made by residents of flood-prone areas. In the second section, various phases of the flood prevention and mitigation strategies are reviewed. The third section presents an empirical example of the usage of indigenous adjustments and coping responses to floods. Finally, a number of policy prescriptions are put forward that include a call for adoption of the "sustainable floodplain development" approach in addressing the problem of flood loss in Bangladesh.

Flood Hazard

Threats and Responses

In Bengali culture, the word "flood" connotes both a blessing and a curse. The territory of Bangladesh is situated on the delta of the Ganges-Brahmaputra river systems with more than 350 other perennial tributaries and distributaries. It lies at the confluence of three of the world's mightiest rivers: the Ganges, the Brahmaputra, and the Meghna. Except for the tertiary hills of the Chittagong Hill Tracts and Sylhet, the elevation of the country is very low, averaging only between 5 meters and 6 meters above sea level. More than one-quarter of Bangladesh experiences a regular annual flood. The country receives an average of 870 million acrefeet (MAF) of river flows from India, China, and Nepal. The net flow to the Bay of Bengal from Bangladesh's rivers (adding an average annual rainfall of 203 MAF and subtracting 120 MAF that account for the estimated evaporation, evapotranspiration and deep percolation) accounts for 953 MAF. This huge volume of water brings down valuable silt, organic materials, and moisture from the Himalayas that are necessary ingredients for production of the country's crops. The term *borsha*, as used by the local people, refers to this normal flood occurrence.

A normal annual flooding is a desirable event for farmers of the region since it comes at the right time for cultivation and lasts long enough to benefit paddy rice and other major crops. Usually, it is also of a limited severity that the local conditions of settlement and housing, agriculture, and physical infrastructure can normally withstand. For centuries, this annual event had played a vital role in maintaining the high fertility of cultivable land and thereby supporting an expanding sedentary population in this region.

However, excess water in the rainy season often endangers human lives, livestock, crops, and other tangible assets. This negative aspect of floods is locally expressed by the term *bonna*, meaning abnormal floods. The socioeconomic impact of such riverine hazards in the region is more extensive and devastating relative to other types of hazards such as droughts or tornadoes. With a population size of 115 million, a per capita GNP of only around US$180, and a predominantly agrarian economy, Bangladesh ranks as one of the poorest countries in the world. Today, the country is one of the most intensively cultivated areas in the world, often supporting more than twelve people per hectare of arable land. The performance of agriculture as well as environmental conditions are thus fundamental to the survival of the people of Bangladesh. While the demographic and socioeconomic setting is already precarious, the high ecological vulnerability of most of the country to abnormal natural events such as cyclones and floods further adds to the insecurity and risks faced by the majority of the population.

The 1987 and 1988 floods, considered by many analysts as the most disastrous in the recorded history of Bangladesh, have caused considerable concerns among many national and international agencies about the possible ways of mitigating the flood problem. The international community is eager to provide technical assistance to help formulate longer-term solutions to Bangladesh's chronic flood problems. The World Bank, the United Nations Development Program (UNDP), national donor agencies from the United States, France and Japan, in collaboration with the Bangladesh government, commissioned a series of flood studies. The resulting reports have offered an array of viewpoints; the most dramatic and costly proposals were made by a French engineering consortium that recommended the construction of more than 3,000 kilometers (km) of high embankments to *prevent* abnormal flooding. On the other hand, the study sponsored by United States Agency for International Development (USAID) has argued in favor of minimal structural intervention into the region's complex deltaic ecology. In 1989, the World Bank, in collaboration with the Government of Bangladesh, prepared an action plan, commonly known as Flood Action Plan (FAP), for flood prevention and control that states that "a high degree of structural protection must be a key element of the long-term strategy for the development of the country" (World Bank 1990).

An assessment of flood-loss mitigating strategies in Bangladesh suggests that solutions to this problem have been monistic—a singleness of preference for eliminating flood by structural-engineering measures (see Zaman 1991). Such a narrow view of the flood problem divests itself from more significant ecological and sociocultural considerations, as well as realistic alternatives that might be employed, and raises serious questions about the long-term viability of only "technological fix" strategies.

Flood-Loss and Vulnerability

The unavailability of systematic time series data on flood damage and loss in Bangladesh precludes a clear picture of the scope. It is, however, possible to review the generalized trend and the extent of flood effects from a number of independent studies. It has been reported that, although the recent floods are not physically different than many previous occurrences (Rogers and others 1989), the degree of economic losses and the vulnerability of the population has dramatically increased in recent decades. This trend is primarily attributed, first, to the increased numbers of the population in perpetual poverty and marginalization, and second, to the growth of tangible resources (such as crops), and physical infrastructure (roads, railways, buildings, factories, and electrical networks) in riverine floodplain areas that are more vulnerable to natural hazards.

Historical records show that there were at least six major floods in the 19th century and there have been fourteen so far this century. While the most devastating flood on record occurred during the late monsoon of 1988, other catastrophic flooding occurred in 1954, 1955, 1977, and 1987. The direct impacts of severe floods can be disastrous and the casualties high; even the moderately severe floods of 1974 caused over 2,000 deaths. The indirect impacts of floods can be even greater; the 1974 flood was followed by a devastating famine that caused more than 30,000 deaths. The 1988 flood inundated 66,360 square kilometers (km^2) or about 46 percent of the country. While several thousand people become homeless during a normal flood season, the 1988 flood uprooted more than 40 million people and over two thousand died. Such periodic large-scale disasters cause lasting disruptions and havoc and the process of reconstruction is slow and expensive. Almost half of the 1988–89 national development budget, for example, was diverted to pay *ad hoc* relief and rehabilitation programs (see Brammer 1990a).

Based on data compiled from various sources, table 10-1 shows the magnitude of major flood damages during the last two decades. It appears that the total seasonal loss of rice production, which is the staple crop of the country, was above one million tons in each of the catastrophic flood years. Also, more than 200,000 tons were lost in each of the other severe flood years. In 1988 alone, the worst flood year of this century, the estimated loss of material damage exceeded US$2 billion (UNDP 1989). According to the report of the Bangladesh Red Cross, among the more than 45 million people directly affected, over two thousand lives were lost and some 172,000 livestock and 7.3 million houses were fully or partially damaged. Besides such immense loss of agricultural components, the growing physical infrastructure was also severely damaged due to the 1988 floods: about 900 bridges and culverts were destroyed and more than 15,000 km of rural and trunk roads were affected.

Flood Prevention and Control Policies

First Phase (1955–1971): Post-Disaster Recovery and la Grande Schemes

The efforts by the public sector for the prevention, control, and mitigation of floods in Bangladesh date back to the 1950s. The overall trend of the water

sector policies of the country can be viewed in terms of some phases. During the first phase (1955-1971), based on only post-disaster recovery strategies, the focus was on building large-scale flood prevention and irrigation schemes. Some specific cases are worth elaborating here. Following the severe flood of 1955, the government of Pakistan sought advice from the United Nations Technical Mission on flood prevention strategies. On the basis of the Krug Mission Report of 1956, a project planning, implementing, and monitoring agency was created in 1959: the East Pakistan Water and Power Development Authority (EPWAPDA). A massive construction work of riverbank and coastal embankment began under the auspices of the EPWAPDA and the guidance of the Krug Mission.

Similarly, after the 1962 floods, the reports of two United Nations consultants (the Hardin Report of 1963 and the Thijsee Report of 1964) examined options for flood control and recommended various types of large-scale engineering works for the confinement of flood waters within the main channels of large rivers. These measures, which included embankment construction, channel improvement by dredging, river training and cut-off, and the construction of by-passes or flood-ways, were

Table 10-1. Losses and Damage Due to Abnormal Floods (bonna), 1971-88

Year	Loss of human lives and livestock		Loss of crop production and housing structure				
	Loss of human lives	Loss of livestock ('000)	Loss of rice production (1000 metric tons)				Houses totally or partially damaged
			Boro	Aus	Ama	Total seasonal	
1971	120	2	n.a.	56	229	285	229
1974*	1,987	46	187	613	562	1,362	6,165
1975	15	n.a.	n.a.	68	25	93	19
1976	54	n.a.	67	351	264	682	89
1980	n.a.	n.a.	4	30	251	285	n.a.
1984*	553	76	373	475	1,299	2,147	536
1987*	1,657	65	n.a.	695	1,341	2,036	2,536
1988*	2,379	172	n.a.	1,357	1,565	2,922	7,179

* More catastrophic flood years.
n.a. Not available.
Source: Mirza 1984; International Red Cross 1988; Brammer 1990b.

incorporated in the Master Plan of the EPWAPDA, in 1964. The Master Plan identified a total of ninety-one projects to address flood problems of what was then East Pakistan. Following the 1962 floods, a review of development policies also led to undertaking some efforts to integrate infrastructure development projects with flood-control efforts. A few such important flood control projects were: Kurigram Embankment, Old Brahmaputra Phase I and II, Belkuchi, Bogra, Chalan Beel, Dhaleshwari and Bangshi Channel Improvement, and Ganga-Kaputakkhya. Other projects included the Southern Rajshahi, Dhaka Southwest, Chandpur, Gorai, Arial Khan, Boral, Haor schemes, Kushiyara, Meghna-Dhangoda, Titas, Gumti, Khowai, Mono and Matamohori (Tarafder 1974).

As a result of this new approach, the Rural Works Program (RWP), which was supported by wheat supply under U.S. Public Law 480, began to construct large scale engineering works such as flood-protection embankments. One of the most impressive structural efforts to control floods was the completion in 1967-68 of the Brahmaputra Right Bank Flood Protection Embankment (BRBFPE). There has been a significant decrease in overbank spillage as a result of the construction of this embankment (Tarafder 1974). Potential flood protection was created for about 2.3 million hectares (ha) of gross acres, of which 157,000 ha of agricultural land were within its immediate vicinity. Production increased by 131,856 tons or more than 68 percent over the pre-project production of 192,650 tons (Rahman 1984).

The first Five Year Plan Document of the Government of Bangladesh reports that, as of the early 1970s, embankment construction had provided flood protection for about 1.2 million ha of land along the coastal areas and floodplains. These works included construction of more than 3,200 km of coastal embankment repelling saline water intrusion and about 320 km of riverbank embankment controlling overbank spills. Irrigation-related physical works included a total of over 1,600 km of main, secondary, and tertiary irrigation canals; some 4,600 sluices and regulators; and 3 major and 85 minor pumping stations (Bangladesh Planning Commission 1973).

The rationale for undertaking large-scale development schemes was rooted in the concept of rapid economic growth to attain the so-called "take-off" stage of development (see Rostow 1960). As Rutton (1986) succinctly states:

There are several reasons for the large-scale infrastructure investments during this period (1950s and 1960s). A major economic rationale was that public benefits exceed private benefits by such a wide margin that only the public sector could afford to undertake them. Spillover or secondary development impacts were believed to substantially exceed the benefits that could be captured in the form of price or user charges.

Second Phase (1971–1988): A Shift to Small-Scale Projects

It was realized in the late 1960s that the proportion of costs to benefits in large-scale projects was higher. Maintenance became a huge uncontrolable task, and rent realization from major irrigation projects was slow and in some cases unsuccessful. Because implementation of large-scale projects required much longer time, the emphasis on the sponsorship of large-scale development projects by public sectors lost their momentum and significance over time. Since the Independence of Bangladesh, concern over the limitations of economically viable large-scale projects has brought about a change in flood control and irrigation strategies. In the early 1970s, World Bank land and water sector studies recommended changes in the strategy, which led the government to shift to small-scale, low-cost, and quick-return projects in flood control, drainage, and irrigation development (World Bank 1970, 1972). Since 1971, with the advent of low-lift pumps, tubewells, and diffusion of dry-season cropping, a shift in policy from major flood control works to more small-scale, quick-yeilding projects took place. This trend continued until the major flood of 1988 that devastated Bangladesh's infrastructural facilities.

Since independence, the focus of development strategy in Bangladesh has been concentrated on achieving self-sufficiency in food supply. Agricultural extension programs, such as irrigation development, and input and credit supplies to the farmers, received utmost priorities in public policy measures. Because the country has had an annual deficit of about two million tons of food grain for the last two decades, the main thrust has always been on increasing food crop production (Hossain 1980; Huq 1980). The problem of natural hazards was considered a secondary issue or only to the extent they might affect the crop production levels. Increasing food grain production towards levels of self-sufficiency was selected as the first priority issue in the First (1973-1978), Second

(1980-1985), and Third Five Year (1985-1990) Plans. Ambitious targets were set in the successive Five Year Plans. The successive regimes in Bangladesh put all out efforts to increase food grain production by setting targets of 6.4 and 7.2 percent growth per year during the Plan periods of 1973–78 and 1980–85, respectively, and an overall agricultural production growth of 5.2 percent per year in the Plan period of 1986–90 (Bangladesh Planning Commission 1973, 1980; World Bank 1987).

The strategies adopted for the above purpose showed some commendable successes in increasing food grain production at a rate faster than population growth. For example, during 1975–1980, food grain production in the country grew at an annual rate of about 3.2 percent compared to a growth in the population of about 2.6 percent. The overall agricultural production grew at an annual rate of 2.8 percent during this period. Remarkable increases in production were made possible by such replacement of long-stem local varieties with the adoption of High Yielding Varieties (HYV). Among the major irrigation, drainage, and flood control projects implemented, the Northern Tube-well Project and the Chandpur Project had the potential for irrigating 28,740 ha and 51,400 ha of land, respectively. Besides developing other infrastructural facilities (such as rural roads and communications), about 3 million ha of agricultural land were protected from floods and a provision was made to irrigate more than 2 million

ha. Overall, given such constraints as the untimely allocation and procurement of funds, and political instability, the number of works completed under different Public Works Projects (PWP), such as RWPs and Food for Works Programs (FFWP), were commendable (Alamgir 1983; BBS 1985; also see table 10-2).

Due to increased impediments to the natural drainage systems caused by the newly placed infrastructure (embankments, dams), and the lack of an ecologically sustainable water resource policy guideline, the country become more vulnerable to abnormal floods. The country lost more than two billion US dollars when the abnormally high floods struck in 1987 and 1988.

Third Phase (1988–1993): The Return of la Grande Schemes

The 1988 floods of Bangladesh received overwhelming attention and responses from the international community. Flood studies were commissioned by the World Bank, the United Nations Development Programme (UNDP), the United States Agency for International Development (USAID), and the national government agencies of France and Japan, in collaboration with the Bangladesh Government. The resulting reports have offered varied viewpoints. The most dramatic and costly proposals were made by the French engineering consortium that recommended the construction of 3,350 km of

Table 10-2. Food for Works Projects and Achievements, 1974/75 - 1983/84

Year	No. of projects implemented	Roads (km)	Embankments (km)	River and canal excavation constructed (km)
1974/75	21,479	3,824	1,402	1,756
1975/76	1,554	1,448	1,246	1,611
1976/77	2,328	1,735	3,067	2,694
1977/78	2,087	2,366	488	3,639
1978/79	2,113	1,770	3,487	3,082
1979/80	2,124	3,301	3,262	4,212
1980/81	3,927	4,981	5,064	6,693
1981/82	3,431	6,910	6,437	1,292
1982/83	3,029	9,213	8,582	1,724
1983/84	4,292	22,083	8,405	3,333

Source: BBS 1985.

high embankment to prevent abnormal flooding. It has been estimated that the implementation of these projects, which may take twenty years to construct, would cost US$10 billion with an annual maintenance cost ranging between US$200 million and $600 million (Bingham 1989). The French consortium of engineering companies is in favor of the construction of embankments to prevent, divert and regulate waters; it has proposed an elaborate and costly set of new constructions along both the Ganges and the Brahmaputra and their four major distributaries, as well as seven other smaller rivers. Flood study teams from the United States and Japan are supportive of a less-grandiose policy strategy, proposing to allow the river to overflow into relatively unimportant or under-populated areas while protecting the important and high-population areas.

It should be pointed out here that total flood prevention would not allow the natural fertility benefits to the soil and the necessary moisture supply to continue. In view of the potential damage and destruction to the existing natural resource base, there was growing opposition to the proposal of the French consortium to construct preventive embankments (Haque 1988; Islam 1989; Rasid 1989; Rogers and others 1989). The major aid donors to Bangladesh discussed the flood mitigation problem at the G-7 summit meeting in Paris in July 1989. They agreed that the World Bank should "coordinate the efforts of the international community so that a sound basis for achieving a real improvement in alleviating the effects of flood can be established."

In 1989, the World Bank prepared an Action Plan for Flood Control in which both the "flood prevention" and "flood control" approaches were accommodated. Actually, the Plan is directed to create preparatory arrangements for the eventual implementation of a Flood Master Plan proposed in the UNDP Policy Study. The Plan apparently represents a "conservative mix" of various studies. Nonetheless, as Boyce (1990) succinctly stated: "[d]espite grave and well founded reservations as to the wisdom of massive embankments, the long-term strategy envisioned in the [World] Bank's action plan incorporates central elements of the French scheme." For instance, although the study did not completely agree to embank four major distributaries of the Ganges and the Brahmaputra-Jamuna and seven smaller rivers, it proposed to build embankments all along the major river courses in Bangladesh. In addition to these structural measures,

the plan intends to create "compartments" inside the main embankments by constructing internal embankments to allow controlled flooding by means of regulators and sluices in both the main and internal embankments.

Ironically, the proposal ignores the fact that local rainfall often leads to high floods, and compartmentalization is rather likely to aggravate the problem of drainage in many cases. Moreover, it has already been observed that the confinement of runoff to river channels intensifies the bank's erosive capacity during the monsoon period in both the Brahmaputra-Jamuna and the Ganges rivers (Haque 1988; Rahman 1984). The Brahmaputra Right Bank Protection Embankment, a 217-km flood control measure, has been cited as a major cause of rapid westward migration of the Brahmaputra-Jamuna channel. Even if the proposed embankment succeeds in achieving flood control purposes, it is probable that the accelerated bank erosion of these braided rivers might outweigh the benefits in this land-scarce country. This is because riverbank erosion hazards affect hundreds of thousands of displaced people, which become a permanent feature compared to the temporary effects of seasonal flooding.

Fourth Phase (1993–Present): The Debate and a Search for New Directions

Concerns about the potential adverse impacts of the Plan have been expressed by many scholars. In a comprehensive review of the issue, Haque and Zaman (1993) suggested that the application of major preventive structural adjustments would create a number of serious problems for Bangladesh. First, the construction of embankments along the major rivers requires a capital cost of as much as US$10 billion (Bingham 1989), as well as annual operating costs on the order of more than US$500,000 (Rogers and others 1988). Since the lion's share of the national development budget continues to come from foreign sources, a costly preventive program will result in a steady rise in the nation's foreign debt burden. Second, preventive embankments tend to provide a false sense of security and, ironically, may actually lead to an increase in flood damage. The findings of a recent study in southern Bangladesh by Stewart (1988) show that the average material damage was worse in areas inside the embankment than in areas outside of it. Third, embankments impede the movement of freshwater fish and cut off their spawning areas, which threatens the livelihood of more than a million fishermen and jeopardizes the already marginal supply of animal protein in the diet of the majority of people. Fourth, the coastal embankments and polder projects have seriously affected shrimp cultivation in the area. The shrimp cultivators, in need of brackish water, are breaking the embankment to allow water to penetrate to their land (Zaman 1991). Finally, embankments deprive the farmers of the beneficial effects of normal seasonal floods.

Normal annual flooding in Bangladesh is part of peasant life; it is a beneficial phenomenon producing the leaching and eluviation processes that have rejuvenated the soil-water properties and soil fertility in the region for centuries (Paul 1984). New inorganic materials from the Himalayan region have drained downstream and alongside floodplains accumulated in this deltaic plain for thousands of years. The silt deposited by floods, however, remains infertile for several years before it begins to improve soil fertility. Brammer (1990b) notes that flood-related soil fertility is generated "from nitrogen-fixing, blue-green algae, from decomposing, submerged, plant remains living in the water, and from the increased availability of phosphorus and other nutrients in the chemically reduced, submerged top-soils."

Since the establishment of the FAP in 1989, the Government of Bangladesh has assigned the management of the Plan to the Flood Plan Coordination Organization (FPCO), which was created as a wing of the Ministry of Irrigation, Water Development and Flood Control. It was decided by the concerned bodies that the final form of the FAP will be based on the results of the twenty-six studies to be taken up by FPCO (for further details see Islam 1993a). Although the FAP's original goals were geared toward structural solutions, it could not ignore the need to explore non-structural, flood proofing responses because of growing academic and policy debates on the long-term economic and environmental implications of the Plan. The debate eventually turned into a dichotomized institutional position between the World Bank and the Government of Bangladesh: the former is in favor of the construction of massive embankments along the major river systems, and the World Bank and other donor agencies are "growing increasingly resistant" to such insistence (Pearce and Tickell 1993).

After experiencing the disaster along the Mississippi River in the summer of 1993 and receiving feed back from the feasibility studies of the FPCO, momentum has already developed toward limited intervention in the Brahmaputra-Ganges flood plain ecosystems. The preliminary results from the three years of feasibility studies into the physical dimensions of the FAP have revealed "the practical impossibility of sealing off the rivers" (Pearce and Tickell 1993). These assessment efforts, before implementing the final plan, cost only US$150 million for the pilot and experimental projects, and undeniably worked as a safety valve for the worth US$10 billion to US$15 billion of capital investment. The overall exercise has provided a very valuable lesson in the environmental assessment (EA) process.

The accumulated results so far of the five regional and other sectoral and supporting projects included an EA component because a mandatory provision for all FAP projects was put in place before the commencement of the pilot studies. The FAP 16, or environmental study, has prepared EA guidelines for ongoing and future flood control and water management projects. The relevant variables were itemized in the first through fifth level impacts (for details see Islam 1993b). The preliminary outcomes of the pilot studies, which largely followed the EA guidelines, offered some significant lessons for policymakers. Although a detailed discussion is beyond the scope of this chapter, the most significant lessions stemming from these exercises were:

• All hazard mitigation and development plans should be flexible and adaptive (that is, the original plans should set up the broader "mission objective" and establish a provision for a series of pilot experiments to identify the best alternative means of achieving the stated goals).

• The specific goals should be formulated through a dynamic process involving feedback from the pilot projects and the changing social, political and economic objectives.

• The incompatibility between the time frame of the economic plans and the ecological processes, which makes the EA process quite difficult, should be recognized during the earlier planning phases.

• Public participation and direct input into the decisionmaking process should be regarded as a vital component in the EA process.

• It should be realized that the outcomes of short-term pilot projects (for example, the three-year experimental schemes) could only demonstrate the *tendencies* of possible impacts of the proposed plans; formulation of the EA with a high degree of confidence would require considerably longer-term ecological research. Generation of longitudinal databases of all major physical, bio-physical, and socioeconomic parameters would be a significant step in this direction.

Exploration into Indigenous Flood-Adjustment Strategies

The principal themes in the current literature on natural disasters not only include the causes of disasters but also the alternative response strategies leading to prevention and mitigation. In this connection, two major paradigms have evolved with regard to what can be done to lessen the impacts of floods. The first of these conceives environmental hazards solely as a nature-generated phenomena requiring structural adjustments; it stresses the application of a technology-biased measure to prevent or modify the physical processes to produce flood mitigation. A second paradigm emphasizes non-structural adjustments to floods (that is, not involving massive engineering works), which include an array of adaptive actions taken by communities before and during floods in order to mitigate loss, as well as other pertinent strategies, such as flood forecasting and early warning systems, flood insurance, and flood relief and rehabilitation. This section discusses the principal non-structural measures that are practiced and used in the region.

The people of the Bengal basin have long been associated with the flooding phenomenon, adopting numerous adjustments to cope with abnormal flooding based on indigenous inventions and innovations, and material and societal resources. As noted above, in contrast to the English meaning of "flood" as a destructive phenomenon, its usage in Bengali refers to both a positive and a negative resource. The term *borsha* refers to normal flooding, and *bonna* implies an abnormal flooding. This literal expression, which is based on real life experience, reflects the awareness and adjustments to flood hazards of the common people of the region. A quantitative analysis of flood loss in Bangladesh also reveals that people are highly adaptive to floods relative to other extreme natural events. For example, whereas more than 200,000 lives were lost from the cyclone-driven storm in November 1970 and over 70,000 lives from the coastal cyclone in May 1985, the direct fatalities by flood occurrences had been limited to roughly two thousand. A firsthand Western observer of the 1988 flood expressed the ability of people to cope with extreme situations. In the midst of the flood period, he reported:

The world has already recognized a catastrophe in a nation where the country's worst floods have left 1,000 dead...and more than 25 million homeless. But Bengalis themselves are coping astonishingly well with the enemy they've always known..."We are all right here", says a women named Sabera, who crept to the edge of her tin roof to talk to a reporter in a boat... Although rice paddies are under several meters of water and the precious jute crop badly damaged, morale among beleaguered Bengalis seem surprisingly high (Johnson 1988).

Hurdus (1988) and Brammer (1990a) further found that during the abnormal flood years, the spread of flood water in extensive areas plays a compensatory role in crop damage. That is, the damage of the two wet season paddies, namely *aus* and *aman*, is largely overcome by better soil moisture conditions, especially for *boro* production (dry season crops; see table 10-3). Consequently, the net loss due to abnormal flood is much less than the superficial estimates.

Does this imply that the impact of floods is nominal? An account for indirect effects of flood reveals that their perpetual progression causes immense socioeconomic and human cost. An extensive survey of the 1974 famine by Alamgir (1980) indicated that the severe flood occurrences leave the poor and marginal peasants much more impoverished. This is because abnormal floods damage their assets, forcing them to draw on past savings while falling further into debt. Among other indirect effects, the demand for agricultural labour decreases drastically as crops are damaged. The capacity to hire labours by landowners is reduced by lower incomes accruing to them. Coupled with the steady increase in seasonal price of food grain and related commodities, the poor peasants and wage laborers become increasingly prone to starvation and famine over time (Rahman 1989). Overall, these perspectives suggest that flood

Table 10-3. Cereal Production in Bangladesh, 1986-1988

Year	Production of cereal (million tons)				
	Aus	Aman	Boro	Wheat	Total
1986/87	3.13	8.27	4.01	1.09	16.50
1987/88	2.99	7.69	4.73	1.05	16.46
1988/89	2.86	6.86	5.80	1.02	16.54

Note: The amounts are excluding minor cereals. Rice production amounts are of milled rice.
Source: Brammer 1990a.

impacts should not be viewed in terms of physical problems but rather in terms of their relevance to social processes and welfare conditions.

In Bangladesh, most of the indigenous adjustments are of the corrective type. Some of them are related to social organization and relationships; others are associated with material responses at an individual level. The concept of resource sharing and income redistribution in ameliorating famine effects in an agrarian economy has been noted by a number of scholars (Sen 1981; Alamgir 1980; Desai 1959); however, attempts at investigating the role of social organizations and other societal forces in mitigating hazard effects has been scanty.

In order to explore the indigenous adjustment strategies and measures, a questionnaire survey was conducted in December 1988 in eight villages of the Sreenagar *Thana* (sub-district) and the Munshiganj district. A sample size of 280 households (primary sampling units) was covered, and a simple random sampling procedure was followed in selecting these units. Only the household heads were directly interviewed to represent their corresponding family units.

The survey showed that majority of the respondents took some corrective measures to minimize flood loss. That is, more than 71 percent of respondents attempted to reduce their loss to floods by selling their land, livestock or belongings; some moved housing structures, livestock, and family members to other safer places (see table 10-4). It is evident that flood victims opted for a number of responses aimed at reducing hazard loss through deliberate measures. Although most of the villagers received some assistance from various sources to cope with flood hazards, less than 12 percent actually were recipients of support from local and national government sources. As indicated in table 10-5, the principal source of assistance to adjustment efforts are relatives (78.6 percent) and other community members (32.9 percent). The items of assistance received from these major sources consist of moral support, free shelter and accommodation, free labor at the time of the move, and cash loans and food. Also, nongovernmental organizations (NGOs) provided a great deal of support to the hazard-mitigating efforts. Of the sampled respondent households, more than 50 percent received food and clothes, housing materials, seeds and loans from them to regain their pre-disaster status. More importantly, this support not only helped the flood victims to survive through the disaster

Table 10-4. Distribution of Adjustment Measures Taken by Respondents during the 1988 Floods in Sreenagar (percent)

Adjustment measures (multiple response possible)	All households (n=280)	Non-members (not involved in institutional network) (n=144)	Members of institutional network (n=136)
Sold land	2.1	4.4	n.a.
Sold livestock	17.1	26.4	7.4
Sold belongings	25.7	33.3	17.6
Mortgaged land	4.3	5.6	2.9
Dismantled housing structure	38.6	30.6	47.1
Borrowed money	39.3	65.3	11.8
Spent previous savings	24.3	44.4	2.9
Moved family to other areas	65.7	79.2	51.5
Moved livestock to other areas	26.4	20.8	32.4

n.a. Not available.
Source: Author's field survey

period, but also to assist in saving many of their belongings, such as utensils, housing materials, and livestock.

More than half of all respondents considered it important to remain within, or to maintain closer ties with, their traditional *samaj* organization during the coping stages with hazards. The *samaj* is an informal but predominant social grouping based on kinship, social, and religious interests of its members. It is the primary forum within which members interact frequently, and are mutually involved in networks of social and ceremonial links and interdependence (Zaman 1986; Haque and Zaman 1989). The *samaj* people are obliged to help in ameliorating difficult situations of its members.

Further evidence of the benefits of institutionalized

networks in the mitigation of hazard loss was revealed in the survey responses (see tables 10-4 and 10-5). Both in terms of hazard preparedness and coping ability, the households that were members of the institutionalized groups demonstrated a better performance compared to their counterparts (non-members). The institutionalized groups were defined as the registered target groups of government and NGOs, such as agricultural cooperatives, credit unions, banks, and integrated rural development programs based on women's groups. These observations support the hypothesis that developing the social and institutional networks can be effectively employed in minimizing hazard effects.

At the individual level, some small-scale structural measures are also employed by the resource users in rural Bangladesh. One of the most common strategies is the construction of homesteads on relatively elevated natural levees. The plinth of houses, locally called *bhiti*, is further raised by digging earth from local depressions (Currey 1979). The rural non-metalled roads (*katcha*), and courtyards of local schools and mosques are often raised to the level of abnormal floods and used as flood shelters. People also build platforms or *machans* using bamboo, straw, water hyacinth, and banana stalks during abnormal flooding years.

The agricultural adjustments to flood hazards is an important part of the indigenous measures in Bangladesh. As Rasid and Paul (1989) cited, farmers of this wet monsoon region have over the centuries made a careful selection of the most adaptive varieties of rice to face the high floods. For instance, certain varieties of *aus* rice are cultivated only in elevated areas (*tans*). Some broadcast and transplanted *aman* grow with floods and are harvested following the recession of flood water. They are grown in the low-lying areas (*dhoabs*) such as backswamps, channel scars, and shallow beds of oxbow lakes. *Chamara*, a broadcast variety of *aman*, can grow more than 15 centimeters a day with the rising flood levels.

Overall, it is evident that, in the context of the rural habitat and agriculture of Bangladesh, flooding is a vital agent to its resources. Although some extreme events turn out to be a serious threat to local resources and human lives, their frequency is measured in the range of the 50 to 100 year event. The floodplain inhabitants would gain little from prevention of such rare events.

An Approach toward a Sustainable Floodplain Development Policy

Because humans strive to produce more resources and to safeguard existing ones, human intervention and modification of the physical environment—such as alluvial floodplains—are growing at a dramatic rate. This trend is expected to continue into the foreseeable future, and with it will come conflicts between flood-prevention activities and the environment. Among many others, Scudder (1991) clearly indicates some of the adverse impacts of African dams on floodplain users and local ecosystems. Rahman (1984) shows many adverse effects of embankments in Bangladesh's floodplains. Minkin (1989) found almost total loss of open water fish in flood control projects in the Ganges-Brahmaputra-Meghna floodplains. Thus, it may be forcefully argued that without significant attention toward more sustainable forms of floodplain development, it is quite probable that severe damage to ecological and cultural habitats will accelerate.

The notion of sustainable development, which was reinforced by Raymond Dasmann while he was with the International Union for the Conservation of Nature and Natural Resources (IUCN) in the 1970s and later promoted by the World Commission on Environment and Development in the 1980s, laid a broad conceptual framework (Dasman, Milton and Freeman 1973; WCED 1987). The Commission defined the concept

Table 10-5. Sources of Assistance Received by Flood Victims during the 1988 Floods in Sreenager (percent)

Sources of assistance (multiple response possible)	All households (n=280)	Non-members (not involved in institutional network) (n=144)	Members of institutional network (n=136)
Relatives	78.6	86.1	70.6
Other villagers	32.9	31.9	33.8
Local government	7.1	8.3	5.9
National government	4.3	4.2	4.4
Relief agencies and other institutions	51.4	18.1	86.8

Source: Author's field survey

as "development that meets the needs of the present without compromising the ability of future generations to meet their own needs" (WCED 1987). This broad theme generated a semantic debate in the literature and is reported elsewhere (Manning 1990; Howarth and Norgaard 1990; Lele 1991). In brief, the overall discussion revealed that the concept underlying sustainable development is an anthropocentric approach to the globe—a human perspective relating to human use of the biosphere. This notion explicitly recognizes interdependencies that exist among environmental, economic, social, and cultural phenomena. The discussion in this chapter concerns two broad areas of public policies regarding flood problems: a holistic approach—unlike the structural strategy—to human aspects of water resource management, and a sustainable floodplain development plan that will ensure benefits to its users.

The annual normal flood has always been beneficial to riverine populations and ecosystems. Indeed, annual flood regimes have historically flourished and sustained the economies of the floodplain users in Bangladesh for generations without any environmental degradation. Thus, flooding *per se* is not an evil but a source of life and livelihood for the vast majority of people in this deltaic landscape. Because flooding is so critical to the economy and society in Bangladesh, a flood prevention policy is definitely *not* the appropriate solution. The need for a structural solution represents a partial view and, perhaps at its best, a somewhat piecemeal solution with all kinds of possible adverse ecological and environmental impacts. In my view, the current emphasis of the Bangladesh flood policy should be changed from flood *prevention* to flood *adaptation*. Such an approach may still require some limited protection of important cities and commercial centers by building new embankments; however, the primary policy objectives should be to encourage and assist the villagers to identify the best ways to protect themselves, their crops, and their livestock by developing improved measures of flood management and preparedness.

Finally, I would like to assert that the flood problem in Bangladesh is not a problem of mere hydraulic dynamics. It is rather "a problem which reaches out to the delicate issues of the economy, ecology, society, demography, settlement pattern, transportation, and even of politics and culture" (Islam 1990). As such, flood issues must be addressed both from sustainability and long-term development perspectives. Since high flood-related loss in the country is related to a number of developmental factors, such as increased population pressure, economic marginalization of rural inhabitants, and ill-conceived infrastructure, addressing disaster impact would require going beyond the concept of sustainable floodplain development. For instance, there would be a need to develop strategies for retaining the unquestioned benefits of annual flooding. The general problem of impoverishment is not a direct product of floods in the riverine plains of Bangladesh, but a significant proportion of floodplain users become marginalized and impoverished due to loss of income, assets, and increased debt burden. The formulation of policies toward rural income diversification is thus needed to address such problems. The generation of capital stock from economic surpluses in agriculture and the redistribution of existing local resources—including land—are fundamental to such policies.

Notes

I am thankful to John R. Rogge, Disaster Research Unit, University of Manitoba, Winnipeg, Canada, for his useful comments and suggestions on an earlier draft of the paper. Special thanks are due to Morshed Alam, Bangladesh Bureau of Statistics, Ministry of Planning, Dhaka, Bangladesh, for his help in obtaining the survey data on the 1988 floods.

References

Alamgir, M. 1980. *Famine in South Asia: Political Economy of Mass Starvation.* Cambridge, Massachusetts: Oelgeschlager, Gunn and Hain.

———. 1983. "A Review of the Public Rural Works Programmes of Bangladesh: 1960-78." *The Bangladesh Development Studies* 11(1 and 2).

Bangladesh Bureau of Statistics (BBS). 1985. *Statistical Pocket Book of Bangladesh, 1984-85.* Statistics Division. Dhaka:Ministry of Planning.

Bangladesh Planning Commission. 1973. *The First Five Year Plan, 1973-78.* Dhaka: Ministry of Planning.

———. 1980. *The Second Five Year Plan 1980-85.* Dhaka: Ministry of Planning.

Bingham, Annette. 1989. "Floods of Aid for Bangladesh." *New Scientist* 1693: 42-46.

Boyce, James. 1990. "Birth of a Megaproject: Political Economy of Flood Control in Bangladesh." *Environmental Management* 14(4):419-428.

Brammer, H. 1990a. "Floods in Bangladesh I. Geographical Background to the 1987 and 1988 Floods." *The Geographical Journal* 156: 12-22.

——. 1990b. "Floods in Bangladesh II. Flood Mitigation and Environmental Aspects." *The Geographical Journal* 156: 158-165.

Currey, Bruce. 1979. "Mapping Areas Liable to Famine in Bangladesh," Ph.D. dissertation, University of Hawaii, Honolulu, Hawaii.

Dasmann, Raymond, F., John P. Milton, and Peter H. Freemon. 1973. *Ecological Principles for Economic Development*. New York: John Wiley and Sons.

Desai, A.R. 1959. *Social Background of Indian Nationalism*. Bombay: Popular Book Depot.

Haque, C.E. 1989. "Impacts of River-Bank Erosion Hazard in the Brahmaputra-Jamuna Floodplain: A Study of Population Displacement and Response Strategies." Ph.D. dissertation, University of Manitoba, Winnipeg, Manitoba.

——. 1980. "Human Adjustments to Riverbank Erosion Hazard in the Jamuna Floodplain, Bangladesh." *Human Ecology* 16(4): 421-437.

Haque, C.E., and M.Q. Zaman. 1989. "Coping with Riverbank Erosion Hazard and Displacement in Bangladesh." *Disasters* 13: 300-314.

——. 1993. "Human Responses to Riverine Hazards in Bangladesh: A Proposal for Sustainable Floodplain Development." *World Development* 21:93-107.

Hossain, Mahabub. 1980. "Foodgrain Production in Bangadesh: Performance, Potential and Constraints." *The Bangladesh Development Studies* 8(1 and 2):39-70.

Howarth, R.B. and R.B. Norgaard. 1990. "Intergenerational Resource Rights, Efficiency, and Social Optimality." *Land Economics* 66: 1-11.

Huq, Mahfuzul. 1980. "Note on Food Policy and National Planning in Bangladesh." *The Bangladesh Development Studies* No. 8.

Hurdus, Alan R. 1988. *Outlook for the 1988/89 Aman Crop and Early Projections for the 1988/89 Wheat and Boro Crops*. Dhaka: Office of Food and Agriculture, USAID.

International Red Cross. 1988. Press Release, Spetember 26. Geneva.

Islam, M.A. 1989. "Floods in Bangladesh: Causes, Consequences, and Adjustments." Proceedings of the International Conference on Bangladesh Floods: What Are the Solutions? International Society of Bangladesh, Montreal.

——. 1993a. "Alternative Strategies for Flood Hazard Mitigation in Bangladesh: Flood Plain Managment Approach." Proceedings of the International Conference on Floods in Bangladesh: An Interdisciplinary Analysis of Alternative Solution Strategies. Working Paper No. 93-007. Center for International Business Education and Research, University of Illinois at Urbana-Cahampaign, Urbana-Champaign, Illinois.

——. 1993b. "Floods Control and Environment in Bangladesh: Experiences and Alternatives." Proceedings of the International Conference on Floods in Bangladesh: An Interdisciplinary Analysis of Alternative Solution Strategies. Working Paper No. 93-007. Center for International Business Education and Research, University of Illinois at Urbana-Cahampaign, Urbana-Champaign, Illinois.

Islam, N. 1990. "Let the Delta be a Delta: An Essay in Dissent on the Flood Problem in Bangladesh." *Journal of Social Studies* 48: 18-41.

Johnson, Bryan. 1988. "Bengalis Coping with Familiar Foe, but Threat of a Lost Harvest Loom." *Globe and Mail (Toronto)*, September 12.

Lele, S.M. 1991. "Sustainable Development: A Critical Review." *World Development*. 19(6): 607-621.

Manning, E.W. 1990. "Conservation Strategies: Providing the Vision for Sustainable Development." *Alternatives* 16:24-29.

Mirza, Munirul Qader. 1984. "Flood has Become a Nightmare." *Bangladesh Today* 2: 26-35.

Paul, Bimal K. 1984. "Perception of And Adjustment to Floods in Jamuna Floodplain, Bangladesh." *Human Ecology* 12:3-19.

Pearce, Fred and Gliver Tickell. 1993. "West Sinks Bangladesh Flood Plan." *New Scientist* 139:4.

Rahman, Atiur. 1989. "Human Responses to Natural Hazards: The Hope Lies in Social Networking." Paper presented at the 23rd Bengal Studies Conference, University of Manitoba, Manitoba, Winnipeg.

Rahman, Shamsur. 1984. "The Brahmaputra Right Bank Flood Embankment: Its Problems and Probable Solutions." Paper presented at the seminar on the Brahmaputra Right Bank Flood Embankment , Bangladesh Academy for Rural Development, Bogra, December 8.

Rasid, Harun. 1989. "Mini-Projects for a Mega-Problem: A Pragmatic Solution for the Flood Problem in Bangladesh." Proceedings of the International Conference on Bangladesh Floods: What Are the Solutions? International Society of Bangladesh, Montreal.

Rasid, Harun, and B.K. Paul. 1989. "Flood Problems in Bangladesh: Is There an Indigenous Solution?" *Environmental Management* 11(2): 155-173.

Rogers, P., Peter Lyndon and David Seckler. 1989. *Eastern Water Study: Strategies to Manage Flood and Drought in the Ganges-Brahmaputra Basin*. Irrigation Support Project for Asia and the Near East, Arlington, Virginia.

Rostow, W.W. 1960. *The Stage of Economic Growth: A Non-Communist Manifesto*. Cambridge, Mass.:Cambridge University Press.

Ruttan, Vernon W. 1986. "Assistance to Expand Agricultural Production." *World Development* 14(1).

Scudder, T. 1991. "The Need for Justification for Maintaining Transboundary Flood Regimes: The African Case." *Natural Resources Journal* 31(1): 75-107.

Sen, A.K. 1981. *Poverty and Famines: An Essay of Entitlement and Deprivation*. Oxford: Clarendon Press.

Stewart, K. 1988. "Post Flood: Assessment and Nutritional

Status of Children in Matlab, Bangladesh." Paper presented at the seminar on Regional and Global Environmental Perspectives, Dhaka, March 4-6.

Tarafdar, M.R. 1974. "Rivers and Flood problems in Bangladesh." in Kamaluddin, ed. *Studies in Bangladesh*. Bangladesh National Geographical Association, Dhaka.

United Nations Development Programme (UNDP). 1989. *Bangladesh Flood Policy Study,* Final Report. Dhaka: UNDP.

World Bank. 1970. *Proposal for an Action Program: East Pakistan Agriculture and Water Development*. Vol. 3. The Water Program, Report No. PS-2a. Washington, DC.

———. 1972. *Bangladesh: Land and Water Resources Sector Study*. Vol. 8. The Flood Problem, Technical Report No.24. Washington, DC.

———. 1987. *Bangladesh: Second Small Scale Flood Control, Drainage and Irrigation Project*. Report No.

6904-BD, Washington, DC.

———. 1990. "Flood Control in Bangladesh: A Plan for Action." World Bank Technical Paper No. 119, Washington, DC.

World Commission on Environment and Development (WCED). 1987. *Our Common Future*. New York: Oxford University Press.

Zaman, M.Q. 1986. "The Role of Social Relations in the Response to Riverbank Erosion Hazards and Population Resettlement in Bangladesh." In Anthony Oliver-Smith. ed., *Studies in Third World Societies*. Special Issue on Natural Disasters and Cultural Responses, College of William and Mary, Williamsburg, Virginia.

———. 1991. "Rivers of Life: Living with Floods in Bangladesh." Paper presented at the University of California at Los Angeles International Conference on the Impact of Natural Disasters, July 10-12. Los Angeles, California.

11

Public Involvement in Environmental Assessment of Tourism

Douglas Earl McLaren

Tourism is one of the fastest growing industries globally. Both industrial and developing countries continue to promote the industry as a tool of economic activity and development. Developing countries see tourism as the opportunity to earn scarce foreign exchange and to generate employment among both skilled and semi-skilled workers. Research indicates that the industry can contribute significantly to the economies of these countries (Lindberg 1991). Growth in tourism has been more rapid in developing countries than in industrial countries. However, decisionmakers and planners may not be fully assessing some of the long-term and potentially negative environmental, socioeconomic, and human impacts of tourism development.

Features of the natural and socio-cultural environment that are important resources for tourism (such as aesthetic and recreational resources) are particularly sensitive to disturbance by human activities. Without careful attention to the balance between the volume and type of tourist activity, on the one hand, and the sensitivities and carrying capacities of the resources being developed on the other, tourism projects can be not only environmentally harmful but also economically self-defeating (Duffield and Walker 1984).

Tourists increase demands on local infrastructure such as transportation, water supply, wastewater collection and treatment, solid waste disposal, and health care facilities as well as a variety of public services that are usually the responsibility of local government. The increased demands on an often unprepared local government can result in the failure of the public sectors in many countries to keep pace with the level of tourism development, as in areas such as Negril in western Jamaica and Cancun on the Mexican coast. In these heavily developed tourist areas, waste treatment and public transportation facilities, to name a few, may currently be overextended.

The failure of government planners to keep pace with rapid development is not limited to developing countries. Many local, community, and development planners in the United States, such as those in northern Virginia, have also failed to provide the necessary infrastructure to keep pace with over-development in their communities. On the positive side, a well-planned ecotourism project can combine conservation of natural and cultural sites with economic and recreational benefits (Lindberg 1991). This chapter will address these issues in the following sections.

Limitations of Current Environmental Assessment Process

General Environmental Issues

The acute unemployment conditions that prevail in many developing countries, approaching 40 percent or more, as well as the dearth of opportunities to earn valuable foreign exchange may blind host governments to many of the potentially negative environmental, social and socioeconomic impacts associated with many project opportunities (Beekuis 1981). Some of the most often overlooked factors in the environmental assessment (EA) process are:

• The carrying capacity of a local community to accommodate the development (that is, availability of health and sanitary facilities, and social services).

• Early and meaningful involvement of local communities.

• Local social and cultural conditions.

• Changes in employment patterns and skills including the immigration of secondary workers.

• Breakdown of traditional methods of social control and discipline.

• The possible rise in the cost of living due to inflation.

In addition to these factors, the unique impact of tourism developments on the environment requires special attention.

Special Environmental Assessment Needs of Tourism Projects

In general, the magnitude and scale of environmental impacts caused by a project depend on the size and type of the development proposed, relative to the fragility of the proposed environment. Notwithstanding, even small tourism projects warrant attention because of the close relationship between tourism and the environment; the many linkages (both economic and social) between tourism development and other sectors of the local community; and the rapid growth in the tourism industry in general and in ecotourism projects in particular.

The impacts of tourism development are not confined solely to the structural changes associated with such developments. They are also related to impacts that occur as a result of large numbers of tourists within a particular community, seasonal variations in the number of visitors, the possibility that the success of the project may eventually overwhelm and dilute the attraction, and the stimulation of indigenous enterprise both to develop and support the industry (Duffield and Walker 1984).

Therefore, a more rigorous and comprehensive approach is needed to assess the environmental and human impacts related to the tourism industry. The symbiotic relationship between tourism, the environment, visitors, and a country's people, mandates the need to also ensure that the local host community perspective is appreciated and factored into the decisionmaking process. Decisionmakers must recognize that the industry is dynamic and interactive with the local community, sensitive to good service delivery and the hospitality of the local community, and very sensitive to local political unrest and social disorder.

Other special issues associated with tourism development include (World Bank 1991):
• Most tourists from industrial countries use more water and other resources and generate more waste per capita than do residents of developing countries.
• Adequate amounts of potable water, and facilities for adequate wastewater treatment and solid waste disposal may not be available in the local community.
• The effect of seasonal population growth on the local community creates the need for additional facilities to meet peak demands that may be underutilized in slow periods.
• Activities such as tours of archaeological sites may conflict with local religious beliefs and practices.

• The influx of large numbers of foreigners into a community and the potential conflict with contrasting life styles can have serious impacts on local cultures.

In general, environmental assessments of tourism projects should also include analyses of the projected social and indirect costs and benefits. Where the benefits of tourism may be assumed to accrue to local residents, it is likely that the residents may incur more of the costs and enjoy fewer of the benefits than visitors, immigrant workers, or commercial intermediaries.

Key Roles and Responsibilities in the Assessment Process

The various roles and responsibilities of local and national host governments for ensuring the implementation of the EA process are outlined in this section. The discussion underscores the need for coordinated planning by government agencies and other groups involved in the development process, mainly the host government, funding agencies, the host community, and the project developer.

The Host Government

National host governments must develop appropriate responses to the pressing needs of new and expanded environmental and socioeconomic assessments. Early steps in this process should include: instilling a national commitment to environmental concerns; setting priorities and formulating policies; establishing the appropriate legal and regulatory framework; implementing an effective administrative structure; providing essential management skills and enhancing institutional support structures; engaging local governments and mandating involvement of the public; providing adequate funding; and ensuring accountability.

INSTILLING A NATIONAL COMMITMENT TO ENVIRONMENTAL CONCERNS. Stopping environmental damage often involves taking rights away from people who may be politically powerful. On the other hand, those who are hurt when the environment is degraded and who stand to gain most from sound policies, are often the poor and the weak. They may be less politically powerful than the polluters the governments must challenge. Enlightened and informed government leadership is essential to correct this imbalance and to establish some environmental equity, nationally. Governments should underscore their commitment to the environment by incorporating environmental planning at all levels of the bureaucracy and by making the commitment publicly.

SETTING PRIORITIES AND FORMULATING POLICIES. The setting of national priorities and formulating policies is essential for making the most of scarce management resources. Top priority must be given to broadening the scope of EAs to include extensive consideration of socioeconomic issues in addition to the consideration of the traditional environmental issues. Environmental planning must not be merely an afterthought; it must be an essential part of the central government planning process. Coordinating and planning environmental activities are essential since environmental issues cut across normal bounds of bureaucratic responsibility. The activities of all government agencies must also be coordinated to be effective and responsive to national, regional, and local environmental concerns.

ESTABLISHING THE APPROPRIATE LEGAL AND REGULATORY FRAMEWORK. It is imperative that the requirement for the preparation of environmental assessments be legislated as a part of the general environmental statutes in order to establish the correct legal framework for implementation. Appropriate flow-down regulations and enforcement measures are also necessary to promote efficient and effective implementation and administration of these statutes. These provisions also need to be integrated into the existing government and judicial procedures and into local customs and practices.

IMPLEMENTING AN EFFECTIVE ADMINISTRATIVE STRUCTURE. Governments need to develop an effective management and administrative structure for implementing and enforcing the new environmental framework. Adequate support services must be in place so that the practices run smoothly. The World Bank asserts that the establishment of a formal high-level agency for setting policies and ensuring implementation across sectors has sharply improved environmental management in Brazil, China, and Nigeria (World Bank 1992b).

Where inter-sectoral decisions need to be made, such as the management of a reservoir catchment area, the conservation of a forest area, and the development of agricultural lands, coordination is required to ensure efficient and cost-effective resource management. As stated earlier, mechanisms for proper coordination are essential.

PROVIDING ESSENTIAL SKILLS AND ENHANCING THE INSTITUTIONAL SUPPORT STRUCTURES. Governments around the world are actively seeking to strengthen their institutional capacity for environmental management. Environmental executing agencies must be given adequately trained staff to manage the various programs. Environmental management requires a wide mix of skills including: natural or biological scientists, social scientists, engineers, and professional managers and planners. In order to provide the necessary technical skills and other resources, environmental nongovernmental organizations (NGOs) and academic institutions, such as local or regional universities, should be utilized.

Academic institutions often possess the technical skills and infrastructure needed to undertake many of the required environmental and social studies and research. They also possess the moral authority and political influence to represent the distributive justice interests of the poor and disadvantaged. In addition, by relying on regional NGOs or academic institutions, the base of relevant skills in a particular geographical area or region can be substantially increased.

ENGAGING LOCAL GOVERNMENTS AND MANDATING INVOLVEMENT OF THE PUBLIC. Once national priorities and policies have been set, it is often cost-effective to solve problems at the local level. Public agencies need training in participatory approaches and a clear indication from senior management of the importance of participation. Day to day program administration can be delegated to local governments. Project developers must be an integral part of this environmental process because they are often the only major group involved in a project at the formulation stages. The flow of authority from national to local governments will empower local leaders to influence project planning and implementation.

PROVIDING ADEQUATE FUNDING. Adequate funding of environmental programs is essential to meeting the objectives of the environmental management program. Host governments should supplement their financial investments in their environmental programs with funding from international donor agencies. Many of the donor agencies already have special funding facilities to support such programs. One such facility is the Global Environment Facility (GEF), which is jointly managed by the United Nations Environment

Programme (UNEP), the United Nations Development Programme (UNDP) and the World Bank. The GEF supports projects in developing countries to reduce global warming, preserve the earth's biological diversity, protect international waters, and prevent further depletion of the ozone layer (World Bank 1992a).

ENSURING ACCOUNTABILITY. Agencies that implement projects should be held accountable for the effects of their actions and should be kept organizationally separate from regulatory and monitoring bodies. The public agencies that implement or regulate programs that may potentially have adverse effects on the environment must be held accountable for the environmental impact of their activities. The same applies to both private and public funding agencies.

Funding Agencies

The availability of either private or public financing may be the major factor that determines whether or not a particular development will ultimately occur in an area. Consequently, the role of financing agencies (whether private investors or lenders, or international development agencies) can be pivotal to the implementation of progressive environmental assessment, management, and mitigation practices. Therefore, a necessary element of any comprehensive environmental legislation should be to make the preparation of an EA a requirement for obtaining either public or private financing for projects over a certain size and complexity. A further requirement for funding would be the commitment by the project proponent or developer to avoid or mitigate adverse impacts. The possibility of lender or investor liability under such environmental statutes would be a compelling incentive for compliance.

International donor agencies should assume a more assertive role in promoting or encouraging comprehensive assessments of project impacts during the sectoral and regional planning stages when considering funding requests. The World Bank has already undertaken bold new steps in this direction. International development institutions such as the United Nations Educational, Scientific, and Cultural Organization (UNESCO), UNDP, and the World Health Organization (WHO) can contribute to the EA exercise by providing expert technical advice *tailored to local needs* in specific areas, such as anthropology, cultural preservation, health, environmental management, and socioeconomic impact assessment and mitigation. Additional

assistance should also be earmarked for technical and management assistance, training, and institutional support.

A key principle of the EA exercise will be the need to solicit and incorporate early and continuous public or local involvement in the EA process. Such involvement will ensure the development of a more viable and sustainable industry.

The Host Community

The balancing of economic and social benefits and environmental costs requires both subjective judgments and detailed knowledge of local circumstances and conditions. Neither governments nor donor agencies are necessarily equipped to judge the priorities of the local populace and the value that they place on their environment. A participatory process is therefore essential. In order to utilize effectively the scarce resources, governments should encourage the involvement of both the private sector and local community leaders and entrepreneurs in the preparation of environmental assessments.

There are many advantages to local participation in a project. These advantages are best articulated by Hudspeth (1982) as follows. First, local participation functions as an early warning system by permitting managers to avoid decisions that would cause animosity between them and the local population. When managers take the time to listen, they enlist confidence, trust, and support from the local population. Studies have shown that people will only support projects that directly benefit them. Including a participation program in the early stage of a project provides the opportunity for the local community to become educated about the purpose and benefits of the project, thereby facilitating support for the project.

Second, public involvement fosters better planning and decisionmaking. Conflicting viewpoints are brought out in the open and resolved during the planning process; additional information is provided that may quantify environmental values; affected persons, often unrecognized, are given a chance to voice their opinion; a wider array of alternatives may be developed from public opinions; and issues, impacts, and management alternatives are better identified. Hence, the expression of differing opinions may be quite beneficial both socially and economically, reducing the likelihood of disruptive community conflict in the future (Coser 1956).

Third, ensuring local input legitimizes the decisionmaking process. The accountability of project managers is reinforced, and local involvement is secured. The involvement of diverse groups with particular concerns or expertise, may elicit relevant information regarding the nature and scope of potential environmental effects and the appropriate mitigation strategies (Drake 1991).

Finally, the active involvement of the public can provide the means to leverage limited technical and human resources to benefit the maximum number of people.

PUBLIC PARTICIPATION IN DEMOCRATIC INDUSTRIAL COUNTRIES. Public consultation is now accepted as an essential part of the EA process in industrial countries. However, the EAs performed in those countries provide little guidance for involving local communities in developing countries. A major premise of public consultation in most industrial countries is that citizens who participate are accustomed to certain protections of free speech and political freedom, and therefore "do not run major personal or political risk in questioning proposed government actions" (World Bank 1991).

In many developing countries, an environmental assessment team cannot operate on these premises because of local cultural constraints, the absence of democratic free speech traditions, and the lack of political and economic power for those most likely to bear the adverse impacts associated with a project. Therefore, the environmental assessment team must be more proactive and persistent in encouraging and eliciting public participation. In other words, the team must actively incorporate the opinions of local citizens into the project's decisionmaking process.

DEVELOPMENT OF A PUBLIC PARTICIPATAION PROGRAM. An environmental assessment program should incorporate local customs and procedures, and develop a working relationship with local citizens at an early stage. Public consultation and the whole EA exercise should be a continuous and iterative process in which new issues are allowed to emerge and insignificant ones are set aside. The underlying theme is participatory decisionmaking, including participation in EA design, ranking of alternatives, and the selection of studies to be undertaken. Some of the relevant questions that should be asked when developing a community participation program are (World Bank 1991):

• Who are the people potentially affected by the project and what are the broad social groups and authority structures present?

• Who are the local community leaders and influential groups in the community?

• How effective are the grassroots organizations or NGOs in the community?

• What is the level of community awareness of the proposed project?

• What roles do political parties and religious or cultural groups play?

• How do government agencies communicate with the local community?

• How effective will the print and electronic media be in informing the public about the project?

Social scientists (anthropologists, sociologists, social workers, and so forth) from the host country have a great deal of expertise regarding their own people, languages, and cultures. These professionals should be consulted on how best to involve people, and they should be made an integral part of the environmental assessment team.

The public participation program should include continued feedback to those consulted. Particular attention should be given to discussing choices and the tentative conclusions of studies and EA drafts, and to explaining how they are being incorporated into project feasibility design and implementation plans. A possible role for the public could be to assist in determining who is responsible for initiating and implementing each action, how each action will be taken, and when the action will be taken. Local citizens could also be involved in the management phase of the project. The support of local business organizations should also be solicited.

INFORMATION, EDUCATION AND COMMUNICATION. A well-designed and implemented community involvement program will incorporate information, education and communication elements. These elements can play a useful role in project development and planning, assessment and mitigation of project impacts, institutional strengthening, and motivation-assimilation into the new project or activity. A successful program will enable information exchange between the local community and the project developer or government agency. This will in return ensure a minimum of social dislocation, development of effective impact mitigation measures, and acceptance of the project in the community.

When the participation process enables two-way communication such that information about the community is obtained from the citizens and, in turn, citizens are educated, the advantages to the project development will outweigh the costs of citizen involvement to the project developers. Lessons learned from existing local public health education programs can be applied to public information, education and communication programs in the environmental area. The print and electronic media are also important elements in providing effective information and influencing opinion.

Finally, by far the most important factor in developing these programs is that they have to start very early on if they are to be meaningful. They must also provide the public with genuine opportunities to influence the decisions that will affect their lives.

The Project Developer

In most instances, environmental assessments are triggered, if at all, during the feasibility stage of a project. However, by this time in the project cycle, the dimensions and specific features of the project (such as site layout and building dimensions) have already been defined and the project concept has developed a constituency of its own. Project changes to accommodate environmental and other considerations then become more difficult, if not impossible, to incorporate.

If EAs are to develop the potential for addressing the full range of environmental and social impacts and the appropriate mitigation measures for a proposed project, then these concerns should be addressed at the earliest possible date. The EA, or at least, a "mini EA," should be initiated during the conceptual or formulation stages by the proponents of the project or by the project developers. In this manner, environmental and social considerations can be incorporated into project formulation and development. Any changes that are prompted by the evaluation of impacts can then be treated as ordinary and necessary project modifications to accommodate site conditions, and not isolated and branded as "costly and time-consuming changes to satisfy the environmentalists."

There is a need to establish a user-friendly and manageable mechanism for project developers to use in their consideration of potential impacts. Project developers must be an integral part of this environmental process because of their potential investment in the project, and the fact that they are often the only major group involved in the project at the formulation stages. The checklist in appendix 11-1 was developed for use by project planners and developers to scope the potential impacts from tourism and other types of projects. This checklist was derived substantially from the State Environmental Quality Review Act, SEQR Handbook (1982) that was developed by the New York State Department of Environmental Conservation, with appropriate modifications. Detailed environmental assessments of potential impacts identified in the checklist should be undertaken as the project evolves.

An Expanded Scope for Impact Assessments

The goals of development projects can be frustrated through unanticipated or unintended negative social or environmental impacts that reduce the desired benefits or even threaten the sustainability of the project. The objective of the EA should be to assess the magnitude of the expected impacts of induced development so that mitigating actions can be planned on an adequate scale. A comprehensive environmental assessment should also identify the social changes, evaluate the social costs of long-term continuation of the project, and formulate strategies to achieve the desired objectives. Such an expanded environmental and social assessment (E&SA) should adequately analyze the nature and effectiveness of the local and regional institutions that may have responsibility for planning and administrative decisions (Branch and others 1984).

Content of the Environmental and Social Assessment

In order to identify and assess social impacts, we need information on the following subjects in addition to the traditional environmental areas: ethnic or tribal affiliation, occupation, socioeconomic status, age and gender. Social information in the above areas can be used to: verify or modify existing assumptions about the local population that may be pivotal in environmental and social assessments; conduct social analysis in order to predict the likely response of local groups to a project; and formulate social strategies for mitigating environmental impacts (World Bank 1991). Many projects also have a potential impact on archaeological sites which are considered part of a country's cultural heritage. Since cultural resources are part of the resource base, it is therefore important that development options be evaluated for potential impacts on cultural property.

Both urban and rural populations depend upon a network of neighbors and relatives to provide a range of low-cost social and socioeconomic support services. These range from child care to diversification of income-earning opportunities to informal credit arrangements. Disruption of these networks due to shifting employment patterns and migration practices places at risk the affected people, particularly women, children and the aged. Consequently, adequate sociological and anthropological studies should be undertaken to assess the resulting project impacts and to develop strategies to overcome them.

Geographic Range of the Assessment

In order to be able to initiate the E&SA process during the formulation stage of a specific project, some mechanism should be instituted to address regional environmental concerns. Familiarity with the physical conditions and requirements of adjoining communities or those sharing common resources (such as water supplies or waste disposal facilities) is essential to address the full range of potential impacts of any project. Therefore, the construction of project support facilities, and other unrelated facilities under consideration or not yet operational within the same geographic region, should be factored into the E&SA process. Without including these areas in the E&SA process, the cumulative burden of these projects cannot be adequately addressed.

A common shortcoming in the design and environmental assessment of such projects is the failure to plan for the influx of a secondary population of workers and their families who take advantage of the new economic opportunities created, and who may also place a burden on the surrounding environment for food, living space, and social services. The construction of facilities by private entrepreneurs in response to the demands of these migrants can cause haphazard development in the community. Such impacts should be taken into account when preparing environmental assessments.

Finally, the migration of workers into the tourist industry may occur at the expense of other productive sectors of the economy, such as agriculture. In many countries, it is very difficult to retain workers in the agricultural sector when other more lucrative and glamorous opportunities are available in a neighboring tourist resort area.

Mitigation Measures

A key element of any E&SA process is the development of a procedure to avoid adverse impacts and to devise appropriate and effective strategies to mitigate these impacts. Such mitigation strategies should address the concerns and incorporate the suggestions of those most affected by the project—namely, residents of the local community. Involvement of the local community in planning appropriate mitigation strategies can resurrect a project concept that may not otherwise be viable, while satisfying the concerns of environmental groups and other interested parties.

Some other mitigation measures that could be considered, depending on the scale and scope of the project, include:

• Providing training for local people, especially for those in less-skilled jobs, and improved transport facilities for workers.

• Promoting investment in local resources to improve the local economic resource base and to capitalize on the expanded economic opportunities.

• Strengthening existing local institutions or developing new ones to undertake long-term development and regional planning, and to provide expanded social services for the public.

• Planning adequate health care, drinking water and sanitary facilities for the benefit of the community.

• Providing the necessary social, psychological and counseling services to cope with socioeconomic changes.

The E&SA team should also develop an ongoing monitoring and evaluation program to periodically assess the impacts of the project that may not be predictable or may not be anticipated at the outset.

The Environmental and Social Assessment Team

As stated earlier, in order to assess the cumulative burden of any project in time for the required design changes to be made, at least a preliminary E&SA must be started during project formulation. The skills required at this stage of project development will be broader and more diversified than those needed, for instance, during the construction and implementation stages. Consequently, the E&SA team should be multi-disciplinary and should be able to address both regional and sectoral concerns in their evaluations of project design options. Depending on the nature of the project and the host environment, the team could include environmental scientists, sociologists, anthropologists, archaeologists, engineers, biological scientists, and community representatives. Such a diversified team, together with an involved public, should be able to assess the environmental and socioeconomic impacts associated with the proposed project and to recommend approaches for avoiding or mitigating anticipated impacts.

Application to Tourism Development Projects

The tourist industry is often perceived as being environmentally benign relative to other industries such as manufacturing or chemical processing. However, if the particular characteristics of tourism projects are acknowledged, many of the impact assessment tools that have been developed for other types of projects may also be applied to that industry. For example, once the transient and seasonal nature of tourism is recognized, the E&SA team may apply traditional assessment methods to assess the negative effects of seasonal demands on resources as well as the corresponding recuperative rates for these resources.

Public participation in tourism development is also essential since it is the local population that must often bear the stress of these seasonal impacts and the cost of providing for peak-load services and resources. Also, because many of these impacts are social in nature, an active public involvement process may help to develop effective solutions to local community concerns. Costs and rewards may be shared more equitably and be more widely appreciated, and in return the industry can be expected to receive greater community support.

The many small entrepreneurs, such as local craftsmen, who tend to be attracted to the industry should also be integrated into the impact assessment and mitigation process. They should be encouraged to participate throughout the process, particularly during the project conceptualization or formulation stages. In this way, it will be possible to broaden community support for developing and implementing impact avoidance and mitigation measures, while encouraging broad-based economic development.

Conclusions

Tourism is a major contributor to the economies of many industrial as well as developing countries. The industry contributes significantly to employment in these areas, particularly in providing lower-skill jobs. Indeed, in certain countries, the industry is the only viable economic activity. Tourism is also a major earner of scarce foreign exchange for many developing countries. Although the industry can contribute to a local economy, it is still important that the potentially negative impacts of developing an industry or specific projects be assessed comprehensively. Specifically, more attention needs to be paid to the assessment of socioeconomic impacts

attributable directly and indirectly to the industry.

There needs to be a more clearly defined role for host governments and the public in the management of their environmental resources, and especially in the assessment of environmental and socioeconomic impacts. Governments need to assume a more assertive role in environmental planning and to establish the appropriate legal and institutional framework for managing these functions. They also need to commit the resources required to monitor and enforce their regulations and programs, and to support public participation in the process. Otherwise, tourism can become a collaborative new form of de facto colonization that exploits resources and does not sustain them for the benefit of the local community.

The environmental function must be thoroughly integrated with other governmental functions and be able to provide state-of-the-art technology and support to the other government agencies, including the development of mitigation strategies. The environmental agency must also promote the concept of E&SA teams combining legal, management, institutional, socioeconomic, technical, and environmental skills. The success of E&SA teams, when assessing tourism projects, depends on recognizing the distinct cyclical nature of the industry, as well as the importance of involving the general public and a broad spectrum of local economic interests in the assessment process.

Funding agencies can promote awareness of environmental concerns by making funding dependent on the preparation of responsive environmental and social assessments and the implementation of effective measures to avoid and mitigate impacts. Legislation to compel compliance by these funding agencies may also be necessary. International donor agencies can contribute to this process by providing long-term financing, technical assistance, training, and management support.

Appendix 11-1. Checklist for Preliminary Assessment of Project Impacts

This is a brief checklist for conducting a preliminary environmental/socioeconomic impact assessment that could be used for tourism and other types of projects. It provides a preliminary determination of potential impacts and the applicability of mitigation measures. The "Proposed Action" is the contemplated activity that may have an impact on the community or the environment.

To assess the magnitude and significance of the impact or effect, consider: the probability of the impact or effect occurring; the duration of the impact or effect; its irreversibility, including permanently lost resources or values; whether the impact or effect can be controlled; the regional consequence of the impact or effect; its potential divergence from local needs and goals; and whether known objections to the project apply to this impact. For each numbered question indicate whether the potential impact is: small to moderate; large; and whether the impact can be reduced or mitigated by a change in the project.

Impact on Land

1. Will the Proposed Action result in a physical change to the project site?
    Examples:
    • Construction on land with a high water table.
    • Construction in or around a designated floodway.
    • Other impacts [omitted hereafter].
    • Mitigation actions [omitted hereafter].
2. Will there be an effect on unique or unusual land forms found on the site (i.e., cliffs, dunes, geological formations, etc.)?
    Examples:
    • Specific Land Forms

Impact on Water

3. Will the Proposed Action affect any protected or non-protected water body?
    Examples:
    • Developable area of site contains a protected water body.
    • Construction of any body of water or increase or decrease in any body of water.
4. Will the Proposed Action affect surface or groundwater quality or quantity?
    Examples:
    • Proposed Actiion requires use of a new source of water (e.g., wells).
    • Construction or operation may cause contamination of water supplies.
    • Proposed Action will adversely affect groundwater.
    • Proposed Action will likely cause siltation or other discharge into an existing body of water.
    • Proposed Action locates facilities that may require new or expansion of existing water, sewer or waste treatment and/or storage facilities.
5. Will the Proposed Action alter drainage flow or patterns, or alter surface water runoff?
    Examples:
    • Proposed Action would change flood water flows and/or may cause substantial erosion.
    • Proposed Action is incompatible with existing drainage patterns.
    • Proposed Action will allow development in a designated floodway.

Impact on Air

6. Will the Proposed Action affect air quality?
    Examples:
    • Proposed Action will have an adverse effect on ambient air quality?

Impact on Plants and Animals

7. Will the Proposed Action affect any threatened or endangered species?
    Examples:
    • Reduction of one or more species using the site, over or near the site, or found on the site.
    • Removal of any portion of a critical or significant wildlife habitat.
8. Will the Proposed Action substantially affect non-threatened or non-endangered species?
    Examples:
    • Proposed Action would substantially interfere with resident or migratory fish, shell fish, or wildlife species.
    • Proposed Action requires the removal of significant acreage of mature forest or other locally important vegetation.

Impact on Agricultural Land Resources

9. Will the Proposed Action affect agricultural land resources?
    Examples:
    • The Proposed Action would limit access to agricultural land or would effectively convert agricultural land to non-agricultural use.

Impact on Aesthetic Resources

10. Will the Proposed Action affect aesthetic resources?
    Examples:
    • Proposed land uses or project components are obviously different from or in sharp contrast to current surrounding land use patterns, or they would significantly reduce or eliminate the aesthetic value of the area.

Impact on Historic and Archaeological Resources

11. Will the Proposed Action impact any site or structure of historic, pre-historic, or paleontological importance?
   Examples:
   • Proposed Action will have an impact on an archaeological site or fossil bed located within the project site.
   • Proposed Action will occur in a sensitive archaeological area.

Impact on Open Space Recreation

12. Will the Proposed Action affect the quantity or quality of existing or future open spaces or recreational opportunities?
   Examples:
   • The permanent foreclosure of a future recreational opportunity or a major reduction of an open space important to the community.

Impact on Transportation

13. Will there be an effect on existing transportation systems?
   Examples:
   • Proposed Action will result in major traffic problems.
   • Proposed Action will result in the need for major construction of roads and other transportation systems.

Impact on Energy

14. Will the Proposed Action affect the community's sources of fuel or its energy supply?
   • Proposed Action will significantly increase the use of any form of energy in the municipality or will require the creation or substantial extension of an energy transmission or supply system for the area.

Noise and Odor Impacts

15. Will there be objectionable odors, noise, or vibrations as a result of the Proposed Action?
   Examples:
   • Odors or vibrations will occur routinely.
   • Proposed Action will produce operating noise exceeding the local ambient noise levels or will remove natural noise barriers.

16. Will the Proposed Action affect public health and safety?
   Examples:
   • Proposed Action may cause a risk of explosion or release of hazardous substances.
   • Proposed Action may result in excavation or other disturbance close to a site used for the disposal of solid or hazardous waste.

Impact on Community or Neighborhood

17. Will the Proposed Action affect the character of the existing community?
   Examples:
   • The permanent population of the city, town, or village in which the project is located is likely to grow by more that 5%.
   • The municipal budget for capital expenditures or operating services will increase by more than 5% per year as a result of this project.
   • Proposed Action will conflict with officially adopted plans or goals.
   • Proposed Action will change the density of land use.
   • Proposed Action will replace or eliminate existing facilities, structures, or areas of historic importance to the community.
   • Development will create a demand for additional community or social and family support services.
   • Proposed Action will set an important precedent for future projects.
   • Proposed Action will create or eliminate employment or will result in diversion of labor and other resources from other productive sectors.

18. Will there be public controversy related to the Proposed Action?

Source: Derived from New York State Department of Environmental Conservation, SEQR Handbook 1982.

References

Beekuis, Jeanne V. 1981. "Tourism in the Caribbean: Impacts on the Economic Social and Natural Environments." *Ambio* 10(6):325-331.

Branch, Kristi, Douglas A. Hooper, James Thompson, and James Creighton. 1984. *Guide to Social Assessment: A Framework for Assessing Social Change*. Boulder, Colorado: Westview Press.

Coser, Lewis A. 1956. *The Functions of Social Conflict*. Glencoe, Illinois: Free Press.

Drake, Susan. 1991. "Development of a Local Participation Plan for Ecotourism Projects." In Jon A. Kusler, ed., *Ecotourism and Resource Conservation*. Second International Symposium, November 27-December 3. Miami Beach, Florida.

Duffield, Brian S., and Susan E. Walker. 1984. "The Assessment of Tourism Impacts." In Brian D. Clark, Alexander Gilad, Ronald Bisset, and Paul Tomlinson, eds., *Perspectives on Environmental Impact Assessment*.

New York: Kumer Academic Press.

Hudspeth, Thomas R. 1982. "Citizen Participation in Revitalization of the Burlington, Vermont Waterfront." Ph.D. dissertation, University of Vermont, Burlington, Vermont.

Lindberg, Kreg. 1991. *Policies for Maximizing Nature Tourism's Ecological Benefits.* Washington, DC: World Resources Institute.

New York State Department of Environmental Conservation, Division of Regulatory Affairs. 1982. *The State Environmental Quality Review Act, SEQR Handbook.* Albany, New York.

World Bank. 1991. *Environmental Assessment Sourcebook.* Vol. I, Policies Procedures and Cross-Sectoral Issues. Technical Paper 139. Vol. 2. Sectoral Guidelines. Technical Paper 140. Vol. 3. Guidelines for Environmental Assessment of Energy and Industry Projects. Technical Paper 154. Washington, DC.

———. 1992a. *Special Report: The World Bank, the Environment and Development.* Washington, DC.

———. 1992b. *World Development Report 1992: Development and the Environment.* New York: Oxford University Press.

Part IV
Environmental Assessment and Sustainability

12

The Sustainable Supply Rule for Economic Evaluation of Natural Capital Depletion

Joachim von Amsberg

In economic evaluations of resource extraction projects, the user or depletion cost is often ignored. Such neglect of the opportunity costs of resource depletion is clearly incorrect and would bias project selection toward extraction projects. When an attempt is made to evaluate nonrenewable resource depletion, however, a broader question is raised about how depletion of natural capital should be treated in cost-benefit analysis. The objective of this chapter is to provide an operational rule for determining a shadow price for the depletion of a natural resource as well as for determining the appropriate compensation of future generations for the depletion.

Natural capital is defined as all the natural resources that, in a broad sense, provide service to humans. Natural capital encompasses all stocks of nonrenewable resources (such as oil, gas and mineral deposits) and renewable resources (such as forests and fisheries). It also includes the biosphere's capacity to sustain human life and economic activities through, for example, provision of clean air, water and a limited capacity to absorb waste products. The term natural capital draws an analogy with humanmade capital: capital, in either case, is the stock of assets from which services can be derived. However, like humanmade capital, natural capital is more than an arbitrary aggregation of stocks of assets. It is a complicated web of interrelations between assets and processes that can provide a wide variety of services to humans. Human activities that use natural capital within its capacity to regenerate are considered sustainable. This chapter deals with other activities that go beyond that limit, that deplete natural capital and hence reduce the earth's capacity to support critical services in the future.

Even though there is growing evidence that we are moving from an "empty world" to a "full world" (Daly 1992), natural capital is still frequently treated as a free good. The indications of long-term, and often irreversible, global environmental impacts from

human economic activities were summarized in the Brundtland Report (WCED 1987). In a increasingly crowded world, the default assumption of natural capital as a free good needs to be replaced. In fact, any unsustainable activity must be replaced by a sustainable activity in the long run.

This chapter shows how economic analysis tools that were developed for an almost empty world can be adjusted for a full world. In the first section, I discuss and summarize deficiencies of conventional analysis of natural capital depletion that cause the cost to be underestimated. The next section argues that intergenerational justice demands adequate compensation of future generations for the depletion of natural capital. The third section discusses sustainability constraints that would overcome the deficiencies of conventional analysis. The next section suggests a practical approach for integrating a sustainability constraint with project analysis. The proposed "sustainable supply rule" would allow derivation of a sustainable price for the depletion of natural capital that should be used as a shadow price in project analysis. Finally, a case study is presented in which the sustainable supply rule is applied to calculate a sustainable price for the depletion of oil in Nigeria.[1]

Deficiencies in Conventional Evaluation of Natural Capital Depletion

In the simplest of all worlds without extraction costs and without uncertainty, conventional analysis of maximizing social benefits from depletion of a nonrenewable resource would require depletion at a rate such that the price of the resource would rise at a rate equal to the economy's interest rate (Hotelling 1931). Correspondingly, the price of a renewable resource would have to change with the interest rate minus the natural rate of growth or regeneration of the resource. The initial price for a nonrenewable resource (or a renewable resource with a growth rate below the interest rate for all stock levels) would be set such that the resource is depleted exactly at the time when the rising price reaches the point where demand is reduced to zero. The inter-temporal resource allocation, resulting from the Hotelling rule, would be efficient since rents derived from the resource could be invested at the rate of interest such that no other resource depletion path would Pareto-dominate the outcome. This implies that earlier generations would have available large quantities of the resource at a low price and could invest a portion of the rents derived from the resource such that no other allocation of the resource would make all generations better off. In a world with perfect markets for natural capital, efficient depletion would be brought about by market mechanisms.

If there were a perfect market for a privately owned resource, the appropriate shadow price for resource extraction would be the market price of the resource in the ground. An extraction project should be undertaken whenever the social benefits from the resource use minus extraction costs exceed the market price of the resource in the ground. If there was no perfect market for the resource, depletion would have to be shadow priced by determining the appropriate user cost. This user cost would be the lesser of the discounted cost of procuring the resource from other sources after depletion and the discounted net benefits from resource use forgone because of depletion. A depletion project would be considered worthwhile whenever the price of the resource is expected to rise at less than the rate of interest. There are a variety of reasons why evaluation of natural capital depletion by conventional resource economic theory is deficient, but basic among them are the market failures that lead to deviations of the market price from the economic value of natural capital and the systematic biases against remedying these market failures.

Lack of Reliable Market Prices for Natural Capital

An owner of humanmade capital would ensure that property rights for the investment be established and that markets existed for the capital and outputs of the investment. By contrast, there is no owner or investor for natural capital to ensure the existence of property rights and markets for such capital. Therefore, property rights are not a prerequisite for the markets for many types of natural capital. Creating markets for natural capital, however, is difficult because many natural resources have public-good characteristics. These resources include fisheries,

public rangelands, groundwater and the absorption capacity of air and water. Without institutions to alleviate the market failure, use of these resources generates external costs that are not considered in individual decisionmaking. However, institutional arrangements are costly. Even where institutional arrangements are made and property rights are assigned, they are often less secure than those for other assets. Furthermore, governments may not have the institutional strength to restrict access to common property resources, resulting in inefficient overuse and underpricing of the resource.

Environmental externalities and the lack of markets can be remedied by, for example, Pigou taxes or trade with emission certificates (Baumol and Oates 1988). However, there are few incentives for policymakers to use these instruments, and they rarely do. Even if Pigou taxes were implemented for all known and proven external costs, the long lag from the time environmental damage occurs to its discovery and then to political recognition and action, would lead to consistent underestimation of external costs. Institutional arrangements for overcoming currently observed market failures is not sufficient. Static consideration of policies to internalize externalities neglects dynamic incentives for the generation of external costs. For utility-maximizing individuals, profit-maximizing corporations, and social welfare-maximizing local or national governments, there is a systematic incentive to generate internal benefits not only by productive activities but also by shifting costs to external entities. Costs of depletion of natural capital can be shifted to outside individuals, corporations or other regions or countries. This pervasive incentive to invent new ways of depleting natural capital without paying for it causes governments to notoriously lag behind in charging for the use of natural capital or securing property rights. Together, these factors explain some of the dramatic deficiencies in environmental policies and the lack of reliable market prices for natural capital.

Even if markets for natural capital exist, the market price is likely to underestimate the social opportunity cost of resource depletion. The opportunity costs of depletion are the discounted future benefits forgone because of depletion. Hence the opportunity cost depends on the discount rate used by the decisionmaker. If the decisionmaker uses a discount rate higher than the social discount rate, the resource would be depleted too fast and prices would be less than the social opportunity cost. An extensive body of literature deals with the complex question whether private and social discount rates do or do not coincide.[2] The main arguments for a difference between the two rates are based on differences between social and individual risk (such as risk of death that is absent from social considerations), taxes, and capital market imperfections. Also, because of external benefits associated with investment in natural capital (such as a forest that provides recreational value, climatic stabilization, soil stabilization and habitat for wildlife) and external costs associated with industrial investment (such as pollution and waste products of an industrial plant), the discount rate of profit-maximizing resource owners is likely to be higher than the social discount rate.

Other reasons for decisionmakers to apply a discount rate higher than the social discount rate are based on resource owner behavior that is inconsistent with profit maximization. The manager of a company who knows more than the shareholders about the value of the natural resource owned by the company would have an incentive to underestimate future opportunity costs in order to boost present profits and his own corresponding compensation. In case of publicly owned resources, the incentives of politicians are similarly distorted. Managers in lending agencies face incentives that are biased toward achieving short-term benefits due to the difficulties involved in introducing a system of personal long-term accountability. While neglect of opportunity costs is acceptable in a marginal project that does not impact on market prices, the aggregate behavior of managers and politicians who ignore or underestimate user costs would have non-marginal effects and depress market prices for natural capital.

Difficulties with Shadow Pricing Natural Capital

Where there are no correct market prices for the depletion of natural capital, shadow pricing is required to evaluate a depletion project. The shadow price of natural capital is its opportunity cost or the value of natural capital in its next best present or future use. Assessing this opportunity cost is a difficult task since for all global resources (such as oceans, atmosphere), non-tradable resources (such as forests) and even tradable resources evaluated from a global perspective (maximizing social welfare on a global and not a national level), the best of all possible alternative uses, now or at any time in the future, has to be determined in order to be able to shadow price the resource. If the depletion of a tradable resource is evaluated from a national point of view, the future price of the resource, after depletion, has to be predicted.

While the opportunity cost of depleting a stock of a natural resource is generally recognized as the user cost, the applicability of the opportunity cost concept to all other types of natural capital depletion is less recognized. Depletion excludes or diminishes the potential benefits from identical or alternative activities now or in the future and hence implies a social opportunity cost that should be reflected in the shadow price. For example, the first factory polluting the air in a specific area may not cause any environmental damage. However, if a second economically feasible factory would cause such damage, the first factory would have caused a social opportunity cost that, for efficiency reasons, should be allocated to that factory as a user charge for a non-marketed production factor (the decreased absorption capacity of the natural environment). As the example shows, in a world with discrete investment opportunities, costs for use of the environment can accrue even in the absence of environmental damage. The opportunity cost concept highlights the pervasiveness of external costs of economic activities in industrial economies and demonstrates that many "free goods" are in fact not free but valuable natural capital.

Besides the difficulty of choosing a social discount rate, other problems seriously impair accurate shadow pricing of natural capital. The services rendered by natural capital are pervasive and very difficult to evaluate completely. The opportunity cost of clear-cutting a forest includes all benefits that could be derived from the free-standing forest in perpetuity: recreational benefits, climatic stabilization, return on sustainable forestry, and so on. While the number of effects to be considered and the information requirements may be overwhelming, more problems arise because of limited knowledge about the functioning of the biosphere. The release of chlorofluorocarbons (CFCs) into the atmosphere could not have been correctly evaluated twenty years ago because the destructive effects on the ozone layer were not yet known. In response to these problems, more sophisticated economic techniques for calculating shadow prices have been developed. For the treatment of uncertainty, the concept of option value (or risk premium) has been developed (Cichetti and Freeman 1971) and for irreversibility, the use of a quasi-option value (Arrow and Fisher 1974).

However, practical applicability of these concepts is still very limited. Moreover, uncertainty about the cultural and technological development of humanity is so great that future economic values of resources are impossible to estimate. Too many unexpected events and potential discoveries lie ahead to make any sensible estimation of resource values hundreds of years ahead. For such Knightian uncertainty, conventional economic tools for decisionmaking under uncertainty, such as expected utility theory, fail.[3]

As a result of the described problems, evaluation of the opportunity costs of natural capital depletion is usually incomplete since only those effects that are already known and understood are included. Our knowledge that there are potential, yet unknown, costs of depletion is not explicitly considered. On the other hand, the benefits from depletion are included more or less completely because they are captured by the market for the output product (steel, pulp, electricity, and others). Thus, conventional shadow pricing of natural capital depletion implies a systematic underestimation of its economic value.

A Better Default Value for Natural Capital

The conventional approach to evaluation implies that the default value of natural capital, in the absence of any knowledge, is zero. If market prices are used, the value is zero unless property rights have been established and can be enforced. As noted, establishment of property rights is often not possible or very costly. If shadow prices are used, the value is zero unless the existence of opportunity costs can be shown explicitly. As discussed above, the pervasiveness of the benefits from natural capital and the deficiency of knowledge would almost always allow parts of the opportunity costs to go unnoticed. This neglect of natural capital in economic evaluation stands in strong conflict with the fact that the earth's natural capital is the result of millions of years of evolution and should be viewed as a proven system that deserves protection. This is not an argument about natural beauty but about prudence. Natural capital is not just an arbitrary accumulation of natural resources but is a complicated web of biological interactions that has successfully emerged from millions of years of evolutionary competition. Although we do not fully understand the functioning of the natural systems, natural capital in its original form deserves considerable benefit of the doubt. Past experiences with interfering with natural systems

and with the unexpected negative consequences (such as ozone layer depletion and deforestation) would suggest that a more cautious attitude toward depleting natural capital is in our own interest. Such a cautious approach would reflect the expectation of unpredictable costs arising from the depletion of natural capital.

A more cautious approach would not imply, however, that all natural capital must be left untouched. Rather, a reversal in the burden of proof is suggested. Conventional evaluation implies that natural capital should be depleted unless it can be shown that depletion makes us worse off. A cautious approach would require that natural capital be left intact unless it can be shown that depletion makes us better off. In a world full of uncertainties, the difference can be significant. In millions of years, life on earth has emerged from co-evolutionary adaptation to the current chemical composition of the atmosphere. Hence, changing the composition of the atmosphere is likely to disrupt the functioning of the biosphere in very fundamental ways. It would be acceptable to change the composition of the atmosphere only if we understood the functioning of the biosphere sufficiently well to be able to show confidently that a change in the composition of the atmosphere would make us better off. On the other hand, conventional analysis would suggest to pollute the atmosphere until we find out that the damage that results from this change in the atmosphere outweighs the benefits. We are currently learning about the functioning of the biosphere by trial and error. Because of the increasing number of human beings populating the earth and our ability to amplify our impacts on the environment through technology, the stakes in this trial and error game have grown so large that the process is generating unacceptable risks. Moreover, many forms of natural capital depletion and thus our possible errors, are irreversible. This increases the risks and provides additional support for a cautious approach and a reversal in the burden of proof.

The mechanism by which I suggest to reflect the reversal in the burden of proof goes back to John Ise's (1925) proposal to evaluate a nonrenewable resource at the price of a renewable substitute. In the absence of better knowledge, the default value for the depletion of natural capital should be the cost of a sustainable substitute. This means depletion of natural capital has to be made as expensive as a sustainable substitute, unless it can be shown that the full economic cost of natural capital depletion is less than the cost of a sustainable substitute. While the default value for resource depletion is set at the cost of a sustainable substitute, we could gradually reduce this default value as our knowledge about the functioning of the world increased, and we concluded that it was to our benefit to deplete natural capital. This is in contrast to conventional analysis that begins with a default value of zero for a presumably free good. As unexpected damage arose and the resource became scarce, the cost of natural capital depletion could be increased gradually. Once all uncertainty was resolved, the resulting value assigned to natural capital would be the same under either approach. The cautious approach leads to a reversal of the default assumption of natural capital as a free good to the assumption that every unsustainable activity must, in the long run, be converted into a sustainable activity.

Some examples can illustrate this change in the default assumption. For the evaluation of depleting an oil field, the cautious approach would imply initial pricing of the energy resource at the cost of a sustainable substitute, such as solar energy. This shadow price would be reduced if it could be shown with reasonable confidence that depletion would not cause unexpected environmental damage, that there are no alternative future high-value uses for oil, and that depletion would lead to an actual Pareto improvement. If a sustainable substitute for natural capital did not exist, the default value for depletion would be infinite and the resource could only be used sustainably. This would, for example, preclude the extinction of species. A renewable resource, such as a forest, would be priced according to its sustainable yield. Cutting trees beyond the sustainable yield would be acceptable only if it could be shown that benefits outweighed all costs arising from reduction of the forest. This cautious approach would help avoid the large costs that arise when an alternative high-value use is discovered after a resource is depleted, for example, as when a very potent cancer fighting drug was discovered in the Pacific yew tree, large numbers of which had already been lost through unsustainable logging.

The Intergenerational Problem

Even more serious concerns about the conventional approach to evaluation of natural capital depletion follow from considering the intergenerational problem: the depletion of natural capital to benefit the present at the expense of the future. Moreover, most of these costs are imposed on those who have no

opportunity to influence decisionmaking in the present. Conventional project analysis implies the use of a universal discount rate for all costs and benefits and, therefore, leads to a short-term focus that ignores intergenerational justice issues. This short-term focus may be justified for many short-lived production projects, but it disregards the possible long-term welfare impacts from depleting natural capital. These intergenerational welfare impacts are at the core of the depletion problem. This section cannot possibly deal with all the complex philosophical questions involved in intergenerational choice (see Berry [1983] for a discussion of some of these issues), but some important arguments and a set of intuitive requirements for the evaluation of natural capital depletion is suggested.

In this section, it is assumed that present individuals do not care at all about the wellbeing of future generations. This assumption is justified since previous studies have shown that the intergenerational justice problem may be alleviated but cannot be overcome by intergenerational altruism alone. Caring for future generation is a public good. Whether individuals care about their own descendants (Daly 1982) or about future generations in general (Marglin 1963), markets would bring about an allocation of resources to future generations that are inefficiently low from the viewpoint of the current generation's preferences.

Intergenerational Justice

Because decisions about depletion of natural capital affect the welfare of future generations, their interest in the decisions made by earlier generations needs to be considered in some way. If the interests of all generations have to be taken into consideration, the focus of economic analysis on efficiency is not justifiable since efficiency requires the assumption that the initial distribution of resources is the desired one. Concentration of economic analysis on efficiency may be justified for *intra*-generational choice because of the existence of more or less effective mechanisms to bring about the socially desired income distribution through government transfer payments. In *inter*-generational choice, on the other hand, there is a fundamental asymmetry between present and future generations since distribution of resources is determined by the present generation alone. Future generations have no influence on current decisions. Pure efficiency criteria would not necessarily prevent any generation from consuming all resources of the planet without compensating future generations at all. Hence, intergenerational justice needs to be explicitly considered.

SOCIAL DISCOUNT RATE. Use of a very low social discount rate has been proposed to address the problems of intergenerational justice. However, the choice of the discount rate for the depletion of natural capital does not lead to unambiguous results. While a lower rate increases the user costs and hence slows down depletion, the same low discount rate leads to increasing development of resources and hence increased demand and supply of the resource. In particular, a low discount rate increases exploration activities because the expected benefits from exploration weigh more against the high exploration costs. Applying different discount rates to different projects would create problems of identification and possible inefficiencies. Norgaard and Howarth (1991) show in an overlapping generations model that the discount rate implied in the competitive equilibrium of trade between generations depends on the transfers previous generations make to the following generations. The result is equivalent to the impact of changing income distribution in a one-period model that, in general, would result in equilibrium price changes. Since discount rates are in part determined by how many resources the present generation allocates to future generations, such a discount rate should not be used to independently determine how many resources should be allocated to the future (for example, by use of the Hotelling rule). Hence the distributional problem has to be solved before an appropriate intergenerational discount rate can be found. Directly adjusting the social discount rate for conservationist objectives is therefore not appropriate.

RESOURCE OWNERSHIP. The intergenerational justice dimension of natural capital depletion is best explained by considering the question of which generation owns the stock of a specific natural resource. Howarth and Norgaard (1990) have shown in a general-equilibrium model with two overlapping generations that for every possible distribution of resource ownership, there is a different efficient depletion path. An increase in the share of the resource owned by the first generation unambiguously reduces welfare of the second generation and vice versa. Hence a self-interested early generation would assume ownership of the full resource stock, leading to gloomy welfare levels for future generations, even though the resource

is depleted efficiently. In a similar model, I show that the efficient resource price for more than two generations would, in general, depend on which generation owned the resource. If the current generation assumes ownership of the full resource stock, future generations would be effectively excluded from bidding on the resource. Since nonadjacent generations cannot trade with each other directly, only a small channel, limited by the wealth of intermediate generations, would exist for all future generations to purchase parts of the resource stock from the early generation that assumes ownership of the resource stock.

While these overlapping-generations models are too simplistic to predict doom for future generations in the real world, they clearly show that efficient markets are not sufficient to ensure a minimum welfare level for future generations. They also show that current resource prices reflect implicit assumptions about which generation owns the resource and would change if the intergenerational welfare criterion is changed. This result corresponds to the useful separation of equity and efficiency issues in standard economic theory. An efficient market equilibrium can only be determined given a certain distribution of initial resources. In intergenerational choice, the same is true.

Although little effort has been expended so far on defining the desired intergenerational distribution of resources, it could be expressed in an intergenerational social welfare function that reflects the desired ethical position (utilitarian, maximin or other forms). From the social welfare function, the optimal distribution of resources to different generations could be derived. However, a social welfare function is hardly operational in an intergenerational context. Besides the uncertainty about the impacts of earlier decisions on the consumption opportunities of later generations, there is uncertainty about the preferences of future generations. Given the assumption that preferences of future generations are like those of the present generation, the present generation would unduly restrict future choices. Other assumptions about future preferences would be completely arbitrary. More operational would be Page's (1983) suggestion that equal opportunities should be required for every generation rather than a specified level of welfare.

Just Distribution of Resources between Generations

Before going further in the discussion of resource distribution between generations, an important issue should be clarified (a point raised by Page [1983]). In cost-benefit analysis, efficiency is commonly used in the sense of the potential Pareto criterion (also Kaldor or compensation criterion). This states that an activity should be undertaken if those who gain from the activity *could* compensate those who lose and still be better off. Since hardly any project is conceivable that does not lead to losses for at least some individuals, projects are justified on efficiency grounds even though they achieve only a potential Pareto improvement and not an actual Pareto improvement. The use of the potential Pareto criterion is quite justifiable in cases where no individuals suffer large losses from a project, where effective income redistribution mechanisms are in place, and where no systematic bias exists against any group. Under these circumstances, it can be expected that compensation can be implicitly achieved by the sum of all projects that, in aggregate, would provide net benefits to every individual.

In intergenerational choice, the conditions that would justify use of the potential Pareto criterion are unlikely to be met. Large losses to specific generations may be possible because long-term discounting diminishes the impact on decisionmaking of possible catastrophic events in the future (such as a nuclear accident). There is no reason to assume that the income distribution between present and future generations is explicitly endorsed. There is a systematic bias against future generations, since politicians responsible for social evaluation are elected by present and not future generations. A systematic bias in favor of activities generating current benefits and future costs is the result. Furthermore, the decision not to compensate losers can be reversed within the same generation. In intergenerational choice, however, gainers will have died by the time the losers live. Hence, the decision to not actually compensate is irreversible. For these reasons, efficiency should be confined to the actual and not the potential Pareto criterion in an intergenerational context. While gains and losses within each generation may still be added, the gains and losses accruing to different generations need to be considered explicitly and actual compensation of losing generations needs to be made.

The discussion of intergenerational equilibrium models has shown that the assumption of ownership of all natural capital by the first generation is unacceptable because it ignores the interests of future generations. Since agreement on an intergenerational social welfare function would be difficult to obtain,

even if it were obtained its operationalization would prove extremely cumbersome. At least some simple rules that every generation could agree on should be used as a guideline for an acceptable intergenerational resource distribution.

First, every generation can use natural capital without depleting it. This would include harvesting the sustainable yield from renewable resources and using the environment as a sink for wastes within the natural capacity for regeneration. Second, adequate compensation of all future generations would be required for any depletion of natural capital because natural capital depletion precludes use by all future generations. The precise nature and quantity of such compensation will be the topic of much of the remainder of this chapter. However, two intuitively appealing requirements for adequate compensation can be established that would let all generations accept the compensation as a substitute for the depleted natural capital. First, the benefits derived from the depletion of natural capital should be shared equally among the depleting and all future generations. Second, later generations must receive compensation at least equal to the benefits they would have received if they had depleted the resource themselves and compensated future generations. This condition is meant to restrict wasteful use of a resource that would be acceptable under the condition of equal rent sharing alone.

Under these guidelines for intergenerational resource distribution, the endowment of every generation would include the sustainable yield of the earth's natural capital plus the benefits from depletion of natural capital if adequate compensation is made to future generations. This requirement of explicit compensation for any unsustainable use of natural capital would imply a major change in our cultural and legal understanding of ownership of land and other natural resources. This is consistent with the conclusion that not all natural capital can be owned by the current generation for intergenerational justice reasons. Owning land would include the right to harvest only the sustainable yield of the land while leaving the capital value intact. Owning a mine would imply the right to exploit the resource only if adequate compensation of future generations is provided. Land ownership would become comparable to trusteeship rather than to ownership of humanmade capital.

The guidelines for intergenerational resource distribution could be implemented through a sustainability constraint to ensure some minimum level for welfare of future generations and a basic stock of natural capital. In fact, consensus appears to be emerging that a sustainability constraint on current economic activities is the preferable approach to addressing the intergenerational problem (Markandya and Pearce 1988). A sustainability constraint would offset the biases of decisionmakers against considering opportunity costs and against actually compensating future generations. A sustainability constraint would become part of the framework within which economic analysis takes place. The constraint would prohibit economic activities that infringe on basic rights of future generations, just as basic individual rights are often considered immune to economic analysis. Intergenerational justice considerations would be reflected in the initial endowments assigned to each generation through the sustainability constraint. The sustainability constraint would lead to different equilibrium prices that were not only efficient but also acceptable in view of intergenerational justice considerations.

Sustainability Constraints on Current Economic Activities

Sustainability has become an almost universally accepted policy objective, but there is little agreement on what it means exactly. Therefore, the discussion of different sustainability definitions, such as in Pezzey (1989), is useful. The purpose of a sustainability constraint is to restrict current economic activities in such a way that a specified variable, such as consumption or utility, can be maintained at its current value in perpetuity. Various definitions of sustainability differ in the variables which they constrain. The controversy between proponents of different sustainability constraints is based on different assumptions about the nature of substitutability between different assets. For example, Daly and Cobb (1989) discuss the distinction between strong and weak sustainability. A weak sustainability constraint only requires that the sum of the values of natural and humanmade capital stock be kept nondeclining. Compensation for natural capital depletion would be an investment in any other form of capital of equal value. On the other hand, a strong sustainability constraint would require nondeclining stocks of humanmade and natural capital, separately. Compensation for the depletion of natural capital would have to be made through investment in natural capital.

Strong and Weak Sustainability

The different sustainability constraints are illustrated in figure 12-1. The stream of human welfare, depicted at the top of the diagram, is the ultimate concern of the economist with an inherently anthropocentric point of view. The weakest sustainability constraint would apply at this highest level of aggregation. It would require that all humanmade and natural capital together be kept intact such that it can support a non-declining stream of welfare in perpetuity. The concept of human welfare is eminently detached from the physical realities of natural capital. Welfare is the result of a variety of consumption streams that are combined in a welfare or utility function. Two representative consumption streams that contribute to welfare are shown at level 2 in figure 12-1. Questioning the assumptions about substitutability between different consumption streams, the next stronger utility constraint would apply to the different consumption streams separately. This sustainability constraint would require that groups of capital that generate different consumption streams be kept intact, such that they can support consumption streams that are all separately non-declining. Similarly, consumption streams are created through a production process that combines various goods. Level 3 would represent sustainability of the supply streams for production. Finally, the strongest sustainability constraint (level 4) would apply at the level of extraction of physical assets. This strongest sustainability constraints would require that the stock of specific assets be left intact as to be able to provide non-declining extraction streams.

The four types of sustainability constraints are representative steps along the continuum between the abstract concept of human welfare and the physical concept of individual resources or assets. They represent a decreasing level of abstraction and an increasing proximity to physical realities. Clearly, a sustainability constraint imposed at a higher level of abstraction restricts the choices of the living generation less than a sustainability constraint imposed at the level of individual resources.

SUSTAINABILITY CONSTRAINTS AND HUMAN WELFARE. The weakest sustainability constraint (level 1 in figure 12-1) requires that every generation limits its activities such that a non-declining level of utility can be obtained by all future generations. Under certainty, every generation would deplete resources such that

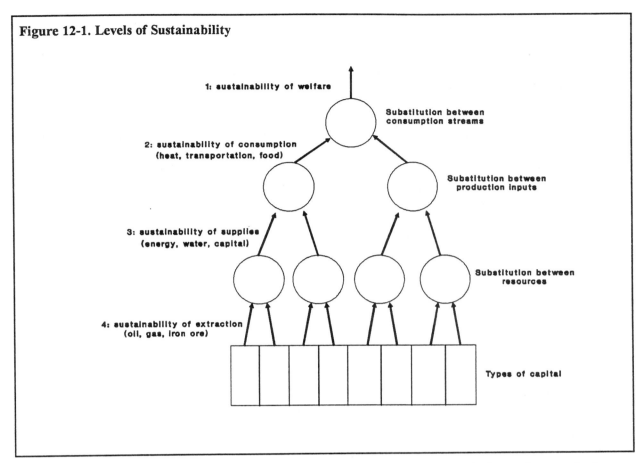

Figure 12-1. Levels of Sustainability

this constraint is just barely met. The maximin welfare path would be the result. Some economists have shown that the maximin welfare path is obtained if net zero investment in the economy is zero (Hartwick 1977; Dixit, Hammond, and Hoel 1980). This means that all competitive profits from resource depletion are invested in reproducible capital (the "Hartwick rule"). Hence to meet the sustainability constraint, every generation would be required to invest all resource profits and leave this investment behind as compensation for future generations. There would be no restriction on the type of compensating investment.

Under complete certainty, the weakest sustainability constraint would be the appropriate one since future economic prices of all goods and all forms of capital could be calculated. If the stock of all capital, aggregated at real future prices is non-declining, utility would be non-declining and a weak sustainability constraint should suffice. However, the uncertainties involved in long-term forecasting of economic prices are numerous. Uncertainty about the economic value of goods in the future can result from uncertainty in demand or supply. Demand

uncertainties can result from changes in income through differing income elasticities. The development of unexpected technological substitutes or additional uses for goods will change demand. Also, preferences of individuals may change, particularly in the long-term. Supply uncertainty can be caused by changes in technology, changes in the quantity of known natural resource deposits, or changes in knowledge about natural system characteristics, such as regeneration capacity of the atmosphere. Considering unquantifiable uncertainties such as the possibility of drastic technological advances, cultural changes, or catastrophic events, providing a sensible distribution function for long-term prices would seem impossible.

In the absence of any reasonable estimate of future economic prices, the weakest sustainability constraint would have to be based on aggregation at present prices. However, using present prices for the valuation of future capital stocks is inappropriate since prices are measures of *marginal* rates of substitution, while depletion of natural capital at the current scale clearly implies *non-marginal* changes in the economy. Such non-marginal changes will lead to changes in relative prices, not just of nonrenewable resources. Investment at present prices is, therefore, unlikely to provide adequate compensation. For example, compensation of future generations for the depletion of oil reserves through investment in a highway system and gasoline-powered vehicles at equal present economic values would clearly be inadequate. Gasoline-powered vehicles and oil are complements and their future values are likely to be negatively correlated. In case oil becomes very valuable, a high compensation for earlier depletion would be required; however, the vehicles or the highway system, intended to serve as compensation, would be worthless because there is not enough oil to use them. Alternatively, if oil proves not to be as scarce as expected, the earlier generation would have compensated excessively and restricted their own consumption unduly.

Under the multidimensional uncertainties of real life, such general investment as compensation would lead to a very high variance in the welfare of future generations. All the uncertainties discussed can affect future rates of substitution at the level of a future generation's welfare function and, hence, the welfare effects of compensatory investment. Either a high risk about the adequacy of compensation would have to be accepted, or compensating investment would have to be made well in excess of the Hartwick rule, to ensure adequacy of the compensation with the desired likelihood. Moreover, a weak sustainability constraint is non-operational under uncertainty: it appears completely impossible to determine the expected welfare of a remote generation resulting from current depletion of natural capital depletion and compensation through general investment. This weak sustainability constraint, therefore, does not satisfy the requirements of intergenerational justice under real life uncertainties.

SUSTAINABILITY CONSTRAINTS AND CONSUMPTION SERVICES. The uncertainty about substitutability of a future generation's welfare can be alleviated by imposing sustainability constraints on the consumption streams that generate welfare (level 2 in figure 12-1). These relevant consumption streams are the services (heat, transportation, nutrition, and so forth) derived from depletion of natural capital. Hence, consumption from a nonsustainable source would be acceptable only if the consumption stream can be obtained at the same real cost in perpetuity. Hence, the stocks of groups of capital providing

certain services (such as energy, water, waste absorption or climatic stabilization), would have to be kept intact. Switching capital would be admissible only within the same group. The consumption streams are the output of a production process that combines natural capital with other forms of capital. The nature of the required compensation would depend on the specific production function. Specific investment that leads to sustainability of the consumption stream would be required as compensation and would increase the efficiency of natural capital use. Sustainability of consumption streams is more operational than sustainability of welfare since the production function is more likely to be known with some confidence than all relative prices in the future. Sustainability of consumption streams is stronger than sustainability of welfare since it requires specific rather than general compensatory investment, and the former is included in the latter. Uncertainty about adequate compensation would be reduced but not eliminated since technological changes may alter production functions in an unexpected way. Therefore, sustainability of consumption streams would be the appropriate constraint if there is sufficient confidence in understanding and predicting the production function but insufficient knowledge of future relative prices.

SUSTAINABILITY CONSTRAINTS AND INPUTS TO PRODUCTION. The next stronger sustainability constraint would apply to resource supplies (level 3 in figure 12-1). This constraint would allow the use of natural capital only if the supply streams entering production can be made sustainable. This constraint would apply separately to the supply of energy, water, the atmosphere's capacity to absorb emissions, and so on. This constraint applies to the inputs to production and is stronger than the one applying to consumption streams, since it does not allow for substitution at the level of the production function. Sustainability of outputs can be achieved through sustainability of inputs but also through substitution between inputs. Compensation under sustainability of resource supplies would have to be made through sustainable substitutes, such as renewable energy sources for nonrenewable ones. Hence, each stock of capital providing certain basic inputs to production such as energy, water, waste absorption or climatic stabilization, would have to remain intact; however, a switch from one to another type of capital within any such a group would be admissible. Sustainability of resource supplies further restricts the choices of earlier generations; however, it is also more operational and further reduces uncertainty about adequate compensation, since the uncertainty about the production function is avoided. However, uncertainty remains about potential alternative high-value uses of individual natural resources. This sustainability constraint would be applicable if there is considerable uncertainty about technological change or the nature of the production function but sufficient confidence that no alternative high-value uses of the depleted resource are possible.

SUSTAINABILITY CONSTRAINTS AND NATURAL CAPITAL EXTRACTION. Finally, the strongest sustainability constraint would require separately sustainability of extraction from all different types of natural capital (level 4 in figure 12-1). Only sustainable yields of renewable resources could be harvested and no nonrenewable resources could be used. The only admissible substitution would be restoration of equal natural capital at another location, for example, relocation of a cultivated forest. This sustainability constraint would eliminate the uncertainties, except for the uncertainty about the size of stocks, harvests and sustainable yields, and would be very operational. However, it would drastically restrict choices and ignores the existence of some substitutability between different resources and, to some degree, between natural resources, technology, and humanmade capital. Since such a strong constraint seems to exclude many activities that would unambiguously benefit all generations, it would be too strong in most instances unless there is a significant possibility for not yet known alternative high-value uses for a resource. The potential future value of genetic material and diversity would require the strongest sustainability for biodiversity that would, for example, preclude the possibility to compensate for the extinction of species.

A sustainability constraint at levels 2 or 3 involves compensation through functional substitutes that provide the same services as the resources they are compensating for. For example, different sources of end-use energy would be functional substitutes. Compensation for the depletion of nonrenewable energy resources would have to be an investment in sustainable energy sources rather than in energy-intensive production facilities. The quantity of such compensating investment has to ensure that the total capital for provision of energy remains intact. This means the capital stock retains the ability to generate the presently consumed amount of energy into infinity. By restricting compensation to functional substitutes, the problem of aggregation weights would be alleviated, since comparison can be made in physical units, such as energy content.

SUSTAINABILITY CONSTRAINTS AND INTER-GENERATIONAL COMPENSATION. The stronger sustainability constraints reflect the intuition that future generations can be more adequately compensated through functional substitutes. The stronger sustainability constraint provides a built-in insurance for future costs of current economic activities. Since the price of functional substitutes is highly correlated, the value of the compensation is high whenever the value of the depleted resource is high and vice versa. The stronger sustainability constraint, therefore, ensures adequate compensation with a high degree of robustness. As a result, compensation through functional substitutes is the cheapest way for current generations to provide adequate compensation. The overly optimistic assumption that technological progress will always increase society's opportunities is unrealistic and should be avoided. Hence, an evaluation of substitution opportunities should be based on currently available technology or foreseeable technological development. This reflects prudent behavior in view of the experience that technology and increasing knowledge can in fact significantly decrease the opportunities of future generations (Daly and Cobb 1989).

The choice between the four sustainability constraints in a particular instance involves considerable judgement and should depend on the degree of risk aversion, the nature and degree of uncertainty about the adequacy of intergenerational compensation, and the availability of substitutes. The search for the appropriate sustainability constraint in a given situation involves the trade-off between the risk of inadequate compensation and expected welfare gains for all generations. The stronger the sustainability constraint, the more it constrains the choices of the current generations. A stronger constraint reflects a more cautious approach involving less interference with the natural support system at the cost of reduced welfare. The less knowledge is available on the nature of substitutability, the stronger the sustainability constraint should be. If no substitute is available at the level of the selected sustainability constraint, the depletion of natural capital would not be permitted. Since intergenerational compensation is a surrogate for voluntary trade where direct trade is not possible, early generations should select the sustainability constraint and provide the compensation they believe will be acceptable to later generations.

The Geographic Scale of Sustainability

The chosen sustainability constraint can be implemented at various geographic scales. Non-declining capital stocks can be required on a global, national, regional or local level. For example, zero net carbon dioxide (CO_2) emissions could be required on a global scale. Alternatively such constraint could be imposed for all countries separately. Even stronger, every city or every project could be required to achieve zero net CO_2 emissions. This decision depends on the substitutability between natural capital at different locations. The atmosphere is a global resource, and reductions of CO_2 emissions at any place in the world are perfect substitutes. For global public resources (atmosphere, oceans) and for tradable resources such as oil, which has a high value compared to transport costs, the sustainability constraint should be implemented on a global scale. Otherwise, the market or shadow prices of natural capital depletion would differ across countries, and the potential gain from equalizing the marginal cost of reducing natural capital depletion across countries would not be realized.

The desirable use of a sustainability constraint on a global scale for global and tradable resources is hampered by the absence of effective mechanisms for international coordination. Therefore, in the absence of global sustainability constraints, individual countries should impose a national or local sustainability constraint even for global and tradable forms of natural capital. In this case, compensatory investment would not be determined on the global scale but would depend on each countries' production or consumption. International lending agencies could play an important role in supporting national sustainability constraints—even for global public resources, where individual countries would face a Prisoners' Dilemma situation. Similarly, if there was not already a sustainability constraint at the national level, it should be imposed at a local or even project level. This process would lead to "bottom up" sustainability without the long delays inherent in national or even global decisionmaking.

Sometimes natural capital cannot be easily substituted by natural capital at another location. Where natural capital is local in nature, a sustainability constraint should naturally be applied at the local level. The services rendered by various watersheds are not readily tradable, hence, each must be kept. Similarly, freshwater on one continent is not a good substitute for freshwater on another continent. In general, since transportation costs are usually prohibitive, sustainable water supplies should be required at the regional level.

Shadow Prices under a Sustainability Constraint

There is no convincing reason why an individual project needs to be sustainable. It is perfectly acceptable to undertake a project that generates positive net benefits over a finite lifetime. However, projects that involve the depletion of natural capital should be evaluated according to the appropriate sustainability constraint (discussed in the previous section) in order to overcome the inherent limitations of conventional evaluation of such projects. If a sustainability constraint was imposed and compensation made at the national or global level, market prices for natural capital would already reflect this sustainability constraint and no further adjustments would be needed. However, if no sustainability constraint was implemented at a higher level (which is probably the case), shadow prices that reflect the appropriate sustainability constraint need to be calculated and used at the project level. Also, compensation needs to be made for natural capital depletion caused by the project. In practice this would mean that (a) the default value for depletion of natural capital would be the price of a sustainable substitute (to overcome the inherent limitations of conventional evaluation); (b) rents derived from depletion would be shared equally with all future generations, and compensation to future generations would be provided through investment in functional substitutes to reduce uncertainty about the adequacy of the compensation; and (c) future generations would be compensated sufficiently for depletion.

The Sustainable Supply Rule

The sustainable supply rule combines elements of a sustainability constraint on a portfolio of projects (Pearce and others 1991) and a tax on resources such that their real price would remain constant over time

(Page 1977). The sustainable supply rule allows the depletion of natural capital only if the depleted natural capital is replaced by investment that functionally substitutes for the depleted capital. Natural capital depletion would be evaluated at the sustainable price of the services derived from it. This sustainable price is the cost at which the services can be provided infinitely through a sustainable substitute if for every unit of depleted natural capital the sustainable price is invested in the substitute. If a functional substitute for the depleted natural capital is not available, natural capital of the same type needs to be restored or depletion of natural capital would not be allowed (the shadow price would be infinite). The sustainable supply rule is applicable for a sustainability constraint at any geographic scale; for instance, for national policymaking, the approach could be used to determine an adequate resource depletion tax.

The intuition of the sustainable supply rule is related to El Serafy's (1989) approach to adjust national income accounts to reflect resource liquidation. However, El Serafy's approach is based on the calculation of revenues or marginal benefits, whereas project evaluation is based on total benefits or rent (producer and consumer rent). Accordingly, all benefits from the depletion of natural capital need to be divided into an income and a compensation component. The compensation component would be allocated as a cost to the resource. When the compensation component is invested in the production of a sustainable substitute for the nonrenewable resource, it would (after exhaustion of the nonrenewable resource) provide an infinite benefit stream from consumption of the sustainable substitute equal to the income component. Benefits from the nonrenewable resource would be shared with all following generations through the steady income component generated through compensatory investment.

SUSTAINABLE SUPPLY CURVE. Figure 12-2 shows the demand for a service that can be provided by a nonrenewable resource or its sustainable substitute. For simplicity, it is assumed that the nonrenewable resource can be extracted at zero cost. The current unit cost of producing the sustainable substitute would be C_s. This is shown through the horizontal supply curve at C_s. The line ABCD represents the demand (or marginal benefit) curve. At the price P_s, no sustainable substitutes would be offered and demand would have to be satisfied with the nonrenewable resource. Market demand at price P_s would equal the distance EK and total benefits from consumption of the resource would be the area under the demand curve up to the quantity used, ACKE. This rent consists of two components: the owner of the resource would receive revenues equalling FCKE; the consumers would receive the rent ACF. The sustainable supply rule requires that the revenues FCKE be the compensation component to be invested and the consumer rent ACF be the income component accruing to the present generation for consumption.

Compensating investment into the sustainable substitute can, in time, reduce the unit cost of the sustainable substitute from its current level C_s. This cost reduction occurs because compensating investment into improvements of technology actually reduces production costs or because compensating investment is used as a free addition to the capital stock for production of the substitute. Now, the sustainable price, P_s, is determined such that the cost of producing the sustainable substitute is reduced to P_s exactly when the nonrenewable resource is depleted. At that time, production of the sustainable substitute will begin. Hence, this procedure ensures that a sustainable price is chosen at which the same quantity of the service from the resource will be provided forever, first from the nonrenewable resource and

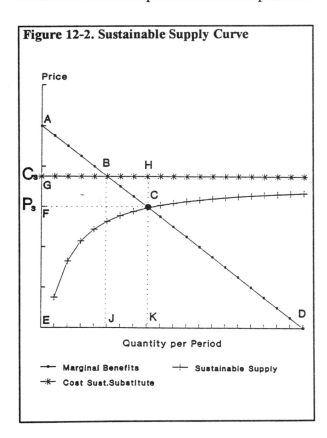

Figure 12-2. Sustainable Supply Curve

Price

Quantity per Period

—•— Marginal Benefits   —+— Sustainable Supply
—*— Cost Sust.Substitute

later from the sustainable substitute. The term sustainable price indicates that the price does not change with depletion of the nonrenewable resource.

For the simplest case of a nonrenewable resource with zero extraction costs and infinitely elastic supply of a perfect sustainable substitute at cost C_s, the sustainable supply rule can be expressed in a simple equation. The compensation component invested throughout the lifetime of the nonrenewable resource must be sufficient to yield an infinite subsidy stream that reduces the cost of the sustainable substitute to the sustainable price for an equal consumption quantity per period. For the quantity of the resource, M, extracted per period the sustainable price, P_s, would have to be set such that $P_s M$ (the area FCKE in figure 12-2) invested in every period until depletion of the nonrenewable resource, would generate a return of $(C_s-P_s) M$ (area GHCF) in every period after depletion. This is the case if the present value of the finite stream of the compensation component equals the infinite stream of the subsidy after resource exhaustion, which occurs after R/M periods. The present value of the compensation component, K, from time zero to R/M is

$$K = \int_0^{\frac{R}{M}} e^{-rt} MP_s \, dt = \frac{MP_s}{r}\left(1 - e^{-r\frac{R}{M}}\right) \quad (1)$$

where r is the return on investment in sustainable substitutes, R is the total stock of the nonrenewable resource and R/M is, therefore, the lifetime of the resource. The present value of the subsidy stream, S, from time R/M until infinity is

$$S = \int_{\frac{R}{M}}^{\infty} e^{-rt} M(C_s - P_s) = e^{-r\frac{R}{M}} \frac{M(C_s - P_s)}{r} \quad (2)$$

equating S and K and dividing both sides by M/r

$$P_s\left(1 - e^{-r\frac{R}{M}}\right) = e^{-r\frac{R}{M}} C_s - P_s \quad (3)$$

This results in the following equation for the sustainable price:

$$P_s = e^{-r\frac{R}{M}} C_s \quad (4)$$

The return to the compensating investment reduces the cost of the sustainable substitute and stabilizes the sustainable price. The quantity M of the resource

will be available at the price P, before depletion from the nonrenewable resource and thereafter from the sustainable substitute.

If the extraction of the nonrenewable resource, M, was increased, the compensation component would have to increase as well, since the reduced lifetime of the resource would leave less time for returns of the compensating investment to compound. The sustainable price would, therefore, have to rise with increases in extraction. Hence, equation (4) describes a positive functional relation between quantity of the service from the resource consumed per period and the sustainable price. The typical shape of the resulting sustainable supply curve is shown in figure 12-2.

The term sustainable supply curve reflects the steady nature of this supply curve as opposed to an imaginary supply curve with Hotelling-depletion, which would shift upward to reflect opportunity costs that would be rising with scarcity of the nonrenewable resource. The sustainable price can be read from this curve with knowledge of annual depletion of the resource. If the resource was supplied according to the sustainable supply curve, point C would be the market equilibrium. The sustainable price would be the shadow price to be used for the valuation of the resource as an input to a project. Under this rule, actual investment of the compensation component (sustainable price times quantity of the resource used) would be required for the project to be acceptable.

Equation (4) is based on highly simplistic assumptions and probably not directly applicable in most instances. However, the assumptions of zero extraction costs for the nonrenewable resource and perfectly elastic supply of the sustainable substitute can be relaxed at the cost of complicating equation (4). Similar equations for sustainable supply can be calculated for rising extraction costs or a situation in which a stock of compensating investment already exists. Also, a similar expression can be found if no perfect sustainable substitute exists. If the service that is to be supplied sustainably is produced from natural capital and another reproducible input, the expression for the sustainable price can be derived from the production function by optimizing the inputs over time such that a constant stream of the service is obtained at least cost.

SUSTAINABLE SUPPLY PRICING. Figure 12-3 compares the price paths resulting from use of the sustainable supply rule and conventional depletion according to

Figure 12-3. Resource Price Comparison

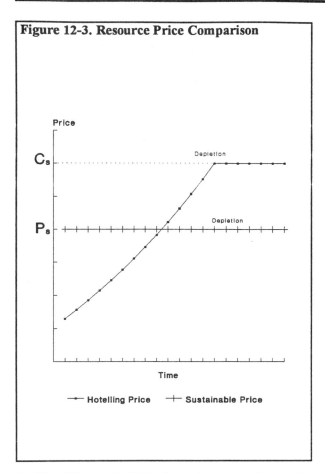

the Hotelling path. With depletion according to the sustainable supply rule, the price would remain constant at level P_s with depletion occurring somewhere along the horizontal line. Optimal depletion in perfect markets without a sustainability constraint would follow the Hotelling rule. C_s would be the cost of a back-stop technology. Therefore, the price of the resource would rise at the interest rate with the initial price set such that depletion occurs exactly when the price reaches C_s as shown in figure 12-3. In the initial years, a larger amount of the resource would be available at a price lower compared to the sustainable supply rule. In the later years, a lesser quantity would be available at a higher price. With conventional depletion, the total rent accruing in the early years would be close to the area ADE in figure 12-2. This rent would fall gradually to ABJE in the last period before depletion. For all periods after depletion, total rent would be only ABG. With the sustainable supply rule, rents would be ACF in all periods. The timing of resource exhaustion under the different regimes would depend on the relation between discount rate and the rate of return on the specific compensating investment.

APPLICATION OF SUSTAINABLE SUPPLY RULE. To apply the sustainable supply rule to, for example, groundwater depletion, a sustainable supply curve for water can be found by considering the compensating investment in a water desalination plant run by solar energy. Again, zero extraction costs are assumed for groundwater and C_s as the present unit cost of producing desalinized seawater at any desired quantity. The sustainable price for groundwater, P_s, would have to be determined such that if an amount equal to P_s times the depletion rate was invested annually in desalination technology, then this investment would be able to provide desalinized seawater of the same quantity at the cost P_s for every year after depletion of groundwater. The sustainable price of groundwater would be calculated by using equation (4) with the current depletion rate, M, total stock left in the ground, R, and rate of return on compensating investment, r. To evaluate a project that uses ground water, the sustainable price of water, P_s, would be subtracted from project benefits as a unit cost for groundwater depletion. Subsequently, the net present value (NPV) of the project could be calculated and the project and the compensating investment implemented in case of a positive NPV.

For pricing of a nonrenewable energy resource, such as oil, C_s would be the cost of producing a sustainable substitute, such as a unit of solar energy. Compensating investment would likely be in research and development in order to increase the efficiency of photovoltaic energy generation. The size of the required compensation component would be determined such that solar energy will be available at the sustainable price of one energy unit from oil in the same quantities after depletion of the oil. Today, oil depletion would be evaluated at the sustainable price. Alternatively, compensating investment could be made in technologies to increase energy use efficiency. An increase in energy use efficiency would decrease the cost of sustainable energy supply in the future accordingly and, thereby, lead to a lower sustainable price per end-use energy unit or per energy service unit from nonrenewable resources.

The sustainable supply rule can be applied to renewable resources as well. If a renewable resource is harvested sustainably, no special problems arise since depletion of natural capital does not occur. Therefore, the appropriate price is the marginal social benefit of the resource at the level of the sustainable yield. For the depletion of a renewable resource, the sustainable supply rule can be applied in analogy to nonrenewable resources. Compensatory investment for depletion has to ensure that the same quantity can be extracted infinitely at the same price. It would be difficult to conceive of a functional substitute for forests. Therefore, compensating investment for harvesting a forest above its sustainable yield would be investment into enlarging the forest area such that the harvested amount would become the sustainable yield of the enlarged forest area. For example, if a forest is harvested at a rate x, leading to depletion after y years, then compensation would take the form of acquiring additional land and investing in afforestation such that this new forest has a sustainable yield of x after y years. The sustainable price of forest depletion would have to cover the costs of expanding the forest area accordingly.

Similarly, there are no functional substitutes available for the services provided by the atmosphere. The composition of the atmosphere constitutes natural capital that is depleted by increasing the concentration of CO_2. Since, there is no known substitute for the atmosphere in its natural composition, compensatory investment would have to maintain the natural capital intact. Hence, a new project that would increase the atmospheric CO_2 concentration would have to bear the costs of investment in, for example, afforestation that would absorb the same amount of CO_2 discharged by the initial project. Alternatively, investment could be undertaken in increased energy efficiency that would lead to the same effect on net carbon emissions. The compensating investment has to be undertaken and the costs are allocated to the initial project. The initial project should only be undertaken if it yields a positive return after subtraction of the cost of the compensating investment.

SUSTAINABLE SUPPLY RULE. The nature of compensating investment and the calculation of the returns on such investment requires further discussion. In principle, any form of compensating investment is acceptable if it leads to the provision of a sustainable supply of the substitute at the sustainable price. The simple case for which equation (4) is derived refers to a situation in which facilities for the sustainable production of the substitute already exist. Then, compensating investment doesn't need to provide the sustainable substitute itself. In cases where technological improvement in the existing sustainable substitute is unlikely, compensating investment should be made in the form of a general sustainable investment in the economy. Proceeds of this investment would be used to subsidize the production of the sustainable substitute in the existing facilities after the nonrenewable resource is depleted. In the more likely case that production facilities for sustainable substitutes do not yet exist, compensating investment would be made to provide them. Only after there is sufficient investment to produce the desired quantity of the substitute, should further investment be made into general sustainable production to subsidize the cost of the sustainable substitute. In any case, r would be the real rate of return on the actual compensating investment undertaken. If the sustainable substitute is a biological resource, the natural growth rate of the resource would be the appropriate rate for r.

In many cases, the most effective investment for the reduction of the cost of a sustainable substitute would be into research and development (R&D). Estimating the return on R&D is simplified since the relevant rate r is the rate of return on R&D measured at the fixed output price C_s. Therefore, uncertainty prevails only about the success of the R&D program in physical and not in economic terms. Measurement of return on R&D in terms of output price C_s explains why R&D into sustainable substitutes might be undertaken that would not be undertaken under a pure market arrangement. There are many reasons to believe that market forces alone will not bring about the efficient level of R&D activities. Since patent protection is rarely complete, private investors could normally not reap the full return on their R&D expenditures. Competitors would imitate the innovation or circumvent the patent which, in turn, would lead to a drop of output prices below C_s.

Use of the sustainable supply rule may lead to the rejection of projects that deplete natural capital but otherwise would be considered desirable. However, other projects that restore natural capital would be more desirable under a sustainability constraint. Imagine a country that uses forests or ground water resources unsustainably. A proposed conservation project that would increase water use efficiency or restore forests would be evaluated, following conventional analysis, by comparing a with-project scenario and a without-project scenario. To justify the project, the pervasive benefits from reforestation would have to be enumerated and evaluated. Under a sustainability constraint, the default assumption would be reversed and the appropriate comparison would be between a with-project scenario and a scenario with the next best project that would achieve sustainability. A reforestation project would be compared with a project providing a sustainable substitute for fuelwood that would be implemented (if it was the least cost alternative for achieving sustainability).

Case Study of Oil Extraction in Nigeria

This section demonstrates the use of the sustainable supply rule by applying it to the Oso Condensate Field Development Project in Nigeria. The purpose of the case study is to show the feasibility of reflecting a sustainability constraint in the economic analysis of projects. The focus is on methodology and not on the precision of individual cost estimates.

The sustainable price of oil depletion is sensitive to the assumed rate of return on compensatory investment. The appropriate rate is the expected real rate of return on actual compensatory investment. The opportunity cost of capital used in the economic evaluation of most projects is between 10 and 12 percent. However, considering a long-term real rate of return on international capital markets in the range of 3 to 5 percent, it is unlikely that a real rate of return of 10 to 12 percent can be realized on long-term investments of very significant amounts. Even if the marginal rate of return in Nigeria was 10–12 percent, it would be unrealistic to expect that significant compensatory investment can be made at this rate. Furthermore, as the worldwide integration of national financial markets progresses, it would be expected that the rate of return on investment would converge to the rates obtained on international markets. Hence, a discount rate of 7 percent, a midpoint estimate between the real rate of return on international financial markets and the opportunity cost of capital, has been selected for the base case calculation. Sustainable prices are also calculated for rates of return of 5 and 10 percent, respectively.

The Project

The Oso Condensate Field Development Project consists of the commercial development of an offshore condensate field (condensate is equivalent to very light crude oil). The main project objective is to increase Nigeria's hydrocarbon exports. The recoverable reserves of the field are estimated at 330 million barrels and would be extracted over the 21-year lifetime of the project. The Oso field comprises about 1.5 percent of Nigeria's oil reserves. Total oil reserves of the country are about 22 billion barrels

including estimated undiscovered reserves. At the current extraction rate of 1.6 million barrel per day. This implies a remaining lifetime of the oil reserves of approximately 38 years. The project was appraised with an economic rate of return of 51 percent. The original economic analysis does not include any user cost or depletion premium. Hence, the economic rate of return reflects the full resource rent without considering the opportunity costs of depletion. The World Bank's oil price projections that were used for the calculation of the economic rate of return are flat for the lifetime of the project (around \$22/bbl in constant 1990 US\$). Since oil prices are not expected to rise at or above the rate of interest, the use of an opportunity cost for depletion, based on these price projections, would not have led to rejection of the project.

The Issues

Two main issues arise with respect to the sustainability of hydrocarbon extraction and its evaluation. First, the extraction of a nonrenewable resource is unsustainable due to the finite reserves. Second, the use of hydrocarbons as energy source is unsustainable, at current consumption, since it leads to increasing CO_2 in the atmosphere. Therefore, according to the sustainable supply rule, depletion needs to be evaluated at the sustainable price derived from the cost of a sustainable substitute. Since condensate is primarily used as an energy commodity, substitution of condensate with another storable energy sources would be acceptable under a sustainability constraint. Other hydrocarbons, such as gas evaluated at its energy content, would be almost perfect substitutes for condensate, but they are finite as well. They can stretch the lifetime of the nonrenewable resource but they cannot substitute for it in perpetuity. There are several renewable energy sources that are almost perfect substitutes for condensate. In this case study, hydrogen produced from solar energy is used as a representative renewable energy source. Hydrogen can be used in much the same way as natural gas and can be produced sustainability by electrolysis from water and photovoltaic electricity. Since it is based on solar energy, the supply of solar hydrogen would be sustainable. The use of solar hydrogen is sustainable since the combustion of hydrogen releases only water and does not contribute to the build-up of CO_2 in the atmosphere. Solar hydrogen is used as a representative sustainable energy source because it has the potential to be the least cost substitute for hydrocarbons in many of their uses, and a variety of cost estimates are available. In reality, however, solar hydrogen is likely to be only one of many renewable energy sources that will be part of a sustainable energy supply system.

Substitution would also be acceptable at the level of production of energy services from primary energy and capital. Within the limits of thermodynamics, capital can substitute for primary energy through increased efficiency in energy use. First, at any given level of technological development, there is some substitutability between capital and energy. Second, investments in research and development can lead to technological progress that would allow production of more energy service from the same amount of capital and primary energy. Clearly, there are limits to the substitution of energy posed by thermodynamic constraints. For example, transport requires some minimum amount of energy regardless of the efficiency of the vehicle. However, in many instances, physical limits have not yet been exploited, allowing for further substitution. The estimation of substitution between capital and energy poses problems because of the many different uses energy is put to and the difficulties inherent in anticipating technological progress. However, reasonable estimates are available that can serve as the basis for sensitivity analysis.

Calculation of Sustainable Prices

The sustainable price for the depletion of condensate should take into account substitution possibilities between different fossil fuels and between nonrenewable and renewable energy sources. It should also reflect possible increases in energy use efficiency and long-term limits on acceptable carbon dioxide emissions. In order to separate the different issues entering the calculation, the sustainable price will be calculated in the following steps: (a) sustainable price for the Oso condensate field; (b) sustainable price for Nigeria's oil reserves; (c) sustainable price for Nigeria's oil and gas reserves; (d) sustainable price taking the expected growth in energy demand into account; (e) sustainable price considering efficiency gains in energy use; and (f) sustainable price considering restrictions on acceptable carbon dioxide emissions.

(a) The sustainable price for depleting Oso Field. According to the production plan, 330 million barrels are to be extracted from the Oso field over twenty-one years. Peak production will be reached in

year 2 with production declining after year 4. To make this individual project sustainable, the average production over the project's lifetime of 15.6 million barrels of condensate per year would have to be replaced by production of an equivalent amount of solar hydrogen after year 21. The cost of solar hydrogen is estimated at $15 per gigajoule (GJ) (see Ogden and Williams 1989). With 6 GJ per barrel of oil, the cost of producing solar hydrogen equivalent in energy content to one barrel of condensate, is $90. The extractions costs for condensate from the Oso field are $4.4 per barrel ($2.4/bl development costs and $2/bl recurrent costs).

The sustainable price is the price that, if paid in perpetuity for every barrel of oil or its sustainable substitute, will cover the costs of oil depletion as well as subsequent production of solar hydrogen. The sustainable price is found by equating the present value of the costs of extraction and producing solar hydrogen with the present value of the revenue stream obtained for the sale of the equivalent of 15.6 million barrels per year in perpetuity. Let R be the present value of the infinite revenue stream resulting from a sustainable price P_s for one barrel of oil equivalent:

$$R = \int_0^{21} e^{-rt} x_t P_s \, dt + \int_{21}^{\infty} e^{-rt} 15.6 * 10^6 P_s \, dt \quad (5)$$

where x_t is the actual extraction rate during the lifetime of the project, and r is the assumed (continuous time) rate of return on investment. Let C be the present value of the costs of extracting oil and producing the sustainable substitute:

$$C = \int_0^{21} e^{-rt} x_t 4.4 \, dt + \int_{21}^{\infty} e^{-rt} 15.6 * 10^6 * 90 \, dt \quad (6)$$

Setting R=C and solving for P_s, at a 7 percent rate of return, the sustainable price is $21.8/bbl. Hence, the depletion premium (sustainable price minus extraction costs) is $17.4/bbl. This means that if $17.4 were invested for every barrel extracted at a real rate of return of 7 percent, this investment would be sufficient to replace the depleted Oso field by production of solar hydrogen to be sold at $21.8 per barrel equivalent.

(b) Sustainable price for depleting Nigeria's total oil reserves. Nigeria has many other yet undeveloped oil reserves. Since other oil reserves are perfect substitutes for the depleted Oso field, those other oil reserves can be depleted before energy supply has to be converted to solar hydrogen as the sustainable substitute. Therefore, a uniform sustainable price for the depletion of all of Nigeria's oil reserves can be calculated and should be used instead of different sustainability premia for the depletion of each individual oil field. Nigeria's oil reserves are estimated at about 22 billion barrels. At the current extraction rate of 1.6 million barrels per day or 584 million barrels per year, these reserves would last 37.7 years. Hence, the energy equivalent of 584 million barrels of oil per year would have to be provided through solar hydrogen after year 38. Assuming $4.4/b as the extraction costs for all of Nigeria's oil reserves, the sustainable price can be calculated as below:

$$R = \int_0^{\overline{\ }} e^{-rt} 584 * 10^6 P_s dt$$

$$C = \int_0^{37.7} e^{-rt} 584 * 10^6 * 4.4 dt + \int_{37.7}^{\overline{\ }} e^{-rt} 584 * 10^6 * 90 dt \quad (7)$$

Setting R=C, the sustainable price is $11.1/bbl. The depletion premium is $6.7/bbl.

(c) SUSTAINABLE PRICE FOR DEPLETING NIGERIA'S TOTAL OIL AND GAS RESERVES. Nigeria also has significant gas reserves estimated at 150 trillion cubic feet (including undiscovered reserves). With 1.1 megajoule (MJ) per cubic feet of natural gas, the gas reserves contain the energy equivalent of 27 billion barrels of oil. Since gas can be considered an almost perfect substitute for oil, a uniform sustainable price should be considered for all of Nigeria's gas and oil reserves. Using the total oil and gas reserves equivalent to 49 billion barrel oil and current extraction of oil and gas equivalent to 612 million barrel per year, the lifetime of oil and gas reserves together would be eighty years. Hence, solar hydrogen would not need to be produced until the year 81. Again, making the assumption of constant and equal extraction costs for gas and oil, the costs and revenues can be calculated:

$$R = \int_0^{\overline{\ }} e^{-rt} 612 * 10^6 P_s dt$$

$$C = \int_0^{80.1} e^{-rt} 612 * 10^6 * 4.4 dt + \int_{80.1}^{\overline{\ }} e^{-rt} 612 * 10^6 * 90 dt \quad (8)$$

The sustainable price would be $4.8/bbl and the depletion premium $0.4/bbl. The effect of compensatory investment accumulating returns over

80 years would, thus, reduce the depletion premium drastically compared to a scenario without gas.

(d) SUSTAINABLE PRICE WITH INCREASING ENERGY DEMAND. The worldwide demand for energy services is expected to rise significantly over the next decades. Both population growth and increasing per capita income would contribute to this increase that is assumed to be 3.7 percent per year. Since the possibility to increase energy use efficiency will be analyzed in the following section, the calculations in this section are based on an equivalent increase in primary energy consumption. If extraction of gas and oil from Nigeria's reserve was rising at 3.7 percent per year, depletion would not occur after 80 years but after 37.5 years. It is assumed that energy demand would remain constant after year 38, and solar hydrogen equivalent to oil and gas extraction in year 37 would have to be provided at the sustainable price in perpetuity. Based on these assumptions, the present value of costs and revenues are calculated:

$$R = \int_0^{37.5} e^{(0.036-r)t} 612 * 10^6 P_s dt + \int_{37.5}^{\overline{\ }} e^{0.036*37.5-rt} 612 \quad (9)$$

$$C = \int_0^{37.5} e^{(0.036-r)t} 612 * 10^6 * 4.4 dt + \int_{37.5}^{\overline{\ }} e^{0.036*37.5-rt} 612$$

Now, the sustainable price would be $19.1/bbl, equivalent to a depletion premium of $14.7/bbl. This calculation implies the assumption that compensatory investment for current depletion would have to provide not only for a constant consumption stream at a constant price but also for an increasing consumption stream. Since the future population is at least partially dependent on current decisions, it is reasonable to assume that we should bear at least some responsibility for satisfying the demands of an increasing human population. Also, taking the large disparities in per capita energy consumption between countries into account, it can be argued that rich nations whose consumption accounts for the largest share of unsustainable energy resource depletion should pay a price for depletion that provides the opportunity for poorer nations to increase their energy consumption at the same low cost currently enjoyed by the high-energy consuming countries.

(e) THE SUSTAINABLE PRICE WITH ENERGY EFFICIENCY INCREASES. Clearly, an increase in primary energy production, assumed in the previous section, is not

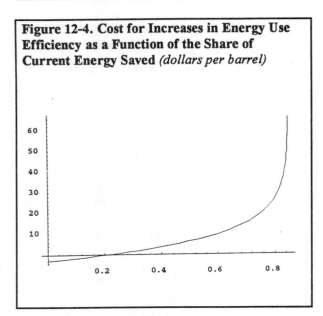

Figure 12-4. Cost for Increases in Energy Use Efficiency as a Function of the Share of Current Energy Saved *(dollars per barrel)*

the least-cost option for satisfying the increasing demand for energy services. Substitution of capital for primary energy and investment in research and development can also satisfy part of the increase for energy services. At this point, only rough cost estimates are provided that should be replaced with more precise calculations as those estimates become available. The cost of increasing energy use efficiency is derived from Lovins's (1990) preliminary estimates of the full technical potential to save U.S. oil consumption. Figure 12-4 shows the cost curve, fitted to Lovins's data. The costs (in dollars per barrel of oil saved) express the present value of the capital investment required to save the specified share of current primary energy input for the production of one unit of energy service. The estimated cost curve is:

$$K = -3 - 10.4 \, Log\left[\frac{E-1+0.85}{0.85}\right]$$

(10)

where K is the marginal cost (in dollars per barrel saved), and E is the share of current primary energy consumption for one unit of energy service. If S is the share of energy saved shown in figure 12-4, with $S=1-E$.

It is clearly unrealistic to expect that any desired level of energy efficiency increase can be achieved immediately. It is estimated that annual increases in energy efficiency of 2 percent are possible over several decades (Worldwatch Institute 1988). This estimate is based on average energy efficiency increases of 1.7 percent per year during the 1973–83

period and the potential to increase these achievements through increased investment. Hence, for the following calculations it is assumed that the annual 3.7 percent increase in demand for energy services is accommodated by 2 percent efficiency increase and 1.7 percent increase in primary energy production. This is consistent with a doubling of primary energy consumption within the next forty years. With an increase in extraction of 1.7 percent per year, Nigeria's gas and oil reserves would be depleted in 50.7 years. It is assumed that efficiency increases can be obtained until the time of depletion and demand would level off after year 51.

The cost for increased energy efficiency per unit of energy service, c_t, is the integral of the cost function depicted in figure 12-4 from zero to the achieved level of energy savings, which, in turn, is a function of time:

$$c_t = \int_0^{1-e^{-0.02t}} -3-10.4\,Log\left[\frac{0.85-S}{0.85}\right]dS =$$
$$-0.026+7.42(1-e^{-0.02t})+10.42(e^{-0.02t}-0.15)\,Log[1.003-1.18(1-e^{-0.02t})]$$

(11)

Now, the price of energy service, not necessarily the price of primary energy, should be sustainable. The sustainable price of energy service is obtained by equating the present value of the cost of extraction (extraction rising at 1.7 percent per year), C_X, the cost of providing solar hydrogen after depletion, C_H, and the assumed expenditures necessary to achieve the 2 percent efficiency increases, C_E, with the present value of revenues, R, received for energy services (rising at 3.7 percent per year) provided at the sustainable price.

$$R = \int_0^{50.7} e^{(0.036-r)t}612*10^6 P_s\,dt + \int_{50.7}^{\infty} e^{0.036*50.7-rt}612*10^6 P_s\,dt$$
$$C_X = \int_0^{50.7} e^{(0.017-r)t}612*10^6*4.4\,dt$$
$$C_H = \int_{50.7}^{\infty} e^{0.017*50.7-rt}612*10^6*90\,dt$$
$$C_E = \int_0^{50.7} e^{(0.036-r)t}612*10^6 c_t\,dt + \int_{50.7}^{\infty} e^{0.036*50.7-rt}612*10^6 c_{50.7}\,dt$$

(12)

The sustainable price for the energy service from 1 barrel of oil today, resulting from $C_X+C_H+C_E=R$, would be \$6.5/bbl and the depletion premium \$2.1/bbl. Under the assumptions made, investments in energy efficiency would be far less costly than accommodation of demand increases by primary energy supply increases. If depletion of fossil fuels was the only concern with respect to the sustainability of the Oso project, $2.1/bbl would be the appropriate depletion premium to be used in evaluating the project.

(f) SUSTAINABLE PRICE WITH RESTRICTIONS ON CO_2 EMISSIONS. The use of hydrocarbons leads to emissions of CO_2 that contribute to the greenhouse effect and global warming. Although what impact increasing concentrations of CO_2 in the atmosphere will have on climate is debated, it is established that burning fossil fuel increases the atmospheric CO_2 concentration. Annual releases of CO_2 are currently estimated at 5.6 billion tons from fossil fuels and 0.6 billion tons from changes in land use (Deutscher Bundestag 1989). It is estimated that 3-4 billion tons of carbon accumulate in the atmosphere annually. Hence, releases of CO_2 would have to be cut roughly in half to stop accumulating CO_2 in the atmosphere. Even if a drastic reduction in carbon emissions is unrealistic in the short term, carbon releases would have to be reduced to the long-run absorption capacity of the atmosphere, which is assumed to be 2-3 billion tons of carbon per year. The following calculations are based on the assumption that global carbon dioxide emissions need to be cut in half by the year 2050. The calculations are easily repeated for alternative carbon dioxide scenarios should new evidence suggests implementation of a different scenario.

The scenario under (e) would imply significant increases in CO_2 emission from the energy produced in Nigeria over the next 50 years. Hence, an alternative scenario is developed under which the extraction of Nigeria's oil and gas reserves is constrained by the requirement that CO_2 emissions from Nigeria's energy sources are gradually reduced to one-half of 1990 levels between 2000 and 2050. Under the

scenario shown in figure 12-5, oil would be depleted until 2050. Gas emits only 65 percent as much CO_2 as oil, compared on an energy content basis. Hence, gas extraction would be increased to the level at which total emissions from gas equal 50 percent of total current CO_2 emissions from gas and oil. All remaining energy demand (as above rising at 1.7 percent per year until year 50) would have to be met with solar hydrogen. Hence, the annual extraction of gas would be constrained by the admissible emissions of CO_2 rather than depletion of the resource. Under this scenario, gas would be depleted after 85.7 years. Thereafter, it would be replaced by hydrogen. Now the sustainable price of energy services can be calculated for this scenario by equating the present value of revenues and costs under constrained extraction of fossil fuels. Revenues and costs of efficiency increases are the same as in equation (12). However, the costs of extracting oil and gas and producing hydrogen would change according to the depletion scenario. The sustainable price of one barrel of oil today would be $14.6/bbl (excluding extraction costs: $10.2/bbl).

The sustainable price of $14.6/bbl reflects the depletion of fossil fuel as well as the carbon dioxide constraint. To separate those two effects, a different scenario is calculated under which unlimited gas reserves are assumed. Hence, the extraction of gas could continue at the rate admissible under the carbon dioxide constraint even after the year 86. The resulting sustainability price is $14.5/bbl. Hence, the depletion premium under the carbon dioxide constraint would be only $0.1/bbl. This reflects the restrictions imposed on the use of fossil fuels by a carbon dioxide constraint. Hence, the appropriate sustainability premium on the depletion of the Oso field would be $10.1/bbl for unsustainable use of the atmosphere as carbon dioxide sink plus $0.1/bbl for unsustainable extraction as depletion premium. In terms of shadow prices, the market price of condensate output needs to be reduced by $10.1/bbl for unsustainable use, while an economic cost of $0.1/bbl for condensate depletion should be included.

Implications of Sustainability Calculations for Project

Table 12-1 summarizes the calculated sustainability premiums for the different approaches used. The CO_2 constraint (f) represents the most comprehensive model including the substitution of condensate with solar hydrogen, efficiency increases in energy use

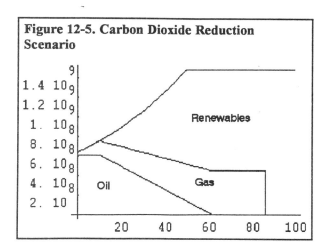

Figure 12-5. Carbon Dioxide Reduction Scenario

Table 12-1. Summary of Sustainability Premiums for Oil Extraction in Nigeria

Evaluation approach	Years until depletion	Sustainability premium ($bbl) (5% ROR)	Sustainability premium ($bbl) (7% ROR)	Sustainability premium ($bbl) (10% ROR)
a. Oso condensate field	21.0	27.5	17.4	8.9
b. Nigeria's oil reserves	37.7	13.6	6.7	2.3
c. Nigeria's oil and gas reserves	80.1	1.7	0.4	0.0
d. Demand growth included	37.5	25.7	14.7	6.1
e. Efficiency increases included	50.7	5.8	2.1	0.0
f. Carbon dioxide constraint included	85.7	13.7	10.2	6.4

Source: Author's analysis of the case study.

and a constraint on admissible carbon dioxide emissions. With an assumed real rate of return on compensatory investment of 7 percent, the sustainability premium is $10.2/bbl of condensate. With this sustainability premium, the project's economic rate of return would be reduced from 51 to 25 percent which is still above the assumed opportunity cost of capital of 12 percent. Hence, under the assumptions made the project would still be acceptable in the base case. However, the sensitivity to oil market price changes would be very large and might lead to the rejection of the project. A drop in oil prices by about $3.8/bbl would be sufficient to reduce the project's economic rate of return (ERR) to 12 percent. This could be considered unacceptable. For a depletion premium of less than $14/bbl, the base case ERR would be above 12 percent. If the project was undertaken, compensatory investment in solar hydrogen technology and energy efficiency would have to be made. Depending on the market prices for energy, some investment would be made by the private sector. The additional investment that would need to be undertaken would be the difference between the sustainability premium multiplied with the extraction under the project and investment undertaken by the private sector.

Two complications arise from the point of view of national welfare maximization. Nigeria clearly has no individual incentive to curtail extraction of hydrocarbons according to a global CO_2 constraint. The decision on a global CO_2 constraint must be taken through international collective action; the sustainable pricing rule would merely be the tool to implement such a decision. Second, Nigeria would

have little incentive to invest parts of the proceeds from the project in energy efficiency increases in other countries (presumably in industrial countries in which most petroleum consumption takes place). However, if all countries agreed on the use of a sustainability constraint, this apparent problem could be solved. If compensatory investment was required for consumption or depletion of natural capital in all countries, it would not matter, in which country compensatory investment is undertaken since the market price would reflect the sustainability premium paid by the producing country. Hence, Nigeria would obtain a higher price for sustainable condensate (for which compensatory investment has been undertaken) than for unsustainable condensate, and compensatory investment would be undertaken in the country in which it yields the highest return.

Conclusions

The sustainable supply rule represents an application of the sustainability principle to the economic evaluation of natural capital depletion. It reflects a model of the economic system as a subsystem of the biosphere and is based on limited substitutability between natural and humanmade capital. This chapter has established the requirements for appropriate shadow prices for natural capital depletion and the need for adequate intergenerational compensation. First, a shadow price below the price of a sustainable substitute should only be used if it can be shown, with reasonable confidence, that the costs are not higher. Second, rents from depletion of natural capital would have to be shared equally with all future generations. Third, sharing of rents should be accommodated through investment in sustainable functional substitutes. Furthermore, in order to be of practice use, the information requirements for the use of such a pricing rule should be limited.

By linking the shadow price of natural capital to the price of a sustainable substitute, the use of the sustainable supply rule would lead to a reversal of the default assumption that natural capital is a free good. Instead, the default assumption is that every unsustainable activity must be eventually converted into a sustainable activity. The rule is suitable as a preemptive measure against biases in evaluating natural capital. Using the sustainable supply rule, differences in relative scarcity of different resources would be appropriately reflected in the sustainable price. The sustainable supply rule alleviates the intergenerational justice problem since the benefits from natural capital depletion are shared equally with all future generations.

The sustainable supply rule is based on a semi-strong sustainability constraint that requires sustainability for groups of functionally substitutable types of capital, assuming that there is far less uncertainty about future functional substitution than about economic substitutability. The suggested rule is based on compensation through investment in sustainable functional substitutes. Finally, a major advantage of the sustainable supply rule is that information requirements for determination of shadow prices for natural capital depletion are moderate. The lifetime of a resource and the price of a sustainable substitute suffice to calculate the sustainable supply curve. Even without knowledge of the demand curve, the sustainable price can be determined iteratively until the market equilibrium lies on the sustainable supply curve. Furthermore, the discount rate used represents the real rate of return on specific compensating investment which can be assessed more objectively and is less likely to be controversial than the appropriate social discount rate.

Use of the sustainable supply rule is clearly preferable to the use of the currently most applied rule: ignore costs of natural capital depletion. However, the justification of the sustainable supply rule does not lie in formal social welfare maximization and it may be possible to show that the sustainable supply rule is inferior to a traditional efficiency approach *if* the conditions for first-best decisionmaking are met. These conditions would be certainty or alternatively complete markets, internalization of all external costs, and profit/social-welfare maximization. The defense of the sustainability rule rests primarily on the assessment that these assumptions are highly unrealistic. However, in those rare cases where market failures and systematic biases are removed and uncertainty about substitutability and inter-dependencies in complex natural systems is sufficiently resolved, the traditional analysis would be preferable as long as actual compensation of future generations is undertaken.

Work in the area of ecological economics is exploratory in nature. A more technical analysis of the involved problems is called for. While the general approach for a sustainable supply rule is presented in this chapter, more work has to follow in order to explore alternatives, resolve theoretical questions, and make the approach more workable for practical evaluation. Theoretical questions concerning the definition of sustainable substitutes and functional substitutability remain. Since there is uncertainty about substitutability, the remaining risk of inadequate compensation needs to be addressed. An interesting extension would involve inquiry into the suitability of the proposed approach for a general shift from taxation of labor to taxation of natural capital, a concept that is intuitively appealing in face of high unemployment and environmental degradation. For this end, the overall impact of universal application of the suggested sustainability constraint on the economy would have to be assessed. Finally, the issue of population growth leaves unresolved questions on the appropriateness of the suggested equal allocation of resources to all generations.

More practical issues to be addressed include the institutional arrangements for implementation of the intergenerational compensation schemes. Who undertakes and supervises the undertaken investment and to whom do the returns to such investment accrue? In a related paper, I try to answer the question whether the allocation of intergenerational property rights and creation of intergenerational markets can bring about the desired compensation through market mechanisms without huge government bureaucracies (von Amsberg 1992b).

The sustainable supply rule needs to be modified for practical cases such as heterogenous resources, substitutes with inelastic supply and gradual phasing-in of the sustainable substitute. While the rule remains applicable in principle, the appropriate equations need to be worked out to guide the practitioner in such instances. Finally, for commonly used natural resources, sustainable substitutes should be identified explicitly and the sustainable price calculated in order to assess the impacts of the suggested rule.

This chapter is intended to stimulate thinking and contribute to the definition and implementation of a sustainable development path for industrial as well as developing nations. If the present generation uses its resources to invest in research, development and implementation of sustainable technologies and initiates the transition toward a sustainable economy, we will not have to bear the responsibility for impoverishing this planet for generations to come. The chapter has not directly addressed the issues of *intra*-generational justice even though implementation of a sustainability constraint would have profound implications for the allocation of resources within the living generation. Most compensating investment would have to be undertaken by industrial countries with the highest amount of unsustainable consumption. On the other hand, many opportunities for compensating investment with the highest return would likely be in developing countries. This could motivate an increased resource flow from industrial to developing countries. More explicitly, the sustainable supply rule could be modified such that a sustainable supply of a resource would be required not at the current level of consumption but at the increasing level of consumption resulting from higher consumption in developing countries. Then, sustainability would ensure that consumption takes place at a level that can theoretically be achieved by all countries and would avoid the ecological disaster likely if all countries consume at the current rate of the industrial nations.

Notes

1. This paper is a slightly modified version of a paper entitled "The Economic Evaluation of Natural Capital Depletion: An Application of the Sustainability Principle" that was prepared for the World Bank's Environment Department. I wish to acknowledge helpful comments of James A. Brander, Herman E. Daly, Salah El Serafy, Robert Goodland, Bryan Routledge and David Wheeler. Of course, I retain responsibility for the expressed opinions and possible errors.

2. For an overview of the arguments see the Introduction in Lind (1982).

3. Knightian uncertainty refers to situations in which even reasonable guesses about the distribution function of a parameter are not available.

References

Ahmad, Yusuf J., Salah El Serafy and Ernst Lutz, eds. 1989. *Environmental Accounting for Sustainable Development*. Washington, DC: World Bank..

Arrow, Kenneth and Anthony C. Fisher. 1974. "Environmental Preservation, Uncertainty and Irreversibility." *Quarterly Journal of Economics* 88: 312-319.

Baumol, William J. and Wallace E. Oates. 1988. *The Theory of Environmental Policy*. 2 ed. New York: Cambridge University Press.

Berry, Brian. 1983. "Intergenerational Justice in Energy Policy." In Douglas MacLean and Peter G. Brown, eds. *Energy and the Future*. Totowa, New Jersey: Rowan and Littlefield.

Cichetti, Carles and A. Myrick Freeman III. 1971. "Option Costanza, Robert, ed. 1991. *Ecological Economics*. New York: Columbia University Press.

Daly, Herman E. 1982. "Chicago School Individualism versus Sexual Reproduction: A Critique of Becker and Tomes." *Journal of Economic Issues* 6(1): 307-12.

——. 1991. "From Empty-World Economics to Full-World Economics." In Robert Goodland, Herman E. Daly and Salah El Serafy, eds. *Population, Technology and Lifestyle: The Transition to Sustainability*. Washington, DC: Island Press.

Daly, Herman E. and John B. Cobb. 1989. *For the Common Good: Redirecting the Economy Toward the Community, the Environment and a Sustainable Future*. Boston: Beacon Press.

Dasgupta, Partha and Geoffrey Heal. 1979. *The Economic Theory and Exhaustible Resources*. Cambridge, England: Cambridge University Press.

Deutscher Bundestag. 1989. *Schutz der Erdatmosphäre, Eine internationale Herausforderung*. Bonn, Germany.

Dixit, A.P. Hammond and M. Hoel. 1980. "On Hartwick's Rule for Regular Maximum Paths of Capital Accumulation and Resource Depletion." *Review of Economic Studies* 47: 551-56.

El Serafy, Salah. 1989. "The Proper Calculation of Income from Depletable Natural Resources." In Yusuf J. Ahmad, Salah El Serafy and Ernst Lutz, eds. *Environmental Accounting for Sustainable Development*. Washington, DC: World Bank.

Georgescu-Roegen, Nicholas. 1971. *The Entropy Law and the Economic Process*. Cambridge, Mass.: Harvard University Press.

Hartwick, John M. 1977. "Intergenerational Equity and the Investing of Rents form Exhaustible Resources." *American Economic Review* 67(5): 972-74.

Hotelling, Harold. 1931. "The Economics of Exhaustible Resources." *Journal of Political Economy* 39:137-175.

Howarth, Richard B. and Richard B. Norgaard. 1990. "Intergenerational Resource Rights, Efficiency and

Social Optimality." *Land Economics* 66(1): 1-11.

Ise, John. 1925. "The Theory of Value as Applied to Natural Resources." *American Economic Review* 15: 284-291.

Lind, Robert C. 1982. *Discounting for Time and Risk in Energy Policy*. Baltimore, MD: Johns Hopkins University Press.

Lovins, Armory B. 1990. "Four Revolutions in Electric Efficiency." *Contemporary Policy Issues* 8 (3): 122-143.

Marglin, Stephen A. 1963. "The Social Rate of Discount and the Optimal Rate of Investment." *Quarterly Journal of Economics* 77: 95-111.

Markandya, Anil and David Pearce. 1988. *Environmental Considerations and the Choice of the Social Discount Rate in Developing Countries*. World Bank Working Paper 3. Washington, DC.

Mikesell, Raymund F. 1991. "Project Evaluation and Sustainable Development." In Robert Goodland, Herman E. Daly and Salah El Serafy, eds. *Population, Technology and Lifestyle: The Transition to Sustainability*. Washington, DC: Island Press.

Norgaard, Richard B. and Richard B. Howarth. 1991. "Sustainability and Discounting the Future." In Robert Costanza, ed., *Ecological Economics: The Science and Management of Sustainability*. New York: Columbia University Press.

Ogden, Joan M. and Robert H. Williams. 1989. *Solar Hydrogen, Moving Beyond Fossil Fuels*, Washington, DC: World Resources Institute.

Page, Talbot. 1977. "Equitable Use of the Resource Base." *Environment and Planning A* 9: 15-22.

———. 1983. "Intergenerational Justice as Opportunity." In Douglas MacLean and Peter G. Brown, eds. *Energy and the Future*. Totowa, New Jersey: Rowan and Littlefield.

Pearce, David W. and R. Kerry Turner. 1989. *Economics of Natural Resources and the Environment*. Baltimore, MD: John Hopkins University Press.

Pearce, David W., Edward Barbier, Anil Markandya, Scott Barrett, R. Kerry Turner and Timothy Swanson. 1991. *Blueprint 2: Greening the World Economy*. London: Earthscan Publications.

Pezzey, John. 1989. *Economic Analysis of Sustainable Growth and Sustainable Development*. Environment Working Paper 15. World Bank, Washington, DC.

Pigou, A.C. 1932. *The Economics of Welfare*. London: Macmillan.

Rawls, John. 1971. *A Theory of Justice*. Cambridge, Mass.: Harvard University Press.

Samuelson, Paul A. and William Samuelson. 1980. *Economics*, 11 ed. New York: McGraw-Hill.

von Amsberg, Joachim. 1992a. "Sustainability and the Depletion of Natural Capital: Intergenerational Welfare Considerations." Discussion Paper. University of British Columbia, Vancouver.

———. 1992b. "A Market Mechanism for Achieving Sustainability." Discussion Paper. University of British Columbia, Vancouver.

———. 1992c. *The Economic Evaluation of Natural Capital Depletion: An Application of the Sustainability Principle*. Environment Department Working Paper 56. World Bank, Washington, DC.

World Commission on the Environment and Development (WCED). 1987. *Our Common Future*. New York: Oxford University Press.

Worldwatch Institute. 1988. *State of the World 1988*. Washington, DC.

13

Operationalizing Sustainable Development by Investing in Natural Capital

Herman Daly

Why Invest in Natural Capital?

Seven Propositions

The following propositions, taken together, build an argument for shifting the focus and active margin of investment in natural capital, for investing (directly, indirectly, actively or passively) in something that, by definition, we do not know how to make.

First, the pre-analytic vision, the foundation, of standard economics is that there is an isolated circular flow of exchange value between firms and households, Nothing enters from the environment nor exits to it. The physical environment is completely abstracted from it. By contrast, the pre-analytic vision of ecological economics is that the economy, in its physical dimensions, is an open subsystem of a finite, nongrowing, and materially closed ecosystem.

Second, the economic subsystem has grown to the extent that remaining natural capital has become scarce relative to manmade capital. This imbalance forces into practical attention three neglected macroeconomic questions: how big *is* the economic subsystem relative to the containing ecosystem? how big *can* it be without destroying the larger sustaining system? and how big *should* it be in order to optimize life enjoyment for human beings (recognizing the instrumental value of the environment) or for humans and other sentient species (recognizing instrumental and intrinsic value)?

Third, although the environment has been abstracted from by standard economics, the concept of sustainability has been recognized and incorporated into the very definition of income as "the maximum amount that a community can consume over some time period and still be as well off at the end of the period as at the beginning" (Hicks 1946). Being as well off means having the same capacity to produce the same income in the next year, that is, maintaining capital intact. The criterion of sustainability is thus explicit in this Hicksian definition of income. But the condition of maintaining capital intact has applied only to manmade capital, since in the past natural capital was abstracted from because it was not scarce. The Hicksian definition of income must in the future apply to total scarce capital—which now includes natural capital as well as manmade.

Fourth, there are two ways to maintain total capital intact: the *sum* of manmade and natural capital can be maintained constant in value, or *each* component can be maintained intact separately. The first way is reasonable if one believes that manmade and natural capital are substitutes. In this view it is totally acceptable to divest natural capital as long as one creates by investment an equivalent value in manmade capital. The second way is reasonable if one believes that manmade and natural capital are complements. The complements must each be maintained intact (separately or jointly in fixed proportion) because the productivity of one depends on the availability of the other. The first case is called "weak sustainability" and the second case "strong sustainability."

Fifth, manmade and natural capital are fundamentally complements and only marginally substitutes. Therefore strong sustainability is ultimately the relevant concept, although weak sustainability is a useful first step. There are reasons for considering manmade and natural capital to be complements more than substitutes:

• To illustrate, one can assume the opposite and show how absurd it is. If manmade capital were a near perfect substitute for natural capital, then natural capital would be a near perfect substitute for manmade capital. But if that were so, there then would have been no reason to accumulate manmade capital in the first place, since we were endowed by nature with a near perfect substitute.

• Manmade capital is itself made from natural resources that come from natural capital, so producing more of the alleged substitute requires more of the very thing being substituted for—a condition very much like complementarity!

• Manmade capital (along with labor) is an agent of transformation of the resource flow from raw material inputs into product outputs. The natural resource flow (and the natural capital stock that generates it) are the *material cause* of production; the capital stock that transforms raw material inputs into product outputs is the *efficient cause* of production. One cannot substitute efficient cause for material cause; one cannot build the same wooden house with half the timber no matter how many saws and hammers one tries to substitute. Also, to process more timber into more wooden houses, in the same time period, requires more saws, hammers, and so forth. Clearly the basic relation of manmade and natural capital is one of complementarity, not substitutability.

The complementarity of manmade and natural capital is made obvious at a concrete and commonsense level by asking what good is a sawmill without a forest, a fishing boat without populations of fish, a refinery without petroleum deposits, or an irrigated farm without an aquifer or river? We have long recognized the complementarity between public infrastructure and private capital—what good is a car or truck without roads to drive on? Following Lotka and Georgescu-Roegen, we can take the concept of natural capital even further and distinguish between endosomatic (within-skin) and exosomatic (outside-skin) natural capital. We can then ask, what good is the private endosomatic capital of our lungs and respiratory system without the complementary exosomatic capital of green plants that take up carbon dioxide in the short run, while in the long run, replenishing the enormous atmospheric stock of oxygen and keeping the atmosphere at the proper mix of gases, that is, the mix to which our respiratory system is adapted and therefore complementary?[1]

Sixth, if we accept that natural and manmade capital are complements rather than substitutes, then what follows? What follows is that *if factors are complements, then the one in shortest supply will be the limiting factor.* If factors are substitutes, then neither can be a limiting factor, since the productivity of one does not much depend on availability of the other. The idea that either natural or manmade capital could be a limiting factor simply cannot arise if the factors are thought to be substitutes. Once we see that they are complements then we must ask which one is the limiting factor, that is, which is in shortest supply?

This proposition gives rise to the following thesis: *that the world is moving from an era in which manmade capital was the limiting factor into an era in which remaining natural capital is the limiting factor.* Nowadays the production of caught fish is limited by remaining fish populations, not by number of fishing boats; timber production is limited by remaining forests, not by saw-mills; barrels of pumped crude oil is limited by petroleum deposits (or perhaps more stringently by the capacity of the atmosphere to absorb CO_2), not by pumping capacity; agricultural production is frequently limited by water availability, not by tractors, harvesters or even land area. We have moved from a world relatively full of natural capital and empty of manmade capital (and people) to a world relatively full of the latter and empty of the former.

Seventh, economic logic requires that we maximize the productivity of the limiting factor in the short run, and invest in increasing its supply in the long run. When the limiting factor changes then behavior that used to be economic becomes uneconomic. Economic logic remains the same, but the pattern of scarcity in the world changes, with the result that behavior must change if it is to remain economic. Instead of maximizing returns to and investing in manmade capital (as was appropriate in an empty world), we must now maximize returns to and invest in natural capital (as is appropriate in a full world). This is not "new economics" but new behavior consistent with "old economics" in a world with a new pattern of scarcity. The fact that much natural capital is outside the market greatly weakens the ability of market prices to reflect this new scarcity. The practice of discounting also greatly diminishes the weight of future scarcity even where markets exist.

Rational Response to Scarcity

Since natural capital has replaced manmade capital as the limiting factor to growth, we should adopt policies that maximize its present productivity and increase its future supply. This conclusion is far from being trivial or irrelevant, because it means that current policies of maximizing the productivity and accumulation of manmade capital are no longer "economic," even in the most traditional sense of the word. In addition, the Hicksian definition of income imposes the condition that capital be maintained intact. If natural capital is the limiting factor then the proper measurement of income requires that natural capital maintenance take priority.

This is not the proclamation of yet another hare-brained "new economics." Rather it is the application of unchanged traditional economics to a changed pattern of scarcity, or the belated application of economic logic to the full world of today instead of the empty world of yesterday.

But how could the pattern of scarcity have changed so dramatically without economists noticing it? Several reasons can be given. First, exponential growth is deceptive. The bottle changes from half full to totally full in the same period of time it went from 1 percent to 2 percent full. Second, economists have considered manmade and natural capital to be substitutes when they are basically complements. If factors are substitutes, then a shortage of one does not limit the productivity of the other. Neither factor can be limiting if they are good substitutes. So even as the world moves from 40 to 80 percent full in the next roughly 35-year doubling time, economists are counting on manmade capital to restore the conditions of relative emptiness by substituting for natural capital.[2] Third, we subconsciously realize that if we cannot continue production growth then the only way to cure poverty is to face up to both sharing and population control. Since these are considered impossible by political realists, it is gratuitously concluded that whatever argument give rise to this conclusion must be wrong. These three biases, I believe, have kept us from seeing the obvious— namely, that the fish catch is limited by remaining populations of fish in the sea, not by the number of fishing boats; timber production is limited by remaining forests, not by saw mills. More saw mills and more fishing boats do not result in more cut timber and more caught fish. For that you need more forests and larger fish populations in the sea. Natural capital and manmade capital are complementary, and natural capital has become the limiting factor. More manmade capital, far from substituting for natural capital, just puts greater complementary demands on it, running it down faster to temporarily support the value of manmade capital, making it all the more limiting in the future.

What is "Investing in Natural Capital"?

Even if the argument is convincing that the focus of investment should shift from manmade to natural capital, a problem remains. Since natural capital is by definition not manmade, it is not immediately obvious what we mean by "investing" in it. Yet the term investment applies because our concept involves the classical notion of "waiting" or refraining from current consumption as the way to invest in natural capital. Before investigating further the meaning of investment in natural capital, we should pause to examine the concept of natural capital itself.

Defining Natural Capital

Natural capital is the stock that yields the flow of natural resources—the population of fish in the ocean that regenerates the flow of cut timber; the petroleum deposits in the ground whose liquidation yields the flow of pumped crude oil. The natural income yielded by natural capital consists of natural services as well as natural resources.[3] Natural capital is of two kinds: renewable (such as fish or trees) and nonrenewable (such as petroleum).

Several difficulties with these definitions should be noticed. First, capital has traditionally been defined as "produced (manmade) means of production," yet natural capital was not and in most cases cannot be produced by man. For the more functional definition, capital is "a stock that yields a flow of useful goods or services into the future," and natural capital fits this conception very well. Also, there is an important category that overlaps natural and manmade capital— such things as plantation forests, fish ponds, herds of cattle bread for certain characteristics, etc.—are not manmade but are significantly modified from their natural state by human action. We will refer to these things as "cultivated natural capital." And, of course, renewable resources can be exploited to extinction and rendered nonrenewable, while nonrenewable resources can be renewed if we are prepared to wait for geological eons to roll by. Subject to these caveats the terms are well defined and are in current use.[4]

We will consider investment in renewable natural capital first and then the more problematic case of nonrenewable natural capital.

Investing in Renewable Natural Capital

For renewable resource management, "waiting" investment simply means constraining the annual offtake. Keeping the annual offtake equal to the annual growth increment (sustainable yield) is equivalent to maintenance investment—that is, to the avoidance of running down the productive stock, equivalent to the Hicksian condition that capital remain intact. Net investment in renewables is simply more waiting—allowing all or a part of the growth increment to be added to the productive stock each year rather than consumed. Investment in natural capital, both maintenance and net investment, is fundamentally passive with respect to natural capital that is simply left alone and allowed to generate. Cultivated natural capital investment also involves waiting, except that it is never really left alone. Even during the waiting period some tending and supervision is required.

Must investment in renewable natural capital be only passive, or can we actively recreate or even design ecosystems? Does Biosphere II out in Arizona stand a chance of working? Beyond its undoubted experimental value on a small scale, is a larger version of such active investment in "natural" capital likely to be a good bet in the future? Can the whole ecosystem become cultivated in natural capital (like a catfish pond), except that it is self-sustaining? I suspect that the answer will ultimately turn out to be "no," but that is just my intuition. What is a fact, however, is that we are currently so far away from the requisite knowledge that policies of active investment can be ruled out as at best quantitatively insignificant and at worst qualitatively dangerous. As Paul Ehrlich has reminded us, ecological economics is a discipline with a time limit. We do not have time to dream of creating Biosphere II. We must save the remnants of Biosphere I and allow them to regenerate by the passive investment of waiting. The term *laissez faire* thus acquires a new and deeper meaning for ecological economists.

Budgeting Nonrenewable Natural Capital

Nonrenewable natural capital cannot be increased either actively or passively. It can only be diminished. We can only divest nonrenewable natural capital itself, even though we invest in the manmade capital equipment that hastens the rate of extraction and divestment. Nonrenewable natural capital is like an inventory of already produced goods, rather than a productive machine or a reproducing population. For nonrenewable natural capital, the question is not how to invest but how best to liquidate the inventory—and what to do with the net wealth realized from that liquidation. Currently, we are counting the liquidated wealth as income, which is clearly wrong because it is not a permanent or sustainable source of consumption.

A better alternative would be to allocate all or part of the net receipts of nonrenewable exploitation for financing waiting investments in renewable natural capital—that is, to allow reduction of the offtake of renewable in order to build up renewable stocks to larger levels, producing larger sustainable yields, that represent true income. The basic idea is to convert nonrenewable natural capital into a renewable substitute, to the extent possible. The general rule would be to deplete nonrenewable at a rate equal to the rate of development of renewable substitutes. Thus, extractive projects based on nonrenewable must be paired in some way with a project that develops the renewable substitute. Net receipts of nonrenewable exploitation are divided into two components (an income component and a capital set-aside) such that the capital set-aside, when invested in a renewable substitute each year, by the time the nonrenewable is depleted, will have grown to a stock size whose sustainable yield is equal to the income component that was being consumed all along. The capital set-side will be greater the lower the growth rate of the renewable substitute (real or biological discount rate) and the shorter the lifetime of the nonrenewable reserves (that is, the reserve stock divided by annual depletion).

The logic and calculations have been worked out by El Serafy (1989) in the context of national income accounting but apply with equal relevance to accounting at the project level. The true rate of return on the project pair would be calculated on the basis of the income component only as net revenue. This differs from the usual cost/benefit evaluation of projects in explicitly costing sustainability by using income (sustainable by definition) rather than cash flow, and by requiring actual rather than hypothetical replacement investment. It does *not* require that the project itself be immortal, nor that nonrenewable should forever remain in the ground, never to benefit anyone.

DEFINING SUBSTITUTES. Difficulties remain concerning how to define "substitute"—whether narrowly or broadly. Probably a broad definition would be indicated initially—at least broad enough to encompass improvements in energy efficiency as a renewable substitute for petroleum depletion and in recycling as a renewable substitute for copper depletion.

In the case of divestment of a renewable resource stock, capital consumption is treated as depreciation of a productive asset (the sacrificed base population that was producing a permanent yield). Depreciation should be deducted from gross income to calculate net income. In the case of nonrenewable, the reduction of stocks is treated as liquidation of existing inventories rather than running down of capacity for future production, and consequently should not even be a part of gross income—as El Serafy rightly insists.

A difficulty in the application of the rule can be easily imagined. Suppose alcohol is the near renewable substitute for gasoline. If one tried to invest all of the capital component of petroleum net revenues in natural capital or cultivated natural capital (wood or sugar cane alcohol), the price of alcohol would rise enormously as large amounts of land would be bid away from food to sugar cane. (This is an indication of how far away we are from sustainability.) The solution would be to begin pricing petroleum energy at the cost of sugar cane energy—namely, at the cost of its long-run renewable substitute. Then as the price of both petroleum and alcohol energy increases, the rate of depletion of petroleum would be slowed; and as depletion is slowed the life expectancy of petroleum reserves will increase, and the percentage of net receipts representing capital will diminish. At some higher price, the amount to be invested will fall. In effect, the difficulty of investing the petroleum capital component will provide the effective limit on the rate of depletion of petroleum. This remains true even if fusion energy rather than sugar cane is taken as the long-run permanent substitute.

This rule is similar to that of economist John Ise (1925) who argued that nonrenewable resources should be priced at the cost of their nearest renewable substitute. In the example, alcohol was treated as the nearest renewable substitute, but other renewable near substitutes may be cheaper (for example, technical improvements in energy efficiency) and should be the effective near substitute as long as they remain least-cost. This last point can be generalized: although we cannot invest in nonrenewables, we can manage their liquidation in such a way as to increase direct passive investment in renewable and indirect active investment in measures that make waiting (throughput reduction) easier.

INDIRECT INVESTMENTS. Any investment that enables us to reduce the volume of throughput needed to maintain a given level of welfare can be considered an indirect investment in natural capital. Two classes of investment for reducing the need for throughput come to mind. The most obvious is investment in reducing population growth—first stopping growth and then gradually reducing numbers of people by reducing birth rates. Investments in female literacy and social security systems, along with contraceptives and delivery systems, offer investment opportunities of this kind. The second class of investment, which

will mainly occupy our attention for the remainder of this chapter, is in increasing the efficiency of use per unit of throughput. More generally, this means increasing the efficiency with which capital, both natural and manmade, is used to provide life-support and life-enhancing services.

EFFICIENCY RATIOS. The efficiency with which we use the world to satisfy our wants depends on two factors: the amount of service gained per unit of manmade capital and the amount of service lost per unit of natural capital converted into manmade capital. This overall ecological-economic efficiency can be stated as the ratio:

$$\frac{MMK\,services\,gained}{NK\,services\,lost}$$

where MMK is manmade capital and NK is natural capital. In an empty world, there is no noticeable sacrifice of NK services required by increases in MMK, so the denominator is irrelevant. In a full world, any increase in MMK comes at a noticeable reduction in NK and its services.

This efficiency ratio can be "unfolded" into four components by means of the identity below.[5] Each term of the identity represents a dimension of efficiency that might be improved by increased investment in knowledge or technique.

$$\frac{MMK\,services\,gained}{NK\,services\,sacrificed} = \frac{MMK\,services\,gained}{MM\,stock} \times \frac{MMK\,stock}{thruput} \times \frac{thruput}{NK\,stock} \times \frac{NK\,stock}{NK\,services\,sacrificed}$$
$$\qquad\qquad\qquad\quad (1)\qquad\quad (2)\qquad (3)\qquad\quad (4)$$

Ratio (1) is the *service efficiency* of the manmade capital stock. It depends on several things: first, the technical design efficiency of the product itself; second, the economic efficiency of resource allocation among the different product uses in conformity with individual preferences and ability to pay, and third, the distributive efficiency among individuals. The first two are straightforward in conformity with standard economics, but the third requires explanation. Usually, distribution is carefully separated from efficiency by the Pareto condition that utility cannot be compared across individuals. Of course, in practice, we do compare utility across individuals, and it does make sense to assume that total social utility is increased when resources are redistributed from the low marginal utility uses of the rich to the high marginal uses of the poor. One can reject the total egalitarianism implicit in carrying this idea to its logical extreme, while at the same time agreeing with Joan Robinson that it is possible to allow too much of the good juice of utility to evaporate from commodities by allowing them to be too unequally distributed. In a full world, investments in distributive efficiency can no longer be ruled out of bounds. Economists have studied these aspects of service efficiency, especially allocative efficiency via the price mechanism, in great detail. Further refinements from deeper study of ratio (1) will probably be less productive than the study of the other three ratios.

Ratio (2) reflects the *maintenance efficiency* or durability of the manmade capital stock. While ratio (1) measures the service intensity per unit of time of the manmade stock, ratio (2) measures the number of units of time over which the stock yields that service. Ratio (2) is the durability of the stock, or the "residence time" of a unit of resource throughput as a part of the manmade capital stock. A slower rate of throughput means reduced depletion and pollution, all else being equal. Maintenance efficiency is increased by designing commodities to be durable, repairable and recyclable, or by designing patterns of living to make certain commodities less necessary to begin with.

Ratio (3) is the *growth efficiency* of natural capital in yielding an increment available for offtake as throughput. Basically, it is determined by the biological growth rate of the population or ecosystem being exploited. For example, pine trees grow faster than mahogany, so in uses where either will do, pine is more efficient. Generally, nature presents a menu of different species growing at different rates. To the extent that we are able to design our technologies and consumption patterns to depend on the faster growing species, that will be more efficient, other things being equal.

As interest in genetic engineering grows, there will be more attempts to speed up growth rates of exploited species (for example, bovine growth hormone). The green revolution involves an attempt to speed up growth rates of wheat and rice. Since an increase in biological growth rate frequently comes at the expense of stability, resilience, resistance to disease or predators, it may be that attempts to speed up reproductive rates will usually end up costing more than they are worth. It is for now surely better for humans to slow down our own biological growth rate than to attempt to speed up the growth rates of all the species we depend upon. Nevertheless, to some degree, we can adapt our pattern of consumption to depend more on naturally faster growing species, where possible.

For sustained-yield exploitation, ratio (3) will vary with the size of the population maintained, according to the familiar inverted-U-shaped function. For any chosen combination of population size and yield, the ratio would remain constant over time under sustained yield management. Maximum sustained yield would of course maximize this dimension of efficiency over the long run (if harvesting costs are constant). In the short run, this ratio can be driven very high by the nonsustainable practice of exceeding renewable rates of harvest and thereby converting permanent stock into one-time throughput.

Ratio (4) measures the amount of natural capital stock that can be exploited for throughput (either as source or sink), per unit of other natural services sacrificed. For example, if we exploit a forest to get maximum sustainable yield of timber (or maximum absorption of CO_2), then we will, to some degree, sacrifice other natural services of the forest (such as wildlife habitat, erosion control and water catchment). We want to minimize the loss of other ecosystem services per unit of natural capital managed with the objective of yielding a single service—usually that of generating raw material throughput. Ratio (4) might be called *ecosystem service efficiency*, reflecting the minimization of loss of other ecosystem services when a population or ecosystem is exploited primarily for one service.

Conclusions

The world is complicated and no simple formula can capture everything. But these four dimensions of ecological-economic efficiency may be helpful to ecological economists in devising ways to invest directly in natural capital. As NK is converted into MMK we want at each step to maximize the service from the increment of MMK and to minimize the loss of ecosystem service from the decrement of NK. But at some point, even if carried out efficiently, this process of conversion of NK into MMK will itself reach an economic limit, an optimal scale of the economic subsystem beyond which further expansion would increase costs faster than benefits. This optimal scale is defined by the usual economic criterion of equating marginal costs and benefits. This criterion assumes that marginal benefits decline and that marginal costs increase, both in a continuous fashion.

It is reasonable to think that marginal benefits decline because humans are sufficiently rational to satisfy their most pressing wants first. But the assumption that marginal costs (sacrificed ecosystem services) increase in a continuous fashion is problematic. As the human niche has expanded, the stresses on the ecosystem have increased, but there has been no rational ordering by human or providential intelligence to ensure that the least important ecosystem services are always sacrificed first. We appear to be sacrificing some vital services rather early. This is another way of saying that ratio (4), ecological service efficiency, has been ignored. If we begin to pay attention to that dimension of efficiency then we may expect human rationality to order ecosystem service sacrifices from least to worst and thus justify economists' usual assumption of gradually rising marginal costs. That would make the optimal scale of the human niche more definable.

The present lack of rational sequencing of ecosystem costs is due both to nonrecognition of the problem and to ignorance of ecosystem functioning. Prudence in the face of large uncertainties about ecosystem costs should lead us to be very conservative about risking any further expansion. But even with complete certainty and a least-cost sequence of environmental costs, there would still be an optimal scale beyond which growth would be uneconomical.

And, of course, this notion of optimal scale is purely anthropocentric, counting all other species only for their instrumental value to human welfare. If we attribute intrinsic value in some degree to other sentient creatures, then the optimal scale of the human niche would be smaller than if only human sentience counted. Investment in natural capital would then have the additional benefit of increasing life support services to nonhuman species whose enjoyment of life would no longer be counted as zero, though it certainly should not be counted as equal to human life enjoyment. To recognize that a sparrow's intrinsic value is greater than zero, does not negate the fact that a human is worth many sparrows. But not even theology can say how many sparrows are worth a human, much less economics.

Notes

1. If natural and manmade capital are obviously complements, how is it that economists have overwhelmingly treated them as substitutes? First, not all economists have—Leontief's input-output economics with its assumption of fixed factor proportions treats all factors

as complements at least in the short run of several years. Second, the formal, mathematical definitions of complementarity and substitutability are such that in the two-factor case the factors must be substitutes. Since most textbooks are written on two-dimensional paper, this case receives most attention. Third, mathematical convenience continues to dominate reality in the general reliance on Cobb-Douglas and other constant elasticity of substitution production functions in which there is near infinite substitutability of factors, in particular of capital for resources. Fourth, exclusive myopic attention to the margin results in marginal substitution obscuring overall relations of complementarity. For example, private expenditure on extra car maintenance may substitute reduced public expenditure on roads. But this marginal element of substitution should not obscure the fact that private cars and roads are basically complementary forms of capital. Fourth, there may well be substitution of capital for resources in aggregate production functions reflecting a change in product mix from resource-intensive to capital-intensive products. But this is an artefact of product aggregation, not factor substitution along a given product isoquant. Also, a new product may be designed that gives the same service with less resource use—e.g., light bulbs that give more lumens per watt. This is technical progress, a qualitative improvement in the state of the art, not the substitution of a quantity of capital for a quantity of resources in the production of a given quantity of a specific product.

No one denies the reality of technical progress, but to call such changes the substitution of capital for resources (or of manmade for natural capital) is a serious confusion. It seems that some economists are counting as "capital" all improvements in knowledge, technology, managerial skills, etc.—in short anything that would increase the efficiency with which resources are used. If this is the usage, then "capital" and resources would by definition be substitutes in the same sense that more efficient use of a resource is a substitute for having more of the resource. But formally to define capital as efficiency would make a mockery of the neoclassical theory of production, where efficiency is a ratio of output to input, and capital is a quantity of input.

2. The measure of "fullness" is taken to be the percentage of the net primary product of photosynthesis that is directly or indirectly preempted for human purposes. For land-based exosystems, the percentage preempted is estimated at 40 percent (see Vitousek and others 1986).

3. Analogous to the public services of infrastructure capital are the life support services of natural capital. Theses include: disposal of wastes and cycling of nutrients; regulation of the hydrologic cycle to provide fresh water; generation and preservation of fertile soils; benign regulation of the mix of gases in the atmosphere; moderation of temperature and weather; filtration of most harmful types of solar radiation; control of vast majority of agricultural pests and disease causing organisms; pollination of many crops; maintenance of sources of forest

products and food from the sea; provision of a "genetic library" of biodiversity containing enormous information on strategies for survival as well as patterns of beauty and delight; and most important of all, the conversion of solar radiation via photosynthesis into forms of energy usable by animals, including ourselves.

Just as infrastructure supports the private sector, so does the "infrastructure" of the natural capital support the entire human economy, both its private and public sectors. As the economic subsystem has grown relative to the finite and nongrowing ecosystem, ecological space has been converted into economic space (natural capital into manmade capital), thus reducing the relative and absolute amount of the total ecosystem functioning as natural capital, and consequently lowering the capacity of the ecosystem to perform the infrastructure services just listed. To the services just listed, one should add the services rendered by forests as capturers of water, controller of erosion, providers of wildlife habitat, as well as enjoyment to campers, hikers, hunters, etc.

4. See Costanza and Daly (1992).

5. See Daly (1991), chapter 4.

References

Daly, Herman E. 1991. *Steady-State Economics*. 2d Ed. Washington, DC: Island Press.

———. 1992. "Allocation, Distribution and Scale: Towards an Economics that is Efficient, Just and Sustainable." *Ecological Economics* 6(3):185-93.

Daly, Herman E., and Robert Costanza. 1992. "On Natural Capital and Sustainable Development," *Conservation Biology* 6(1):27-46.

Daly, Herman E., and K. Townsend, eds. 1993. *Valuing the Earth: Economics, Ecology, Ethics*. Cambridge, MA: MIT Press.

El Serafy, Salah. 1989. "The Proper Calculation of Income from Depletable Natural Resources." In Y. Ahmad, S. El Serafy, and E. Lutz, eds., *Environmental Accounting for Sustainable Development*. Washington, DC: World Bank.

Goodland, Robert, and Herman E. Daly. 1991. "Environmental Assessment and Sustainability in the World Bank." *Sustainable Development* 1(1): 12-23.

Hicks, J.R. 1946. *Value and Capital*. Oxford: Oxford University Press.

Ise, John. 1925. "The Theory of Value as Applied to Natural Resources." *American Economic Review*.

Vitousek, P.M., P.R. Ehrlich, A.H. Ehrlich, and P.A. Matson. 1986. "Human Appropriation of the Products of Photosynthesis." *BioScience* 34(May):368-73.